THE EVALUATION OF SEXUAL DISORDERS:

Psychological and Medical Aspects

THE EVALUATION OF SEXUAL DISORDERS:
Psychological and Medical Aspects

Helen Singer Kaplan, M.D., Ph.D.

with chapters by

Melvin Horwith, M.D.,
Julianne Imperato-McGinley, M.D.,
Sherwin A. Kaufman, M.D.,
Elliot Leiter, M.D.,
Arnold Melman, M.D., and
Jon M. Reckler, M.D.

BRUNNER/MAZEL, *Publishers* • New York

SECOND PRINTING

Library of Congress Cataloging in Publication Data

Kaplan, Helen Singer, 1929–
  The evaluation of sexual disorders.

  Includes index.
  1. Sexual disorders. I. Horwith, Melvin.
II. Title. [DNLM: 1. Sex disorders. 2. Sex
disorders—Psychology. WM 611 K17e]
RC556.K3193 1983   616.6'9   83-2749
ISBN 0-87630-329-7

CONTENTS

LIST OF CASE STUDIES

LIST OF TABLES

Chapter 10

CONTRIBUTORS

HELEN SINGER KAPLAN, M.D., Ph.D.

Dr. Kaplan is Clinical Professor of Psychiatry at the New York Hospital-Cornell Medical Center and the founder and director of the Human Sexual Teaching program at that institution. She also heads the Helen S. Kaplan Group for the Evaluation and Treatment of Sexual Disorders in New York City.

MELVIN HORWITH, M.D.

Dr. Horwith, Professor of Clinical Medicine (Endocrinology), heads the Department of Endocrinology at the New York Hospital-Cornell Medical Center, New York.

JULIANNE IMPERATO-McGINLEY, M.D.

Dr. Imperato-McGinley is Associate Professor of Medicine and in charge of the endocrine clinic at New York Hospital-Cornell Medical College, New York.

SHERWIN A. KAUFMAN, M.D.

Dr. Kaufman is Clinical Associate Professor of Obstetrics/Gynecology at New York Medical College, and Director of the Infertility Clinic at Lenox Hill Hospital, New York.

ELLIOT LEITER, M.D.

Dr. Leiter is Professor and Director of the Department of Urology at the Mt. Sinai School of Medicine, New York.

ARNOLD MELMAN, M.D.

Dr. Melman is Associate Professor of Urology at the Mt. Sinai School of Medicine, New York, and physician-in-charge of the Center for Male Sexual Dysfunction at the Beth Israel Hospital, New York.

JON RECKLER, M.D.

Dr. Reckler is Clinical Assistant Professor of Surgery (Urology) on the staff of the Department of Urology at the New York Hospital-Cornell Medical Center.

THE EVALUATION OF SEXUAL DISORDERS:

Psychological and Medical Aspects

INTRODUCTION
The New Sexual Medicine:
Implications for Evaluation

Diagnosis is the single most important function of the clinician who deals with sexual complaints. Correct diagnosis leads to appropriate treatment. Incorrect diagnosis leads to inappropriate and unsuccessful treatment. Accurate assessment is, of course, key in all of medicine, but assumes particular importance with sexual disorders because so many diverse psychological and biological stressors can produce identical symptoms. As yet, the differential diagnosis of sexual disorders is not widely understood, and many treatment failures can be traced to faulty evaluation procedures and to a lack of understanding of psychosexual medicine on the part of those engaged in the process.

The patient who is impotent because subtle arteriosclerotic changes in the small blood vessels of his penis have impaired the delicate erectile mechanism is examined by his internist. Because his physical exam is normal and there are no pathological laboratory findings, he is given a "clean bill of health." But the doctor is wrong. This common cause of impotence may occur in otherwise healthy men and often can be detected only by special tests of the penile circulation, which are not yet in common use. Thus, erroneously presuming that his patient is suffering from a psychogenic disorder, the internist refers him to a sex therapist, who prescribes sensate focus exercises and confronts him with his inability to communicate and his intimacy problems with women.

The happily married anorgastic woman is an "orgasm watcher" who inhibits her orgasm reflex by obsessively wondering if she will come. Because of false traditional beliefs that all psychosexual disorders are the product of major neurotic conflicts, she is psychoanalyzed. For three years, four times a week, she explores her unconscious (which may be beneficial in enhancing the quality of her life in other respects, but has only a slim chance of facilitating her orgastic response).

The premature ejaculator, desperate for a cure, becomes a victim of a similar diagnostic error. His psychotherapist sees that the marital relationship is stormy and falsely concludes that the rapid ejaculations are a reflection of the couple's deeply neurotic power struggles. On this assumption he recommends psychodynamically oriented couples therapy. There the husband attains insight into his unconscious ambivalence towards mother figures. The wife resolves her anger. Their marital relationship improves, but he still comes rapidly.

At least in the last two cases the diagnosis of the psychogenicity was correctly made. However, such gross diagnostic distinctions, while necessary, are not sufficient for successful treatment. The current and immediate psychologic antecedents of the sexual symptoms were *not* identified correctly during the evaluation. Consequently, those patients were treated with modalities which are appropriate to the resolution of major unconscious neurotic conflicts, but do not include the specific behavioral interventions that are required for correcting the minor anxieties and the immediate psychological causes which are the "common final pathway" now causing their sexual symptoms. Unless the specific immediate causes that are currently disrupting the patient's sexual reflexes are modified, sexual difficulties are likely to persist, even when deeper intrapsychic conflicts and relationship problems which may have been the ultimate source of the symptom are successfully resolved.

The depressed middle-aged husband trapped in a destructive marriage by his history, his passivity, his guilt, and his wife's manipulations is given a series of testosterone injections on the erroneous assumption that his lack of interest has a physical basis. When hormones fail to increase his desire, he feels that his life has passed him by and sinks further into a state of hopelessness.

The wife who avoids kisses and touching and abhors physical intimacy of any kind, to the point of dreading her husband's return from work each night, is misdiagnosed by a series of professionals. First it is assumed that her sexual avoidance grows out of marital problems. She undergoes Transactional Analysis (Berne, 1961) type of couples therapy and gains insight about the Child within her who struggles with the Child within her husband; but still she avoids sex, and her sense of hopelessness deepens. Next, she is accepted by a behaviorally oriented sex therapy program. With new hope she attempts to carry out her sexual exercises. But these mainly serve to heighten her fears; in addition, she now feels that she is hopelessly sick. Her next attempt is psychoanalysis. She comes to value herself more as a woman, but she still panics in the sexual situation.

All this good therapy was of no avail in terms of the target symptoms because the essential pathogenic determinant was not identified correctly and therefore could not be treated appropriately. This patient's *panic disorder*, which gave rise to her sexual phobia with its elaborate network of crippling avoidances, was not recognized by any of the therapists she had consulted — a pity, because although this syndrome fails to improve with any sort of psychological intervention, the outcome is excellent when anti-panic medication is combined with appropriate sex therapy (Kaplan, Fyer, & Novick, 1982).

Sexual medicine has advanced to the point where a significant proportion of patients with sexual problems can be treated successfully — providing, of course, that the etiologic agents are accurately identified. The patient who is impotent on an organic basis should be informed about the physical and irreversible nature of his erectile difficulty and spared the frustration and expense of useless psychological or hormonal treatments. However, he need not give up his sex life. When erectile difficulties are secondary to circulation problems, libido and orgasm are not impaired and the couple can be offered viable choices. He is an appropriate candidate for a penile prosthesis or he and his wife can be taught to enjoy pleasurable and gratifying sex without penetration if they find this acceptable.

There is an excellent probability that the anorgastic woman can learn to have orgasm in a relatively few sessions, if treatment is focused on modifying the specific and immediate cause of her orgasm inhibition. No amount of insight into her relationship with her mother and father will automatically accomplish this. However, modern behavioral techniques can help stop her obsessive self-observations, her "spectatoring," while she is making love. And only this will enable her to experience a climax.

The man whose ejaculatory control is inadequate (premature ejaculation) also has a highly favorable prognosis. He has an excellent chance of attaining control in response to brief sex therapy, which will teach him to relax during sex and to focus his attention on the pleasurable erotic sensations premonitory to orgasm (Kaplan, 1974). Behaviorally oriented sex therapy can often successfully cure orgasm disorders even though the patient gains no insight into any deeper emotional problems.

On the other hand, behavior modification will *not* help the depressed husband. He clearly needs to confront and resolve his unconscious fear of pleasure and his infantile transferences towards women, which have entrapped him into a paralyzed and asexual existence and entangled him hopelessly with his ambivalent partner. Psychoanalysis or one of the modified psychotherapeutic techniques capable of fostering insight into and resolution of his unconscious neurotic conflicts is the appropriate treatment in this case. Injections of testosterone will merely be conjugated in his liver and discarded with his urine.

Psychoanalysis will not help the impotent man whose wife demands an instant erection which must last until she is satisfied. To restore that patient's potency, the therapist will have to work with the couple conjointly to change the destructive marital system.

I do not mean to imply that every sexual disorder can now be cured. Some are caused by deep and tenacious psychological conflict, by serious marital problems, and by illness or injury that damages the sexual apparatus irreversibly. These are difficult if not impossible to cure, even with today's great advances in sexual medicine. However, we now understand that many disabling sexual complaints grow out of minor and readily reversible causes. These have an excellent prognosis with effective psychological and medical treatments.

THE METHOD

The method of evaluation described in this volume grew out of my experience of evaluating and treating thousands of patients with sexual complaints over the last 12 years. I have found this system useful in clinical practice, as well as for training clinicians in these skills.

The traditional methods of assessment — the psychiatric examination, behavioral analysis, and the standard sexual history used in research — were not developed for diagnosing sexual disorders. Valuable as these methods are in other respects, they are of limited usefulness for evaluating impotent or anorgastic patients for treatment.

Further, the examiner cannot always rely on a standard medical examination to rule out or accurately diagnose the organic aspects of a sexual problem. The consideration of the effects of illness and drugs on sexual functioning is very new, and the art of medical diagnosis was developed when knowledge about sexual medicine was still rudimentary. Therefore, the usual medical, urologic, and gynecological evaluations can be expected to detect the sexual disorders caused by obvious and serious disease states, but may miss the more subtle organic sexual problems which are just now coming to the attention of the medical profession.

The diagnostic system described here is a hybrid. It retains the useful elements of the diagnostic procedures used in psychiatry, psychology, sex research, and medicine, but it was especially adapted and developed for the clinical evaluation of sexual disorders.

The cornerstone of diagnosis is the clinical interview. A major portion of the book is devoted to describing our specially structured, problem-centered diagnostic interview, which is supplemented, when necessary for making the differential diagnosis between organicity and psychogenicity, by physical examinations, laboratory tests, and the new special diagnostic procedures used in sexual medicine.

The method integrates the psychological and the medical aspects of the diagnosis. It works on a comprehensive but selective system: The examination must be comprehensive enough to obtain all the information required for clinical decision-making, while selectively focusing on only the material which is necessary for this purpose.

THE BOOK

The main emphasis of this book is on evaluation of the *psychosexual dysfunctions*, because these syndromes are among the most prevalent and distressing medical complaints of modern times and, when correctly diagnosed, have on the whole an excellent prognosis with the rapid treatment methods.

The discussion is organized according to the *triphasic concept* of the sexual response, which classifies the sexual dysfunctions into separate syndromes involving disturbance of the orgasm, excitement, and desire phases of the sexual response cycle. The triphasic model of the sexual disorders represents a significant advance over the old concepts, which regarded all sexual symptoms as variants of a single pathological entity. In women this was labeled "frigidity," while its male analogue was termed "impotence" (Kaplan, 1979). The new approach makes good clinical and theoretical sense because it recognizes that orgasm, excitement, and desire phase impairments are separate diseases and, since they are each associated with a different set of causes, respond to different and specific therapeutic interventions.

The Diagnostic and Statistical Manual of the American Psychiatric Association (DSM-III) (APA, 1980) uses the triphasic model as the basis for its classification of the psychosexual disorders, and this book corresponds for the most part with DSM-III. However, I have also included several additional types of sexual complaints which are not mentioned in DSM-III, in particular, *partially retarded ejaculation* (Kaplan, 1974), *unconsummated marriage*, and *sexual phobias.**

Sexual phobias and sexual avoidance, which are not strictly speaking sexual disorders, are included as separate syndromes in the discussion on evaluation because patients suffering from sexual phobias make up a substantial proportion of the population who seek help for their sexual difficulties. Also, phobic patients are highly amenable to sex therapy methods, which, when indicated, may be combined with anti-panic medication (Kaplan et al., 1982).

The paraphilias and (ego-dystonic) homosexuality, which are classified in two separate subgroups in DSM-III, have been included within the category of (situationally) inhibited sexual desire, because these conditions all share essential features and sometimes respond to similar therapeutic interventions (Kaplan, 1982). Despite traditional pessimism about the outcome of the treatment, recent evidence indicates that highly motivated homosexuals can often successfully increase their heterosexual capacities with sex therapies, among other modalities (Bieber et al., 1962; Feldman & MacCulloch, 1971; Masters & Johnson, 1979). For this reason, a growing number of homosexuals are seeking professional help, and the clinician who sees sexual problems should be knowledgeable about the evaluation of these individuals.

THE CONTENTS

The book is divided into three sections. Section I describes the differential diagnosis and the psychological aspects of assessment. The medical evaluation of the sexual disorders is discussed in Section II; and the psychological and medical components of the evaluation are brought together and integrated in Section III.

---

*DSM-III does not provide a specific category for sexual phobias. These disorders can be included under: "Psychosexual Dysfunctions, not elsewhere classified."

Section I, The Psychosexual Evaluation, was prepared by the editor (HSK) and is comprised of two chapters. Chapter 1 on *The Data* explains the nature and the purposes of the information that must be elicited during the evaluation in order to differentiate between organic and psychogenic causes and to evaluate the psychological aspects of the problem. The sequence in which data can be collected systematically is also discussed and summarized in flow charts which depict the information-gathering and decision-making process.

Chapter 2 on *The Method* presents the complex data-gathering and analytic process involved in assessing sexual problems, which must fit within the brief time frame of the diagnostic interview(s) and must be done with sufficient warmth and skill to ensure that the experience is constructive for both partners. Another objective of the initial interview is to establish rapport with the patient or couple and engage them in the treatment process. The method that I have found useful for obtaining this information rapidly and in an organized way still leaves room for sensitivity to patients' feelings. The techniques we use to screen out and, if present, to evaluate medical, psychiatric, and marital causes of sexual difficulties are also described in Chapter 2.

The rest of the chapter deals with the psychological aspects of the evaluation, with special emphasis on assessing patients for sex therapy. Because psychosexual disorders can result from *minor* and/or *major intrapsychic* problems and/or from difficulties in the *marital system*, the psychological aspect of the evaluation is integrated to encompass these three levels of causation.

The *sexual status examination* is an important part of the diagnostic interview, which is essentially a detailed analysis of the patient's current sexual experience, including physical functioning, sexual behavior, and interactions with the partner. This information is crucial for planning the *behavioral interventions* of sex therapy. Other portions of the diagnostic interview are designed to elicit data about the deeper roots of the patient's sexual difficulty and also about the role played by the couple's relationship and their sexual interactions. That information enables the examiner to understand the patient in depth and formulate the *psychodynamic and systems aspects* of the treatment.

Section II is devoted to *The Medical Aspects of Evaluation* of sexual disorders. This material cannot yet be found in standard medical texts. The medical evaluation has also been organized according to the triphasic concept of sexuality, because this material gains clarity when disorders of orgasm, excitement, and libido and syndromes which are marked by sexual pain are conceptualized as separate and different disease states. The three phases involve separate anatomic structures and physiologic systems;

moreover, different drugs and illnesses are associated with loss of libido, impotence, retarded ejaculation, and ejaculatory pain. It is therefore necessary to pursue different causes and to utilize different and specific diagnostic examinations and procedures for the medical evaluation of each of these disorders.

To add to this complexity, male and female sexual disorders should also be considered as separate clinical entities, since male and female reproductive physiology and anatomy are different, and the sexual syndromes of males and females are the product of different pathogenic determinants. For example, the physical causes of *excitement phase disorders of females*, which are marked by deficient vaginal lubrication, often involve estrogen deficiency. But *impotence* (excitement phase disorder of the male or erectile dysfunction) requires that entirely different etiologic factors be investigated. These include reduced blood flow in the penis, diabetes, deficiencies in testosterone, prolactin secreting pituitary adenomas, and the use of antihypertensive medications (among others).

For these reasons separate chapters in Section II were prepared by specialists in urology and gynecology. These describe the medical evaluation of orgasm and excitement disorders and conditions producing sexual pain in males and females. Since the organic disturbances of libido are not gender specific to the same degree, the medical and endocrinological evaluation of disorders of male and female sexual desire is described in a single chapter.

Section III, The Comprehensive Evaluation of the Psychosexual Disorders, integrates the methods presented in earlier chapters. Sexual dysfunctions are multidetermined psychosomatic disorders which cannot be evaluated effectively by the mere *addition* of psychological and medical diagnostic methods. A routine medical examination *plus* a standard psychiatric history and mental status evaluation will give the clinician very little information that is useful for managing an impotent or anorgastic patient or a couple who cannot consummate their marriage. The proper assessment of such disorders requires that medical and psychological concepts and diagnostic procedures be integrated in a comprehensive manner.

In the last section of the book the evaluation of the psychosexual disorders is discussed from such a holistic perspective. Chapter 10 summarizes and integrates the psychological and medical aspects of the evaluation of every syndrome. In addition, the diagnostic criteria and clinical features of each psychosexual disorder are outlined so that the clinician will know what signs and symptoms to look for during the evaluation.

Only enough basic information on treatment is presented in Chapter 10 to enable the clinician who is not familiar with the sexual disorders to make sense of the material on evaluation. Those who wish to read about the sexual disorders, their causes and treatments in more detail and greater depth are referred to Volumes I and II of *The New Sex Therapy* (Kaplan, 1974, 1979).

H.S.K.

REFERENCES

American Psychiatric Association. *Diagnostic and statistical manual.* Third Edition. Washington, D.C.: American Psychiatric Association, 1980.

Berne, E. *Transactional analysis in psychotherapy.* New York: Grove Press, 1961.

Bieber, I., Dain, J. J., Diuce, P. R., Drelich, M. G., Grand, H. G., Grundlach, R. H., Kremer, M. W., Rifkin, A. H., Wilbur, C. B., & Bieber, T. B. *Homosexuality.* New York: Basic Books, 1962.

Feldman, M. P., & MacCulloch, M. J. *Homosexual behavior.* Oxford: Pergamon Press, 1971.

Kaplan, H. S. *The new sex therapy, vol. I.* New York: Brunner/Mazel, 1974.

Kaplan, H. S. *Disorders of sexual desire: The new sex therapy, vol. II.* New York: Brunner/ Mazel, 1979.

Kaplan, H. S. *ISD: A model for the treatment of egodystonic homosexuality.* Presented at the 2nd Symposium in the Integrative Psychiatry Series, N.Y. Medical College, Jan. 1982 (Unpublished).

Kaplan, H. S., Fyer, A. J., & Novick, A. The treatment of sexual phobias: The combined use of anti-panic medication and sex therapy. *Journal of Sex and Marital Therapy*, 1982, 8, 3–28.

Masters, W. H., & Johnson, V. *Homosexuality in Perspective.* Boston: Little Brown, 1979.

SECTION I
THE PSYCHOSEXUAL EVALUATION

The material on the evaluation of sexual disorders has been divided into two separate chapters. In Chapter 1 on The Data, *the nature and significance of the medical and psychological information needed to understand sexual problems and to formulate appropriate treatment strategies are discussed. Chapter 2 describes* The Method *useful for collecting this information.*

1

THE DATA

Helen Singer Kaplan, M.D., Ph.D.

In order to understand a sexual problem, to formulate the treatment of choice and to estimate the prognosis, the examiner must clarify the *chief complaint*, establish an accurate *diagnosis* and determine the *etiology* of the problem. The latter requires two kinds of data: the *differential diagnosis* between organic and psychological causes and an *analysis of the psychological elements* of the problem. In order to obtain this information the following questions must be answered during the evaluation:

1) Does the patient really have a sexual disorder?
2) What is the diagnosis?
3) The differential diagnosis: Is the symptom organic or psychogenic?
4) Is the symptom secondary to another psychiatric disorder?
5) What are the immediate psychological causes?
6) Are there deeper psychological causes? What are they?
7) How severe are the psychological causes?
8) What are the relationship factors?

1) DOES THE PATIENT REALLY HAVE A SEXUAL DISORDER?

Many persons whose sexual function is actually normal present with a variety of concerns about their sexuality, and the first question that the examiner must ask is whether or not there is anything really wrong with the patient's sexual functioning. One may well ask why a sexually adequate person should become obsessed with his sexuality, but emotional issues that range from trivial to serious lie beneath unrealistic sexual concerns. The examiner cannot assume that all persons who seek his help have a real sexual dysfunction.

When psychosexual complaints are the product of minor anxieties, inexperience, and unrealistic expectations and occur in a basically healthy person, a little reassurance or practical advice is all that is needed to solve the problem. The worried couple in their sixties need to be told that his slower response is due to the normal aging process and not to a physical impairment or the wife's diminished attractiveness. They should be reassured that with some changes they will be able to continue to enjoy their sexuality together. Similar considerations apply to the young woman who fears she is abnormal because her first intercourse was disappointing.

The astute recognition that a patient does not have a serious sexual problem provides the exceedingly valuable service of sparing him unnecessary tests and treatments, while at the same time providing realistic reassurance and guidance. Such couples or patients always find their consultation exceedingly worthwhile.

Sometimes an unrealistic or obsessive concern about sex represents displacement of a more serious emotional problem that should not be neglected. For example, some people are overly concerned about their sexual functioning because of *unconscious insecurities* and *latent anxieties about their sexual adequacy*. Some suffer from *excessive separation anxieties* and *rejection sensitivity*. Persons who are insecure about their partner's affections may try to explain their uneasiness on the basis of imaginary or exaggerated deficiencies in his or her sexual functioning. Actually, an *obsessive* person may "turn off" his partner just because he is too insecure and too anxious to please. However, such individuals are unaware of just how unattractive they are making themselves and focus instead on their performance. They urgently want to become better sexual partners. They seek treatment for coital anorgasmia, for better ejaculatory control or harder erections, with the unrealistic hope of securing through a better sexual performance the obsessively desired love object. Characteristically, such patients have no insight into the real causes of their *obsession* with their sexual adequacy.

Many kinds of unconscious *neurotic anxieties* and *conflicts* are hidden beneath unfounded concerns about sexual functioning. These may also mask an underlying *depression*.

Couples whose sexual responses are essentially normal but who are incompatible for other reasons may seek sex therapy in an attempt to *deny*

TABLE 1
Information and Decisions in the Evaluation of Sexual Disorders

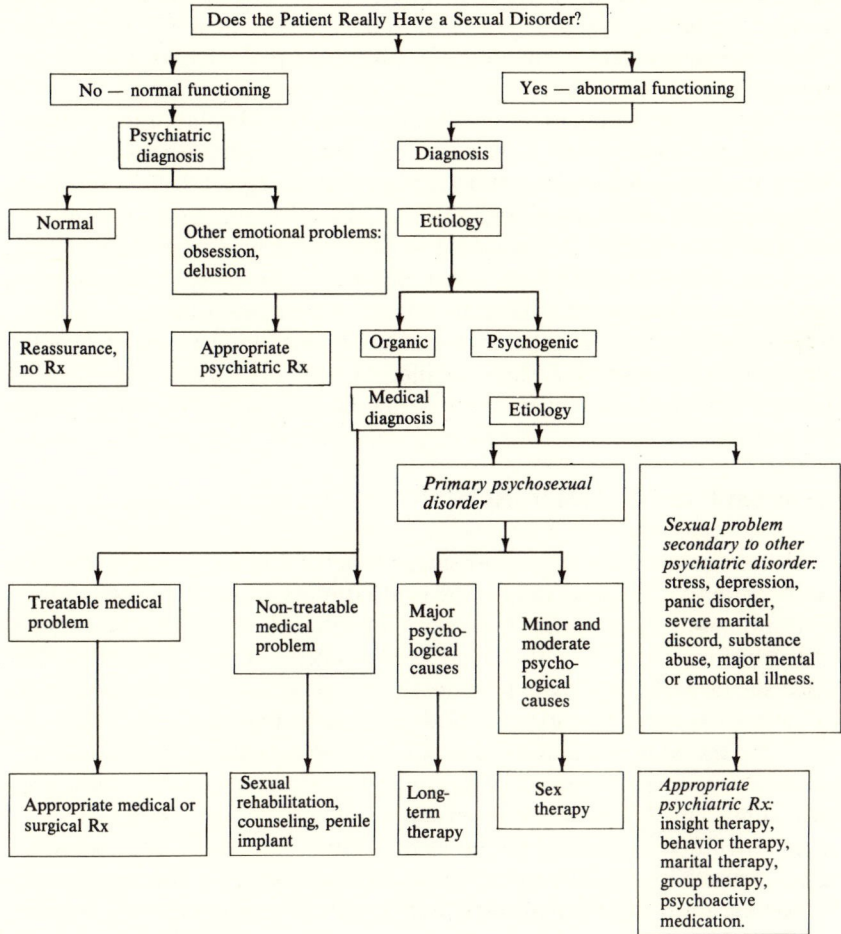

their *marital problems* or in the hopes of *saving* a *moribund relationship.* Sometimes one partner is in love with someone else. Sometimes a person will seek treatment in the attempt to conjure up sexual feelings for someone who does not basically attract him or her, but whom he/she does not want to leave for other reasons.

At times, *schizophrenic patients* present themselves for sexual therapy with bizarre sexual complaints. For instance, one delusional patient complained that his semen was poisonous. Another that people "knew" he was impotent and were mocking him. Mentally ill patients often have an irrational need to cling to their delusions of sexual inadequacy and will not accept reassurance even by means of physical proof such as hormone determinations or sleep tests.

If the analysis of a patient's sexual response reveals that his or her functioning is essentially normal and that the complaint represents a displacement of other emotional or relationship problems which he has not faced, the patient should be reassured about his sexual normalcy and, of course, not accepted for sexual therapy. The other problems, especially if these are profound and could endanger the patient or others, should be taken seriously and evaluated so that appropriate treatment can be provided.

In order to determine whether the patient's sexual functioning falls within the limits of normalcy, the examiner needs to have a clear and detailed picture of his/her current sexual experience.

2) WHAT IS THE DIAGNOSIS?

When the patient's or couple's sexual functioning has in fact been found to be deficient, the next step in the evaluation is to place the sexual disorder into its correct diagnostic category. It will no longer do to label all sexually dysfunctional patients "frigid" or "impotent" since it is now clear that each sexual symptom is the product of different physical and psychological stressors requiring different kinds of intervention. The precise diagnosis of the sexual problem thus narrows down the organic and psychological causes that must be explored during the evaluation and, because some syndromes are frequently caused by drugs and illness while others are overwhelmingly psychogenic, helps to differentiate organic from psychogenic causes. Identifying the specific disorder is also necessary for formulating an appropriate treatment plan when the problem is psychogenic, since the different psychosexual syndromes respond to different and specific treatment strategies (Kaplan, 1974, 1975, 1979).

In order to arrive at an accurate diagnosis, it is necessary to know *which phase* of the sexual response is impaired, what the nature of the impairment is, and how this affects the patient's sexual experience. A detailed description of the chief complaint, together with an analysis of the patient's current sexual functioning (sexual status) will yield this information.

TABLE 2
The Sexual Dysfunctions: Physiology, Clinical Features, and Causes

	Male	Female
1. *Orgasm Phase Disorders*		
The Physiology of Orgasm	*Phase 1 — Emission:* contraction of smooth muscles or internal male reproductive organs collects ejaculate in the posterior urethra	No female emission phase*
	Phase 2 — Ejaculation: 0.8/sec. contractions of striated perineal muscles, propels semen out of urethra. Pleasurable.	*Phase 2 —* Orgasm: 0.8/sec. contractions of striated perineal muscles; pleasurable
Clinical Features	*Premature ejaculation (PE):* inadequate control of ejaculation reflex	No clinical female analogue
	Retarded ejaculation (RE): delayed or absent ejaculation	Inhibited female orgasm; delayed or absent orgasm
	Partial retarded ejaculation: inhibition of emission phase only; no pleasure	"Missed" female orgasm
Common Organic Causes	1) There are no *common* organic causes of primary ejaculatory disorders	1) There are no *common* organic causes of primary anorgasmia
	2) Secondary ejaculatory disorders: a) radical abdominal and pelvic surgery; trauma and diseases of the lower spinal cord b) alpha adrenergic blocking drugs; thioridazine	2) Secondary anorgasmia: a) advanced diabetes b) MAO inhibitor drugs
Psychological Causes	*PE:* failure to perceive or register erotic sensations premonitory to orgasm	
A) Immediate Causes	*RE* (and partial RE): 1) Obsessive self-observation during sex 2) inability to "let go"	*Inhibited female orgasm:* 1) obsessive self-observation during sex 2) inability to "let go" 3) insufficient stimulation

*Claims for "female ejaculation" (Gräfenberg, 1950, Ladas, Whipple, & Perry, 1982) have not been substantiated.

(continued)

TABLE 2 *(continued)*

	Male	Female
B) Deeper Intrapsychic and Relationship Causes	*PE:* tend to be mild *RE:* variable — sometimes associated with hostility towards women	*Inhibited female orgasm:* tend to be mild

2. *Excitement Phase Disorders*

	Male	Female
Physiology of Excitement	*Genital Vasocongestion:* Dilation of penile arteries increases inflow of blood, while outflow is diminished. This creates a high pressure system in the cavernous sinuses of the penis which produces *erection*.	*Genital Vasocongestion:* Diffuse dilation of blood vessels in labia and around vagina produces *genital swelling* and *vaginal lubrication*.
Clinical Features	Impotence	Vaginal dryness, Painful coitus
Common Organic Causes	1) diabetes 2) penile circulatory problems 3) endocrine problems (low testosterone, high prolactin) 4) drugs: antihypertensives, beta blockers, alcohol	Estrogen deficiency (menopause)
Psychological Causes		
A) Immediate Causes	performance anxiety partner pressure overconcern with pleasing partner	?
B) Deeper Causes	not specific — vary from mild performance anxiety to severe neurosis *intrapsychic* — oedipal problems, cultural guilt about sex *relationship* — ambivalence towards partner, overconcern with pleasing partner, fear of rejection	Ambivalence about intercourse

3. *Desire Phase Disorders*

	Male	Female
Physiology of	Activation of sex circuits in	Same as male, requires lower

TABLE 2 (*continued*)

	Male	Female
Desire	brain — mediated by *testosterone.*	level of testosterone.
Clinical Features	1) total loss of desire 2) loss of desire in specific situation only	Same
Common Organic Causes	1) disease states that reduce testosterone 2) depression 3) severe stress 4) drugs that impair the sex circuits of the brain: beta blockers, narcotics, alcohol	Same
Psychological Causes		
A) Immediate Causes	1) "anti-fantasies" — focus on negative aspects of partner or sexual situation 2) avoidance of erotic stimulation 3) avoidance of erotic fantasies	Same
B) Deeper Causes	Often severe, not specific 1) *Intrapsychic* — fear of intimacy and commitment 2) *Relationship* — anger at partner	Same

4. *Sexual Disorders Associated with Genital Muscle Spasm*

Clinical Features	ejaculatory pain → secondary avoidance	vaginismus → dyspareunia + secondary avoidance
Common Organic Causes	infections of the urogenital tract, e.g., prostatitis, vesiculitis, herpes, etc.	painful gynecologic conditions, e.g., pelvic inflammatory disease, endometriosis, hymenal obstruction, painful hymenal remnants, herpes, etc.
Pathology	conditioned involuntary painful spasm of cremasteric or perineal muscles or muscles of internal reproductive organs	conditioned involuntary spasm of the circumvaginal muscles
Psychological Causes	ambivalence about ejaculating	variable — ranges from simple conditioned guarding reaction

(*continued*)

TABLE 2 (*continued*)

	Male	Female
		to severe neurosis and relationship problems

5. *Functional Dyspareunia*

Clinical Features	pain on erection, intromission or ejaculation	pain on entry, deep thrusting, orgasm
Organic Causes	pain is *more often organic than psychogenic* and organic cause must be ruled out in each case	Same
Psychological Mechanisms (Psychogenic Dyspareunia)	1) hypochondriacal overreaction to normal sensations 2) hysterical pain 3) pain-depression syndrome 4) intractable schizophrenic pain 5) functional genital muscle spasm 6) brutal sexual intercourse	Same Also, vaginismus

6. *Phobic Avoidance of Sex*

Clinical Features	Phobic avoidance of sex	Same
Cause	1) associated with panic disorder 2) simple sexual phobia — conditioning and neurotic processes	Same

3) THE DIFFERENTIAL DIAGNOSIS: IS THE SYMPTOM ORGANIC OR PSYCHOGENIC?

The determination of *causes* is the most important aspect of the evaluation. The *differential diagnosis* between organicity and psychogenicity is the first and crucial step in this process. If organic factors are ruled out, then the detailed *analysis of the psychological causes* completes the evaluation.

In the past, it was believed that 95 percent of sexual disorders had a psychological basis. However recent evidence indicates that this figure is too high (Spark et al., 1980). Illness and drugs must be carefully ruled out when evaluating patients, especially those over the age of 40, with complaints that carry a high risk of organicity.

Awareness of the effects of illness and drugs on sexual functioning is relatively recent, and unfortunately, the time has not yet arrived when the examiner can always count on a routine medical, gynecological, or urological examination to detect the subtler organic causes of his patient's sexual symptom. For these reasons, it is up to the clinician who undertakes to treat sexual disorders to learn the principles of the medical aspects of the evaluation and to see to it that the differentiation between organicity and psychogenicity has been properly made.

The differential diagnosis between organic and psychogenic sexual problems is made first and foremost on the basis of the diagnostic interview. Only when this does not clearly establish psychogenicity are further diagnostic examinations and tests necessary or appropriate. The following points of information will aid in differentiating psychogenic from organic sexual symptoms:

Is the Symptom Global or Situational?

This is the most important point of information for making a differential diagnosis. *If the symptom is clearly situational, psychogenicity is established and, conversely, drugs and illness are ruled out as causative factors.* * When the interview indicates unequivocally that a patient's symptom occurs only in specific circumstances, that patient may be spared the expense and trouble of further medical examinations and diagnostic procedures.

What is the Nature of the Sexual Symptom?

- Which phase(s) of the sexual response cycle is impaired?
- What is the nature of the impairment?
- Does this disorder carry a high or low risk (probability) of organicity?

---

*There are rare exceptions, e.g., the "steal" syndrome, where impotence occurs in the male superior position only, because blood needed for erection is diverted away from the penis under certain hemodynamic conditions (Wagner & Green, 1982).

*Sexual disorders frequently associated with organic causes**

The following dysfunctions, when they are *global*, that is, when they occur in all circumstances, in contrast to situational symptoms that fluctuate with specific emotional circumstances, are caused at least in part by illness or drugs so frequently that organicity *should always be carefully ruled out* before commencing psychological treatment:

1) impotence
2) dyspareunia in males and females
3) vaginismus
4) unconsummated marriage
5) low or absent libido
6) secondary anorgasmia in males and females
7) secondary premature ejaculation
8) secondary retarded ejaculation

Sexual disorders seldom associated with organic causes

The following dysfunctions are associated with physical causes infrequently, even when they are global.

1) primary premature ejaculation
2) primary impairment of female orgasm (anorgasmia)
3) primary retarded ejaculation

Organic etiology is especially unlikely when these symptoms occur in a healthy and otherwise medically asymptomatic individual. To subject each patient with these diagnoses to a complete medical, neurological, and gynecological evaluation would be impractical, uneconomic, and quite unnecessary. Often, a brief trial of sex therapy is the most sensible diagnostic procedure with these patients, as the risk of missing significant illness is small. However, it should be remembered that none of these syndromes is exclusively psychogenic, since biological organs that are subject to disease are involved. The examiner must use his clinical judgment about how thoroughly the potential medical causes need to be analyzed in each individual case.

---

*Studies have just begun to yield reliable information about the prevalence of medical factors in impotence, but there is a dearth of hard data regarding the prevalence of physical determinants for the other dysfunctions. The following discussion is based primarily on impressions gained by clinical experience and awaits correction as more reliable information is accumulated.

TABLE 3
Reversible and Irreversible Organic Causes of Sexual Disorders

a) *Potentially reversible conditions*

1) *Loss of libido* due to endocrine deficiencies: testosterone deficiency (common in older males); thyroid deficiency (rare). (*Treatment:* hormone replacement)

2) *Loss of libido* due to endocrine secreting tumors: prolactin secreting tumors of the pituitary (relatively common); estrogen secreting tumors of the testes and adrenals (rare). (*Treatment:* medical, surgical and nuclear treatment of the tumor)

3) *Loss of libido* due to depression and stress (common). (*Treatment:* antidepressant medication, psychotherapy, ECT)

4) *Loss of libido* due to substances (common): centrally acting beta adrenergic blockers, centrally acting antihypertensive agents, excessive alcohol and narcotics. (*Treatment:* beta blockers which penetrate the blood-brain barrier to a lesser extent can be substitutes; calcium channel blockers can be used at times; peripherally acting antihypertensive agents can sometimes be substituted for centrally acting ones; treatment of substance abuse)

5) *Vaginal dryness* and/or atrophy and discomfort on intercourse due to estrogen deficiency (very common in postmenopausal women). (*Treatment:* estrogen replacement, oral or local, dilation and use of lubricants)

6) *Impotence* due to antihypertensive drugs (very common). (*Treatment:* reversible only if blood pressure can be controlled by diet, exercise and lifestyle changes and the substitution of antihypertensive agents with lesser sexual side-effects)

7) *Impotence* due to blockage of *large vessels* supplying the penis (rare). (*Treatment:* vascular surgery)

8) *Impotence* due to deficits in the tunica albuginea of the penis (rare) (Wagner & Green, 1982). (*Treatment:* reparative surgery)

9) *Irreversible organic impotence.* (*Treatment:* can be helped with surgically implanted prosthesis)

10) *Vaginal obstructions* due to vaginal agenesis, imperforate or rigid hymen. (*Treatment:* surgery)

11) *Female dyspareunia* due to vaginal infections, bladder infections, PID. (*Treatment:* antibiotics) Endometriosis. (*Treatment:* hormonal, surgical) Painful hymenal tags, episiotomy scars. (*Treatment:* surgery)

12) *Male dyspareunia* due to prostate infection, vesicular infection, urethral infection and tumors, hernia, chordee, penile infections, herpes. (*Treatment:* antibiotics, surgery)

13) *Orgasm and excitement phase impairments* due to reversible neurological conditions caused by a) vitamin deficiencies. (*Treatment:* vitamin replacement); b) neurotropic viral infections. (*Treatment:* supportive management)

14) *Delayed or absent orgasm* due to MAO inhibitor medication. (*Treatment:* substitution of tricyclic or tetracyclic antidepressants, or trazodone)

b) *Medical conditions which are not reversible but which should be actively managed or treated in order to prevent further progression of the disease and further deterioration of the sexual response*

(continued)

TABLE 3 *(continued)*

1) *Diabetes*, attention to glucose control (impotence in males, anorgasmia in females)

2) *Hypertension*, with its high risk of arteriosclerosis of the small blood vessels (impotence — it is theoretically possible in some cases to prevent progression of penile arteriosclerosis by attention to blood pressure, exercise, low cholesterol and salt diet, and cessation of tobacco smoking)

3) *Vaginal atrophy*, secondary to pelvic irradiation and surgery. (*Treatment:* dilation and frequent sexual intercourse; estrogen cream when not medically contraindicated)

c) *Common conditions that are not reversible or controllable with present methods*

1) *Small vessel arteriosclerosis* of the penile vessels and corpora cavernosa (very common)

2) *Diabetic damage* to vessels and nerves involved in the erection and orgasm reflex (very common)

3) *Degenerative neurological diseases* and injury to the central nervous system and surgical trauma to the nerves and anatomic structure involved in the genital reflexes (rare)

4) *Impotence* and diminished libido associated with renal dialysis (rare)

5) *Drug-related impotence* when no effective substitute without sexual side-effects is available.

Sexual disorders not associated with medical causes

The following disorders are almost always psychogenic. Patients presenting with these problems do not generally require a medical evaluation beyond the medical screening questions which form the part of the diagnostic interview of all patients.

1) all situational sexual symptoms, including homosexuality and the paraphilias (situational ISD)

2) sexual phobias and avoidances*

A minor qualification is required. Sometimes latent homosexual and/or paraphiliac tendencies will emerge as part of a person's effort to overcome

---

*The drug-responsive panic and anxiety disorders may, in fact, have a physiological basis. Some patients with panic disorders respond with symptoms of panic when infused with sodium lactate on an experimental basis (Gorman, Fyer, Glicklich, King, & Klein, 1981). However, to date, no biological tests are available to the clinician which will identify these patients.

a partially defective libido or an erectile mechanism which has become impaired on an organic basis. For these reasons, when an older person complains of late emerging and unwelcome variant sexual appetites, he (it is usually a male) should be worked up medically like any other patient with secondary or late appearing libido and erectile problems.

Is the Clinical Pattern Characteristic
of a Specific Medical Condition?
Is the Symptom Primary or Secondary?
Was Its Onset Precipitous or Gradual?

As a general rule, a *primary* sexual symptom, that is, one which has always been present, is more likely to be psychogenic than a *secondary* disability that occurs after a period of good functioning, especially in the absence of emotional stress or trauma. Thus, for example, it is highly probable that a man who has always been a premature ejaculator or a woman who has never had an orgasm has a psychogenic problem. (Providing, of course, that he/she does not suffer from an exceedingly rare congenital abnormality, and did not sustain physical trauma to the genital organs before becoming sexually active). On the other hand, organic causes should be suspected if ejaculatory control deteriorates or orgasm becomes delayed in a person whose sexual functioning had been normal for a significant period of time.

When erection, orgasm, or libido becomes impaired precipitously (in the absence of significant trauma and stress), one looks for drugs with sexual side-effects or injury to the genital organs as possible causes. Gradually progressive conditions like diabetes and arteriosclerosis of the small penile blood vessels would be suspect in patients who complain of slowly progressive impotence. The estrogen deficiency of menopause is characterized by gradually increasing vaginal dryness, while a slowly diminishing libido in a male could be associated with age-related diminution of testosterone or a slowly growing pituitary adenoma.

The Evaluation of the Organic Cause(s): What Drug or Illness is Causing the Problem?

After the differential diagnosis has been made, we need to find out precisely which drug or illness is causing the problem and how extensive the impairment is.

Specific questions that must be answered during the evaluation include:

- Does the patient have a diagnosed illness or injury which could be causing his sexual symptom?
- Does he have signs and symptoms of such an illness or injury?
- Have these been properly evaluated and treated?
- Is he taking any drug or substance that has sexual side-effects?

The examiner should be knowledgeable about the sexual side-effects of commonly used drugs and understand which illnesses and injuries damage the sexual organs or impair their functioning. Armed with this knowledge, he can be alert to organicity, when, for example, an impotent patient tells him that he has diabetes or is taking antihypertensive medication or when a postmenopausal woman complains about vaginal dryness and dyspareunia.

Can the Condition be Cured?

For sexual counseling, and rehabilitation, the clinician needs to know whether the patient's underlying medical condition is treatable or irreversible; whether the disability is stable or progressive so that the patient must be prepared to face further deterioration of his sexual capability. Many illnesses that cause sexual problems can be cured or arrested with modern medical and surgical treatment, and substitutes can often be found for drugs with sexual side-effects. It is particularly important to detect *treatable conditions* during the evaluation so that the problem can be corrected and efforts be made to prevent further progression of the damage. Table 2 lists irreversible and reversible organic causes of sexual impairment and also indicates the appropriate treatment.

How Extensive is the Sexual Impairment?
What Has Been Spared and What Has Been Lost?

The basic principle of sexual therapy and rehabilitation with a sexually handicapped person is to build upon his remaining capabilities and to help him compensate for his deficits. Very often illness and drugs will damage one phase of the sexual response cycle only and spare the others; therefore, in order to plan appropriate management it is important to analyze the physical parameters of the patient's current sexual response precisely. Is the post irradiation patient still orgastic and interested in sex, even though vaginal atrophy has made penetration impossible? Has the impotent patient who has undergone radical pelvic surgery retained his sex drive? Can he still ejaculate? There are the kinds of issues that arise in evaluating the sexually handicapped patient.

Evaluating the Psychological Aspects of
Organic Sexual Problems

Since sexual symptoms frequently result from an interplay between organic and psychological factors, an attempt must be made to sort out the relative contributions of each. Organic disease can occur in people with previous psychological problems and their anxious response to even mild organic deficiencies will complicate the clinical picture enormously. Therefore, for the management and/or rehabilitation of patients with organic or partial organic problems, the assessment of psychological reactions is extremely important. How does the patient handle his deficit? How does his partner feel? Are they aggravating the problem unnecessarily? Are they emotionally stable enough to benefit from sexual counseling?

Mild physiological deficits are common in the aging population. In the past a man might have been accustomed to becoming erect immediately in response to the psychic stimulation of seeing his wife take off her clothes. He did not need any physical stimulation of his genitals. Formerly he might have been able to function even though he was tired and upset. But as he grows older, he notices with alarm that he no longer becomes erect instantly and sometimes his erections are not quite as firm as they were. If he is fatigued, he may not be able to function at all. If he is insecure, the sense of diminishing sexual power may trouble him to the extent of escalating the minor partial deficit into a total and severe disability.

The partner's responses and attitudes are of equal importance in determining the ultimate clinical picture and must be carefully noted during the evaluation. If a wife misconstrues her husband's slower sexual response (which is really due to minor age-related circulatory disorder) as evidence that she is losing her attractiveness, she is likely to become anxious, demanding and critical in bed. She may reject his attempts to compensate for his diminished response by requesting oral and manual stimulation of his penis or suddenly coming home with erotica. Her reactions will only aggravate her husband's problem. In such cases the symptomatic patient might best be helped by the therapist's working with the partner to modify her negative attitude or seeing the couple conjointly to improve their sexual system.

In sum, when a partial impairment occurs in a person who is anxious about his or her sexual performance or whose partner is insecure about his or her sexual desirability, a serious sexual avoidance and/or dysfunction may result. On the other hand, a sexually secure couple with an identical physical loss will be open to the therapist's suggestions that they explore alternative ways of stimulation and gratification. *As long as libido is re-*

tained, the possibilities for exploiting a couple's remaining sexual capacities are excellent.

A dramatic example of these principles is illustrated in the case recently reported by Witkin and Kaplan (1982). A 50-year-old man underwent penectomy for cancer of the urethra. Enough of the anatomic structures necessary for ejaculation were left intact (the internal male reproductive organs and some of the muscles of the penile crura) to allow him to experience orgasm after surgery. His libido, which had always been strong, was not affected by the procedure. He was fortunate in having a most supportive wife who found him attractive despite his disability. Both were sexually unconflicted and loving to each other. With the aid of therapy they were able to work out a mutually gratifying sexual relationship that incorporated clitoral stimulation and fantasy, and included ejaculations for him and orgasms for her, despite the loss of the penis.

4) IS THE SYMPTOM SECONDARY TO ANOTHER PSYCHIATRIC DISORDER?

Many persons who suffer from sexual problems function well in other respects and are free of serious psychopathology. However, others and/or their spouses are psychotic, depressed, obsessive, phobic, or alcoholic. Or they are trying to cope with severe stress or are involved in relationships that are so stormy that it would be absurd to expect good sex.

During the evaluation of the patient with a sexual disorder, it is important to detect and screen out other psychiatric disorders on two counts. First, when a sexual symptom is secondary to another psychiatric disorder, it may not be appropriate to treat the sexual symptom directly. Second, significant psychological difficulties in either spouse may constitute a contraindication to sex therapy because of the risk of aggravating the emotional problem.

When the interview reveals that the symptomatic patient or the spouse is suffering from a major psychiatric disorder, a complete psychiatric examination must be done for each in order to answer the following questions:

- What is the psychiatric diagnosis?
- Is sex therapy appropriate?
- Is sex therapy safe?
- How does the other psychiatric disorder affect the treatment of the sexual problem?
- Is the patient receiving appropriate treatment for the psychiatric disorder?

Stress Reactions

The examiner will need to ask the following questions related to stress:

- Is the patient dealing with major stress?
- Should this be resolved first or is he/she ready for sex therapy now?
- What pathological processes were set in motion by the crisis?
- Are these still actively interfering with the patient's sexual functioning?

When a person is enmeshed in a crisis, when he is on the firing line and feels unable to cope, asexuality is a normal reaction. We mammals are programmed so that survival has priority over reproduction and the sexual reflexes simply do not work in highly stressful situations. Even the person whose sexuality is fundamentally sound may experience difficulty making love on the battlefield, during a divorce, after the death of a spouse or a child, during financial, legal, and career crises, or in the midst of severe marital fights.

The sexually dysfunctional patient who is currently trying to cope with overwhelming stress should be guided towards appropriate crisis intervention, psychotherapy, marital therapy, psychotropic drugs, etc. — but not sex therapy. The patient's sexual status may be evaluated when the crisis is under control.

Schizophrenia

Schizophrenics are capable of having perfectly normal sexual responses, and they are also subject to all the psychosexual dysfunctions. The decision of who to treat and how is a sensitive one which requires an understanding of the schizophrenic process and the dynamics of sex therapy.

The patient's sexual complaint may be the product of performance anxieties that are not dynamically related to the schizophrenic illness; then, the couple can safely be treated. On the other hand, the sexual symptom may constitute a defense against the underlying psychotic process which should not be tampered with, or the sexual disability may serve a defensive function for the compensated schizophrenic spouse, requiring great caution lest a delicate balance be disturbed. Thus, when one evaluates patients with sexual problems, the question is *not* simply: Is the patient or his spouse schizophrenic? Further exploration is required to ascertain what relationship the sexual symptom bears to the schizophrenic process:

- Does the patient have a psychological need to avoid sex?
- What role does the sexual symptom play in the couple's relationship?

- Does he or she have the resources to tolerate active and rapid sex therapy?
- Can they benefit from treatment?

Overtly psychotic patients or couples wherein the spouse is actively psychotic are clearly not appropriate candidates for sex therapy, even when they have a real sexual problem. When a major thought disorder is detected in the course of the diagnostic interview, the examiner should ensure that the patients are receiving appropriate psychiatric treatment in the form of medication, psychotherapy, and, in some cases, hospitalization. When the patient recovers from the acute phase of the psychosis, the sexual difficulty may be reevaluated.

Sex therapy is not contraindicated for all persons with a history of schizophrenia. On the contrary, many patients who are in a quiescent or compensated phase of a major psychiatric illness have been successfully treated with sex therapy and have actually benefited greatly in terms of their overall psychological well-being and their sense of mastery and success (Kaplan, 1974). Nevertheless, sexually dysfunctional patients and their spouses who are in the remission or latent phases of schizophrenia may pose difficult decisions for the examiner.

The process and/or the outcome of sex therapy poses a danger only when it disrupts either spouse's defenses against disorganization. The following case histories illustrate these points.

CASE 1: SCHIZOPHRENIC PATIENT WHO WAS SUCCESSFULLY
TREATED FOR HER SEXUAL PROBLEM

Jack and Jill S, who had been married for six years, consulted me with complaints of sexual avoidance, vaginismus, and unconsummated marriage. Jill reported that she had had three overt schizophrenic episodes for which she had been hospitalized. At the time of evaluation, she was in remission, taking 50 mg. of Mellaril (thioridazine) HS and participating in group therapy with an exceptionally talented therapist. Her husband, a gentle and supportive man, was free of major psychopathology and seemed to have no stake in his wife's sexual problem.

The patient was taking no drugs and had no illness to account for her symptoms. (Mellaril does not cause sexual avoidance or vaginismus). Her menstrual periods were regular. Vaginal examination revealed that there was no physical obstruction; however, her vaginal muscles were tightly closed and she was obviously frightened of the examination.

The patient's ideas about sex were appropriate and she recognized that her fear of penetration had no basis in reality. No sexually destructive trauma or dynamic forces were revealed by her history.

It appeared that Jill's vaginismus did not represent a defense against her psychotic process. To the contrary, she had been working hard at being "normal." She hated her "sick" role and had made a good deal of progress in developing normal patterns of behavior, which included the acquisition of effective work and social skills. Most important, both she and Jack had responded positively to each forward step of therapy. Her inability to have a normal sexual relationship with her husband made her feel "abnormal and weird" and she was highly motivated to remedy this, as she had done in other areas of previously poor functioning.

The couple was accepted for sex therapy and Jill did very well. With the caring support of her husband, she slowly and gently proceeded with dilation exercises to extinguish the vaginal muscle spasms. Little resistance was encountered. When she finally achieved intercourse, both she and Jack felt gratified about their success.

CASE 2: SCHIZOPHRENIC SPOUSE WITH AN
ADVERSE REACTION TO SEX THERAPY

In contrast, Joyce X, who also had a history of schizophrenia, developed a flare-up of her psychotic process in response to her husband's improvement in sex therapy.

Jim X was a 52-year-old butcher who had always been a premature ejaculator. He made excellent progress through the stages of treatment, which involved manual stimulation of the penis by his wife. The trouble began when treatment progressed to vaginal containment. At that point, Joyce became agitated and angry and accused me (the therapist) of "being against her." She developed the delusion that her husband was having an affair with their sister-in-law and that I was encouraging this.

The behavioral aspects of sex therapy were immediately discontinued and treatment was shifted to Joyce's psychosis. She was reassured that I wished to help her develop a pleasurable relationship with her husband. She was given antipsychotic medication and her irrational fears were explored in depth. Apparently, her husband's symptom of sexual inadequacy had served as an important defense for Joyce. Irrationally, she had felt that she could never hold the love of a potent man and that Jim stayed with her primarily because she tolerated his inadequacy. His growing sexual potency and the possibility of a more complete and adult sexual relationship had mobilized old irrational fears, as well as intense rage still unresolved from childhood. She had never formed a trusting identification with her mother, still blamed her for all her frustrations, and harbored angry, envious feelings towards her. She projected and transferred those feelings to me and irrationally feared my (mother's) retaliation if she were to have a successful pleasurable adult relationship with her husband (father). Joyce simply could not believe that I wanted her to be a sexually adequate and successful woman.

This patient eventually did fairly well in that her acute symptoms subsided and she learned to trust me. However, she never quite resolved her insecurity about her husband. Sex therapy was not resumed with this couple and Jim remained a premature ejaculator.*

Depression

If the patient with a sexual problem is also depressed, the examiner needs to evaluate the severity of his/her depression and seek to clarify its history:

- Was the patient depressed before he/she had the sexual problem?
- Has he/she had previous depressive or manic episodes?
- Is there a pattern?
- Is he/she now or has he/she ever been suicidal?
- Have previous depressions also been associated with sexual problems?

Global loss of libido, secondary impotence, and dyspareunia are frequently secondary to affective disorders. The diagnosis of depression in patients with these syndromes raises questions about the relationship of the depression to the sexual complaint:

- Which came first — the depression or the sexual symptom?
- Did the patient's underlying depression cause him to lose his sexual appetite, or did his sexual inadequacy cause him to become depressed and discouraged?
- Is this woman's discomfort on intercourse a sign of the depression/pain syndrome, or did her sexual problem precipitate her depression?

---

*Jim rapidly attained ejaculatory control with a new partner after his wife died, six years after treatment.

The signs of depressive illness include vegetative symptoms, as well as sadness and pessimistic thoughts. There may be disturbances of the functions regulated by the autonomic nervous system, including sleep, sex, and appetite. The differential diagnosis is complicated by the fact that a sexual deficiency may be extremely threatening and often precipitates feelings of depression.

The accurate assessment of the depression-dysfunction sequence will determine if the patient should receive antidepressant medication, psychotherapy, or sex therapy. A primary depression should be treated before all else. When the depression has lifted, the patient's sexual status should be reevaluated. Often sexual functioning and libido will improve spontaneously along with the waning of depression, but in other cases the sexual symptoms persist after the patient has recovered from his depression. Then sex therapy is indicated. When the diagnostic interview reveals that the patient became depressed in reaction to the sexual disability, the order of treatment is reversed. The sexual symptom is treated first and the patient's mood disorder is reevaluated and, if necessary, treated after sexual functioning improves.

Anxiety Disorders, Panics and Phobias

The assessment of the patient's general anxiety level and his specific anxiety about sex is an essential part of the evaluation of all patients with sexual disorders, but it is especially important to detect panic disorders (or phobic anxiety syndrome) in such patients because most will not get better without anti-panic medication. Persons afflicted with this syndrome have an abnormally low panic threshold, probably on a constitutional basis (Klein, 1964, 1980). They behave as though their "alarm" sensor is set at too sensitive a level and their "panic button" discharges too easily. Thus, they react excessively and inappropriately to minor hazards and separations. Such patients run a high risk of developing panics, phobias, and avoidances, which paralyze them and may constrict their lives.

Phobias and avoidances of sex are commonly seen in this population and tend to be particularly damaging. Frequently the sexual problem is the presenting complaint of patients who are afflicted with panic disorders.

The recognition of this syndrome is relatively new and phobic anxiety can easily be confused with neurotic forms of anxiety and personality disorders. For these reasons, the diagnosis is often missed. Yet, it is extremely important to identify these patients because, while they are refractory to all kinds of psychological treatment, 80 to 85 percent improve if anti-panic drugs are included in the treatment regimen (Klein, 1980). The drugs are probably not curative in themselves, but they protect the patient against his panic so that he can benefit from sex therapy and psychotherapy. Patients with simple phobias who have a normal panic threshold do not benefit from medication.

Neurotic Conflicts, Personality Disorders, and Borderline States

When evaluating the sexual complaints of patients with these psychopathological states, the following questions should be kept in mind by the interviewer:

- Is the sexual symptom a product of or does it serve as a defense against the neurotic process?
- Is it incidental, a product of performance anxiety?
- Are the patient's emotional conflicts too severe for rapid treatment?
- Will it take profound psychic reconstruction for this patient to be able to function sexually?

Psychoanalytic theory predicts that all neurotic individuals and those suffering from personality disorders (character disorders) will have sexual difficulties, but extensive clinical experience with this patient population has taught us that many neurotics and persons with severe personality and borderline disorders enjoy excellent sexual functioning. Of course, many other patients with neurotic problems do, in fact, also suffer from psychosexual dysfunctions. Sometimes the sexual symptom in a neurotic person is coincidental and not dynamically connected to the neurotic process and/or the partner's neurosis. This can happen, for example, when an obsessive/compulsive patient who had previously functioned well sexually develops impotence purely on the basis of performance anxiety, but this symptom does not serve as a defense against deeper sexual conflicts. Case 6 (p. 52) illustrates this clinical situation. More often, the sexual problem is enmeshed in the couple's deeper neurotic processes, as, for example, when impotence serves to defend the borderline patient against the psychic dangers posed to him by intimacy with and commitment to a partner.

It is important to differentiate between sexual symptoms which are "pure" and those that have arisen from unconscious neurotic conflicts, since the latter may mobilize defenses against their rapid removal during sex therapy. Often, such unconscious conflicts can be bypassed in therapy. That is, the direct treatment of the symptom is possible without complete resolution of the underlying neurotic conflict. This clinical situation is demonstrated in the Case of John and Mary which is discussed in Chapter 2. At other times, a certain amount of insight and resolution of the unconscious conflict must occur within the psychosexual treatment process before the patient can tolerate and accept his new sexual adequacy. Case 4 (p. 47) illustrates this situation. When the neurotic process is severe and dynamically connected to the sexual symptom, the patient is not amenable to brief sex therapy and may be better off with lengthier therapeutic interventions which foster insight and resolution of the underlying unconscious conflict. Case 5 (p. 50) is an example of this kind.

Neurotic *obsessive reactions* pose special problems in sexual therapy. For one, patients with obsessive personality disorders are especially likely to develop obsessive fears about their sexual performance that are disruptive to sexual functioning. Performance anxiety in an obsessive personality is often very intense and for this reason difficult to diminish in brief treatment.

Also, obsessive persons are apt to "turn off" their sexual partners. A spouse's obsessiveness in bed is a frequent cause of inhibited sexual desire (ISD). Even if a person really loves her partner, it is difficult to summon great desire when faced with his panic and tension in bed. It is, therefore, often mandatory to first treat the *partner's* obsessive performance fears when dealing with ISD and sexual avoidance.

The evaluation of the obviously neurotic patient and his partner poses the most subtle diagnostic problem in this field. One must not only determine whether the patient or his partner has a neurosis or personality disorder, but also assess whether the neurotic process poses an obstacle to the brief direct treatment of the sexual symptom and just how this can be handled in the most effective, economic, and efficient manner. It is easy to recommend psychoanalysis for all neurotic patients with sexual problems, but often this is not the most beneficial approach. Brief psychosexual therapy, combining the direct, rapid treatment of the sexual symptom with a certain amount of insight therapy, has more to offer some neurotic patients.

Alcoholism and Substance Abuse

Use of alcohol and other drugs should be evaluated:

- Is the patient or his partner abusing alcohol, narcotics, or stimulants?
- Has he sustained permanent physical damage?
- If he is detoxified and abstinent at the time of evaluation, is he in a constructive and stable state suitable for the treatment of sexual problems?

A person who is currently addicted to drugs and/or alcohol is not a suitable candidate for sex therapy until he has been detoxified and is abstinent or off the drug.* Many addictive substances have biologically detrimental effects on the sex drive and potency. It is therefore difficult but important to sort out the psychological and organic elements involved in alcohol or drug use and to delineate the patient's physical deficits precisely, so that realistic treatment goals can be set.

From the psychological perspective, patients who are currently abusing substances seldom possess the integration, self-love, and constructive motivation required for the demanding process of treatment. They are often too self-destructive to participate actively in a program designed to improve the quality of their lives.

Alcoholism and drug abuse can have devastating effects on a marriage and sexual relationship, and frequently sexual functioning does not improve spontaneously when the addiction is under control. Therefore, *rehabilitated alcoholics and former drug users* are often very much in need of and can benefit greatly from marital and sexual therapy to repair the damage that was sustained during the active periods of their addiction.

For these reasons, it is important to ascertain whether the alcoholic patient and his partner are in a psychologically constructive state. In addition, with male alcoholics it is often necessary to assess their physical capabilities with nocturnal penile tumescence monitoring, because chronic alcohol usage may permanently and irreversibly damage their sexual capability.

Mental Retardation

Many mentally retarded individuals, especially those with borderline to moderate impairment, are physically normal and have *normal sexual urges.* Sexual problems in the mentally retarded are likely to involve inappropriate sexual expression and unwanted pregnancy, as well as problems associated with fear of sex and lack of information about sex.

When assessing sexual problems of this patient population, the examiner must determine whether the retarded person has the capacity to benefit from treatment. More specifically, three points of information should be investigated: the nature of the retarded person's current sexual experience; his or her intellectual capacity; and the attitudes of the responsible family members and/or institutions.

---

*Methadone, which is sometimes used to aid the withdrawal of narcotics addicts, is a long-acting narcotic substance which also depresses the sexual response. Therefore, patients on methadone maintenance programs are not suitable candidates for sex therapy.

It is frequently helpful to counsel male retardates with strong sex drives on masturbatory techniques, but this should only be done if self-stimulation is acceptable to this patient's family. Similar considerations apply to contraceptive counseling for retarded females. Evidently, intellectual capacity is not an important ingredient in female sexual attractiveness and unwanted pregnancy is a significant problem with these women. Tubal ligation and insertion of an IUD make the fewest intellectual demands on these women and are therefore preferred methods of contraception.

We have successfully counseled couples in which the female partner was mildly retarded and anorgastic. Such women have normal sex drives and with patience and understanding can come to enjoy sex and make very good sexual partners to men with certain kinds of needs. The reverse situation, involving male retardates and normal women, is more unusual.

Assessment of the family or caretaker is an important part of the evaluation of mentally retarded persons with sexual problems, because the manner in which they handle their sex drive must fit the requirements of the system in which they live.

Is Sex Therapy Safe for this Couple?

The *structured sexual interactions* assigned to the couple include experiences which they have previously avoided because they are threatening. They are not mechanical exercises but *psychologically potent experiences* that may confront patients with their deepest and most hidden fears and wishes. This represents a significant hazard if sexual avoidance is a defense against an underlying psychosis or panic disorder.

In the therapy sessions, couples are encouraged and supported, but they are also *actively confronted* with their avoidance of sexuality, their denial, and their defenses against erotic pleasure, love, and intimacy. This process can also be extremely threatening and may place intolerable strains on the vulnerable patient's tenuous defenses.

Not only the *process* but also the *outcome* of sex therapy may be hazardous for the vulnerable individual. If he or she fails to improve, the patient or the partner's depression and sense of helplessness may deepen. But paradoxically, treatment *success* can also jeopardize the emotional stability of the vulnerable patient and his partner. If he is not emotionally prepared, the rapid pace of sexual improvement which is often seen in sex therapy, together with the emotional crises that result from the disruption of defenses against underlying neurotic conflicts, make this a risky procedure for the potentially suicidal, the depressed, panicky, the insecure, and the tenuously compensated patient.

The partner is even more vulnerable than the symptomatic patient. The latter can "resist" treatment and slow down progress when the pace is too much for him. The spouse, however, is more helpless and is in trouble if she cannot handle her partner's rapid improvement. In clinical practice, we more often see emotional problems in the spouse when a couple improves rapidly; consequently, the partner's "ego" strength and the symbolic meaning that her spouse's symptom has for her must be assessed at least as carefully during the evaluation as the symptomatic patient's. Case 2 (p. 33) illustrates the traumatic potential for the partner of a rapid change in a previously stable sexual system.

The best insurance against adversive reactions to sex therapy is for the clinician to be alert to this possibility. One guards against adverse reactions by detecting and screening out seriously disturbed patients during the evaluation and clarifying the relationship between the sexual symptom and their illness. Some patients with sexual problems are so fragile that they are clearly not suitable candidates for sex therapy. They might be far better off with slower, more supportive, and less confrontive psychotherapeutic modalities which provide more time for the emergence and integration of newly acquired sexual responses. Those who are somewhat better integrated can be accepted for sex therapy and often do very well, provided the therapist is sensitive to and accommodates the special needs of such vulnerable patients. This might involve the judicious use of psychoactive medication, softening of the confrontations, and slowing the pace of treatment.

Beyond these general guidelines, I am not able to list specific criteria for the appropriateness and safety of sex therapy of patients with concomitant serious psychiatric problems. The judgment of whom to treat and how to deal with their vulnerability is largely intuitive and can best be made by a clinician who is experienced in treating difficult patients.

The *refusal to treat* a patient for his sexual difficulty carries its own special hazards. Depressed and schizophrenic patients and their partners may misinterpret the examiner's motivation for discouraging sex therapy (which is really caution and concern for their welfare) as a rejection or as evidence that they are not worthy of sexual gratification or capable of sexual adequacy. In dealing with emotionally troubled persons, exquisite sensitivity is required to ensure that the evaluation has a constructive impact on both partners. If a patient is deemed too fragile for sex therapy, this must be conveyed to him or her in a sensitive and helpful manner.

It is the responsibility of the clinician who undertakes the evaluation of sexual disorders to detect major psychiatric problems and to see to it that they are properly evaluated and treated.

The Analysis of the Psychological Causes

Up to this point, the data-gathering process has been concerned with detecting pseudosexual complaints, making the differential diagnosis between organic and psychogenic sexual complaints, and screening out sexual problems that are secondary to major psychiatric disorders, stress, or serious marital problems. It is of utmost importance to filter out these patients because they are not amenable to sex therapy and may require other kinds of intervention. In my experience, approximately one-half of the patients evaluated for sexual complaints fall into these categories.* The rest have true *psychosexual disorders* caused by specific conflicts about sex and ineffective interactions with their sexual partners; these patients are appropriate candidates for sex therapy.

For the clinician who is interested in treating psychosexual problems, the most fascinating aspect of evaluation begins at this juncture when the psychological elements of the difficulty are analyzed in detail for the purpose of formulating the precise individualized strategies of sex therapy.

The evaluation of a patient or couple for brief treatment poses special challenges. One cannot reconstruct and repair everything in sex therapy, but sometimes a well-planned, simple intervention can produce a significant difference in a complex system.

Getting the wife to accept her husband's use of erotica without feeling demeaned thereby, raising a husband's consciousness about his wife's legitimate need for clitoral stimulation, a little improvement in a couple's communication of their vulnerabilities to each other, a bit more confidence and trust — these are small changes, but they can sometimes make the difference between impotence and potency.

During the evaluation of a multifaceted sexual problem, which may involve the intrapsychic conflicts of both partners in the context of an unworkable sexual system, it is the examiner's task to seek out and select the most economic and efficient points of intervention. I have found it useful to conceptualize the psychological causes of the sexual dysfunctions as operating at different layers or levels of experience (Kaplan, 1979). The distinction between "superficial" and "deeper" determinants is crucial to the integrated treatment of psychosexual disorders. According to this model, *behavioral*

---

*This proportion will vary with the community from which the patients are drawn and with the source of referrals.

techniques are used to modify the causes that operate at an immediate and current level, while deeper intrapsychic conflicts and relationship problems are treated with *psychotherapeutic interventions*. When evaluating patients for sex therapy, both kinds of causes are analyzed separately.

5) WHAT ARE THE IMMEDIATE CAUSES?

The *immediate psychological causes or antecedents* of the sexual symptom are comprised of the patient's current ineffective sexual behavior and destructive interactions with his sexual partner and the obsessive thoughts and fearful or angry emotions which he experiences just prior to the occurrence of the sexual impairment. *These cognitive and emotional processes are specifically instrumental in disrupting the individual's erotic feelings and sexual reflexes and so produce the symptom in the here and now*; they constitute the final defenses, the ultimate instruments for the avoidance of the normal and joyful expression of sexuality. *Psychosexual symptoms may be conceptualized as the resultant of the interaction of these immediate psychobehavioral antecedents and the physiologic phase of the sexual response which they disrupt* (Kaplan, 1979).

The success of treatment depends on eliminating or modifying the immediate, currently operating psychobehavioral antecedents which are impairing the patient's functioning. This is the crucial ingredient for cure and the basic strategy of sex therapy. When therapy succeeds in modifying the immediate cause of the patient's symptom, his sexual functioning will improve no matter what other psychological or relationship problems remain. On the other hand, unless the immediate cause is eliminated, the sexual symptom will persist no matter what other benefits the patient gains from therapy.

Specific immediate causes are associated with each syndrome. However, every patient experiences these in highly individual ways. All premature ejaculators, for example, fail to register their erotic sensations premonitory to orgasm, which they need to do in order to learn control. However, this happens to one patient because he becomes obsessed with the fear that he will come too rapidly to please his partner, while the next is simply unaware of his anxiety level and grimly attempts to function no matter how tense he is. A third fails to perceive the sensations because his partner's increasing excitement triggers an erotic fantasy which impairs his concentration. The specific immediate psychological causes that are associated with each psychosexual dysfunction are briefly described in Chapter 10, where

TABLE 4
Information and Decisions in Evaluating
Patients for Sex Therapy

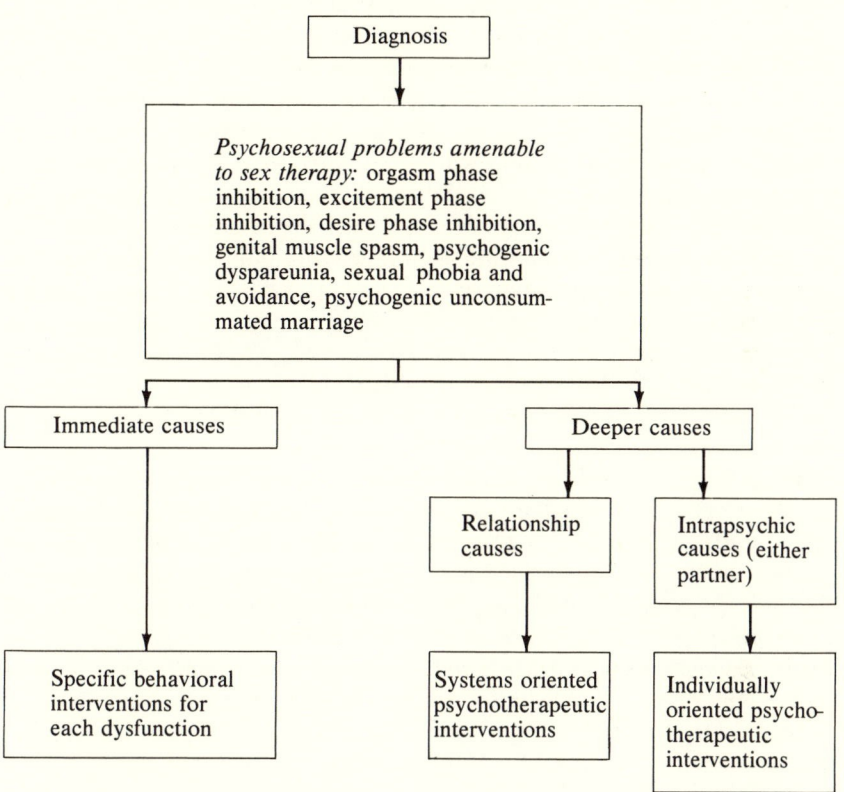

the clinical aspects and the causes of each syndrome are reviewed; this material is also summarized in Table 4.*

Because the immediate psychopathological mechanism of each dysfunction differs, highly specific behavioral strategies have been developed for every syndrome. For example, the "homework" assigned to anorgastic women is entirely different from the sequence of erotic tasks prescribed for

---

*Volumes I and II of *The New Sex Therapy* (Kaplan, 1974, 1979) contain more detailed descriptions of the causes and treatment of psychosexual disorders.

the couple whose complaint involves sexual avoidance. Anorgastic women usually learn to stimulate themselves to orgasm before the partner is involved in treatment, while the therapy of couples who avoid sex emphasizes their working together to improve their sexual interactions. But there are nuances of difference in each patient's immediate defenses and for maximum effectiveness the behavioral tasks should be specifically tailored to each patient's unique requirements (Kaplan, 1974, 1975, 1979).

For these reasons, the psychosexual evaluation places a great deal of emphasis on the analysis of the immediate and current causes of the patient's sexual symptom. Every patient who is evaluated for a sexual disorder must receive a detailed and complete analysis of his current sexual behavior, experience, and functioning which will reveal the immediate causes of his disability. It is simply impossible to understand and treat a psychosexual disorder without such an analysis.

6) ARE THERE "DEEPER" CAUSES? WHAT ARE THEY?

It is not a question of whether superficial *or* deeper causes are making the patient impotent. Immediate antecedents are instrumental in *all* psychosexual dysfunctions, but sometimes these are the sole and final cause of the psychosexual problem. In such cases, brief behavioral forms of intervention may succeed in curing the patient. In other cases, however, these immediate mechanisms operate in the service of deeper *neurotic needs to avoid sexual pleasure and adequacy.* When such deeper emotional dynamics are operative, they must also be assessed during the evaluation in order to prepare the therapist for the psychodynamic aspect of treatment, which is often the key to a successful outcome with these patients.

When deeper sexual conflicts are associated with the symptom or when asexuality plays a dynamic role in the relationship, the therapist can expect resistances to the structured erotic interactions comprising the behavioral aspects of sex therapy. The patient (or the partner) with an intrapsychic conflict may be ambivalent about giving up his sexual symptom and doing the "homework assignment," and/or the very success of treatment may increase his anxiety. It is at this point that psychotherapeutic interventions are used to work through the couple's resistances to behavioral modification.*

---

*The proportion of patients requiring extensive psychotherapeutic work along with the behavioral aspects of treatment will vary with the patient population. Dr. Harold Lief (Lief,

The following questions should be explored when the patient's sexual symptoms have deeper *emotional roots:*

- Does the patient have a neurotic conflict about sex?
- What are the psychodynamics?
- Is he guilty about sexual pleasure because of negative religious or cultural messages?
- Can these dynamics be "bypassed" by direct behavioral modification of the sexual symptom or should these deeper issues be confronted and resolved in treatment?
- What kind of resistances can be expected?
- How extensively must the person or the relationship change before sexual adequacy can be restored?

The deeper psychodynamic infrastructure of the psychosexual problem cannot be measured objectively or assessed by direct questioning because neurotic processes operate outside of the patient's conscious awareness. The patient does not understand that he is driven by his own unrecognized fears of sexual success, growing out of childhood problems long forgotten. He is consciously aware only of his current desperate wish for sexual adequacy. In fact, he may be puzzled by his compulsive and repetitive self-destructive behavior. He cannot tell you why he is seized by performance anxiety only when he is with the woman he desires most, the woman who is his ideal, while he is perfectly calm, cool, and functional when with a prostitute who does not interest him in the least. He has no insight into the fact that only the "ideal" woman arouses his oedipal conflicts, that intimacy with her reminds him of the mother he once longed for, loved, was afraid of, hated, struggled with, wanted to be close to, was desperately afraid to lose — feelings and memories that he buried long ago.

The deeper psychopathological dynamics must be *inferred* from the analysis of the problems the patient experiences in his current and past romantic relationships, while the family and psychosexual history will provide information about the *genesis* of the neurotic process.

1982) has estimated that in "30-40 percent of sexually dysfunctional patients improvement will occur without major psychodynamic changes." He divides the remaining 60 percent as follows: "Ten percent need individual therapy, 20 percent need marital therapy, setting aside sex therapy until much later, and 30 percent need a combination of sex and marital therapy." For the most part, this agrees with my experience, except that some patients receive a combination of sex and individual therapy, and approximately 20 percent of our patients require a combination of psychoactive medication and sex therapy.

The following clinical examples illustrate the integrated evaluation of superficial and deep causes when assessing patients for sexual therapy.

CASE 3: ANORGASMIA CAUSED BY SUPERFICIAL
CONSCIOUSLY RECOGNIZED ANXIETY ONLY

Roseanne is a 36-year-old married woman who has one child. Her chief complaint is anorgasmia. She has never in her life had an orgasm, although her husband tries to stimulate her and she has, on the advice of friends, tried to masturbate.

The analysis of her current sexual experience reveals that Roseanne enjoys sex only to a "certain point." At higher levels of erotic arousal she becomes tense and complains that she "cuts off" and obsessive thoughts enter her mind: "Is he getting tired? Will I ever come?" She loves her husband and is attracted to him. He is a sensitive and skilled lover and, until she reaches the point of inhibition, Roseanne feels pleasure and lubricates during lovemaking. Partner rejection and inadequate stimulation, two common "immediate" causes of anorgasmia, can be ruled out in this case.

Roseanne has no illness and is taking no drugs with sexual side-effects. Her periods are regular and her genitalia normal. Organic factors do not play a role in this case.

She is an attractive, vital woman who loves her husband and enjoys mothering her little girl. She did very well in school, is active in community affairs and projects, enjoys a rich social life and athletics, and is free of emotional and mental symptoms. Her problem is not secondary to another psychiatric disorder.

Her father is a successful banker in a small southern city. It is her impression that her mother and father love each other and their children as well. Roseanne has a warm relationship with her mother. This is an important diagnostic point. Many women with sexual difficulties have ambivalent relationships with their mothers, and a history of good mothering makes for a good prognosis. She loves her father but he seems somewhat distant and overly involved with his work. The parents are traditional and highly religious. Her grandfather and maternal uncle were Baptist ministers.

Coming from this conservative background, as a child and adolescent Roseanne received strongly negative messages about pleasure and sex: "Sex is sin," "sex is evil," "good women don't," and "don't indulge yourself." Roseanne was a very "good girl" who tried to please her parents and teachers. Although she functions well in other spheres of life, her early antisexual and antipleasure programming had taken its toll. Even now she tends to control her impulses, and is much more at ease "giving" than "receiving" pleasure.

The *immediate cause* of this patient's symptom is obsessive self-observation and self-judgment, which she experiences when she reaches moderately high levels of sexual arousal. Probing for deeper conflicts revealed *no evidence of neurotic conflict or of ambivalence towards her husband.* Her husband's evaluation indicated that he received *no conscious or unconscious gain from his wife's sexual problem.*

The deeper cause of this patient's sexual anxiety had *sociocultural* and *religious* roots which she consciously recognized.

This was clearly an appropriate case for sex therapy. Roseanne was assigned to a brief sex therapy group, where she could undergo a program of behaviorally oriented sexual therapy and also have the opportunity to see how other people of different sociocultural backgrounds and values deal with similar sexual problems. Treatment was designed to modify her obsessive defenses against sexual abandonment. Roseanne was instructed and encouraged to stimulate herself while distracted by erotic imagery. Her "new family," the group, supported every step of her sexual improvement, and her negative attitudes about sex and their origins were confronted.

When the group ended after 10 sessions, Roseanne was able to have orgasms by herself comfortably and without guilt. Then, she and her husband were seen together for three more sessions and Roseanne learned to have orgasms together with him. Treatment proceeded without notable resistance from either partner and they were both delighted by the successful outcome.

Unfortunately (or perhaps fortunately), such simple cases are no longer as common in our society as they were a decade ago. The next case, that of Peter, who suffers from increasingly severe impotence, presents the more complex clinical picture which is more common in large urban centers today. Such cases are more difficult to treat because the sexual symptom serves as a defense against deeper unconscious conflicts.

CASE 4: IMPOTENCE DYNAMICALLY RELATED TO SUCCESS ANXIETY

Peter, a 37-year-old physician who had been married for 11 years, complained of increasingly severe impotence over the past year. He was not a seriously disturbed person, but he did have a history of "ups and downs" in his career that is typical of patients that are governed by unconscious neurotic ambivalence about success (Kaplan, 1979). In his first year in medical school, he earned top grades, only to be placed on probation in his second year. He managed to graduate and his considerable charm and social skills got him a placement in a first-rate surgical residency program. However, he was asked to leave after his second year because he behaved provocatively with his attendings and was unreliable about his clinical responsibilities. He finished training at a less prestigious institution and then started a private practice in plastic surgery. After a very rocky beginning, his practice became successful and exceedingly profitable.

About this time, his tennis game (of which he was very proud — he was a ranked amateur player) deteriorated and he also began to experience erectile problems.

Although the patient denied illness or use of drugs with sexual side-effects, organic factors had to be ruled out because he remembered no morning or spontaneous erections and his potency problem appeared to be global. A sleep test was ordered and this revealed a nocturnal pattern of erections which were normal in frequency, architecture, and duration. This situational pattern of erectile impairment established psychogenicity.

The analysis of this couple's current behavior indicated that on an *immediate and current level,* Peter's erectile difficulty was being caused by his critical thoughts about his wife, which emerged whenever lovemaking was contemplated: "She is too anxious, she is too clumsy, she is too flat chested." These negative mental processes effectively interfered with the generation of erotic feeling. He then complicated the problem by compulsively trying to "perform" without being fully excited and obsessively worrying about his sexual performance. His critical attitude together with his increasing performance difficulties made his wife, Perl, who was already unsure of herself, increasingly apprehensive and "turned off"; this became another factor in the escalating cycle of Peter's impotence.

On a psychodynamic level it could be speculated that Peter was "trading off" career success for sexual failure. His history of "ups and downs" raised the questions:

- Did success in both spheres make him too anxious?
- Was the neurotic success anxiety dynamically related to his potency problem?
- Did it serve as a defense against the psychic dangers of "too much success?"

- Could this be bypassed?
- Would it need to be resolved?
- Was his obsessive concern about his sexual performance related to this issue?
- Why did he develop performance anxiety only when things were going well?

The *deeper roots* of Peter's ambivalence about being "a winner" could be traced to his family background. He was raised in a warm cohesive family which was dominated by a highly ambitious and competitive mother. Peter's father, a sweet gentle man, was not very successful in material terms, much to his wife's frustration and despair. Peter's mother was warm and supportive to the children, but exceedingly envious of her two sisters, who had married hard-driving, competitive men, who were much more successful than Peter's father. Maybe she didn't win the "family Olympics" (Friedman, 1981), but her sons would. Her approval of the boys was conditional on their excellence and outstanding performance. She was like a coach, drilling them for achievement. When they "failed," they were "out." When they succeeded, they were "in." Peter, the brighter of the two brothers, was her favorite. He was (unconsciously) torn between wishing to please his mother by "winning" and his guilt about besting his gentle father and his less gifted brother.

The following data elicited during the evaluation led to the decision to attempt to treat Peter's sexual problem directly (behaviorally) with brief treatment, despite his obvious psychological problems: 1) Peter was free of major psychopathology and his "ego strength" was basically sound. He had demonstrated adaptability and resiliency by conquering past problems. For example, after he "self-destructed" during his residency, he compensated and managed to develop an alternative pathway to career success. 2) His wife, Perl, while she had problems of her own, loved Peter, and, most important, had no psychic investment in her husband's potency problem. This meant that she could be counted on to cooperate fully in the therapeutic process. The couple was accepted for sex therapy, with the awareness that this would *not* be a simple case and that the behavioral measures would probably have to be buttressed by insight-fostering techniques.

Their response to treatment confirmed these hypotheses. The behavioral aspect of therapy was designed to reduce Peter's performance fears and his obsessive critical thoughts. The exercises consisted of non-demanding erotic stimulation, first of the non-genital parts of the body, then of the genitals. Peter was also encouraged to make liberal use of fantasy to distract him from his obsessive performance concerns. At the same time Perl was helped with her fears of pleasure and feelings of sexual inadequacy. She became a better and more exciting sexual partner, and no longer allowed Peter to "set her up" when he became anxious.

In the initial stages of treatment, Peter was ambivalent about and resisted doing the assigned tasks and undermined his wife's emerging sexual self-confidence. His success anxiety could not be bypassed so easily. Some measure of insight into and resolution of his ambivalence were necessary for treatment to move forward.

Peter was confronted with his success anxiety and its dynamic connection with his sexual symptom. He came to recognize his tendency to become anxious when he was successful and to sabotage his victories. Further, he gained insight into the early genesis of his neurotic fears of success. This psychotherapeutic work was done during the office sessions with Peter alone. He progressed rapidly and began to function better in his work. Sex therapy proceeded more smoothly to a successful conclusion. As a bonus, his tennis game improved!

Cases in which the sexual symptom has a dynamic connection with intrapsychic and/or interpersonal problems can often be treated successfully with sex therapy if these emotional issues are dealt with in treatment. However, the examiner must also be prepared for the more difficult patient with major sexual conflicts and more serious psychopathology, who is not amenable to brief treatment.

CASE 5: IMPOTENCE AND RETARDED EJACULATION CAUSED BY MAJOR
SEXUAL CONFLICT AND AMBIVALENCE TOWARDS WOMEN THAT ORIGINATED
FROM A PATHOLOGICAL RELATIONSHIP WITH HIS MOTHER

Jeff is a 34-year-old bachelor who complained of chronic and recurring impotence with his numerous sexual partners. He feels intense sexual desire and has good erections and ejaculates normally when he masturbates with sadistic fantasies; however, with a woman his erections are partial and insufficient for penetration. Moreover, he finds it extremely difficult to climax in the presence of a partner and has never ejaculated inside a woman's vagina. He attempts to heighten his sexual feelings by acting out mildly sadistic scenes (tying up his partners, anal penetration with his finger, mock rape scenes), but frequently even these measures do not work and he is completely impotent. After an unsuccessful attempt, Jeff becomes enraged and remains depressed and irritable for as long as a week.

Jeff is in good health and has no illnesses and is taking no medication which could account for his sexual symptom. He uses marijuana heavily,* but the *situational pattern* of his sexual symptom indicates that THC is not a cause of this problem and rules out organicity.

This patient's psychiatric history reveals longstanding serious emotional difficulties. He was subject to violent rages as a child and had a history of truancy. He has suffered from recurrent depressions, but denies suicidal ideas. As an adolescent he was referred for psychiatric treatment because of his violent arguments with his mother, which sometimes entailed physical combat. He also reported a single episode of exhibitionism. There is no special stress at this time, but Jeff's life is always in a turmoil.

Jeff is an accountant. Although he is very bright, he has been fired from several good jobs because of his violent arguments with his superiors and his surliness to clients. He feels demeaned by his profession; his life's ambition is to be an attorney. He has attempted to enter law school many times; however, he panics each time he tries to take his law boards and, although he knows his material exceedingly well, knowing more law than most lawyers, he has never been able to complete the examination. He is so envious of lawyers that, when he encounters one in the course of his work, he experiences violent murderous impulses.

Jeff's problems have their roots in his pathological family history. His father died when he was eight and he has no memory of him. His relationship with his mother was and still is ambivalent and stormy, with a strong sadomasochistic flavor. An aggressive, controlling woman, she demeaned Jeff, an only child, and gave him the message that he did not have the ability to become a successful attorney like her uncle, her hero.

As a child, Jeff alternately tried to please her and rebelled against her control. To this day, he is provocative and at the same time attempts to attain his mother's love and approval. He calls her, insults her, and then tells her about one of his new accomplishments. She punishes him by criticizing him and withholds positive comment.

When she insults him and fails to give him attention, as she invar-

---

*The heavy chronic use of THC has been implicated in male sexual dysfunctions (Kolodny, Jacobs, Masters, Toro, & Daughaday, 1972).

iably does, he becomes enraged and screams and vows never to speak to her again. He then lapses into a profound depression, which is similar in character to what he experiences after a frustrating sexual encounter. As soon as he feels better, he calls her again and the pattern is repeated.

Jeff has no intimate friends. When he does not have a date, he spends his weekends smoking pot, masturbating, and watching erotic tapes on his video player.

The analysis of Jeff's current sexual experiences reveals that his obsessive performance anxiety and "orgasm watching" are the *immediate causes* of his impotence and retarded ejaculation. From his history it may be inferred that on a *deeper level,* his obsessive sexual symptom serves to defend him from experiencing intolerable oedipal memories and impulses. His sexual inadequacy prevents him from being close to a woman and from giving her pleasure. He needs this distance because when he becomes intimate with a sexual partner he experiences the same violent ambivalence that he once felt and still feels towards his mother. To him, sex is not a natural sensous pleasure to which he feels entitled. It is not an experience of sharing and love, but an incestuous violent act, an act of vengeance and conquest. He can only achieve sexual release when he is alone, "safe" from the company of women, and when he bypasses his conflicts with sadistic imagery.

Because of the serious emotional problems revealed during Jeff's evaluation and clear evidence that his sexual symptom plays a central role in his neurosis, I could not anticipate a quick sex therapy cure and tried to prepare him for a difficult and lengthy course of reconstructive psychotherapy.

A neurotic person can acquire anxiety about sexual performance on a cultural basis or learn it by chance, entirely independent of his other problems. It cannot be automatically assumed that such patients are not amenable to sex therapy. The following case history illustrates this point.

CASE 6: A NEUROTIC COUPLE AMENABLE TO SEX THERAPY

Sy, a 37-year-old diamond dealer, called me repeatedly and obsessively until he could get an appointment for the evaluation of his premature ejaculation. For six years, he had been married to Sheila, age 32, who had been complaining bitterly about his lack of ejaculatory control. Sy's premature ejaculation was severe. He ejaculated upon entry or within one to three strokes. He had experienced the same difficulty with several partners before his marriage.

The couple had been seeing a marriage counselor for the past year and a half. When this failed to relieve the sexual symptom, Sheila announced that she was ready to leave and Sy panicked.

Sy was a healthy young man with a strong sex drive and no erectile difficulty. He had no illness and was taking no medication that could account for his symptom.

Sy was the product of a highly pathological family. He was the only son of two concentration camp survivors. He was born while his parents were in a detention camp shortly after liberation. The parents were ambivalent about his birth, about bringing a child into a cruel and destructive world. His mother was both overprotective and demanding and transmitted her many fears, her pessimism, and suspiciousness to the child. His father, a bitter and withdrawn man who worked exceedingly hard, ruled his family in a tyrannical manner. He shouted orders at the boy in his hardly intelligible English; if Sy did not obey instantly (he often could not understand what his father wanted), he would be punished severely. Sy did not remember hearing any discussion about sex in his house. His family was not religious and did not equate sex and sin.

Sy had nightmares as a child and did only fair work in school, despite his obvious intelligence. He bit his nails and developed a tick. He worried obsessively about everything, as he does to this day.

Sheila's background was no healthier than Sy's. Her mother was and still is a severe agoraphobic and one of her sisters had been hospitalized for what appeared to be a panic episode. The father assumed a central and caretaking role and Sheila adored and overidealized him. The whole family had been extensively psychoanalyzed. Sheila had a hysterical personality and suffered from multiple psychosomatic complaints. She had psychoanalytic explanations for everything. She lamented her lack of coital orgasms, to which she attributed most of her many problems. Before her marriage, Shelia had numerous sexual relationships. While these were erotically satisfying, they were always with men who were highly unsuitable and inappropriate for her.

In sum, the evaluation revealed that the husband and wife were both highly neurotic, that he had a longstanding, severely disabling sexual symptom, and that the outcome of this marriage depended on the result of treatment. Hardly a promising case for sex therapy!

However, this patient's premature ejaculation did not seem related to his other neurotic conflicts. A detailed analysis of this patient's behavior and mental processes was very instructive. As a child he had learned to focus on what was demanded of him and to ignore or suppress his own feelings and sensations, which would only have interfered with his compliance to his father's wishes. With this history, it is not surprising that Sy did not perceive when he was tense or feel the level of his sexual arousal. He was not in touch with his sensations — this was the *immediate cause* of his inadequate ejaculatory control. However, his psychosexual development was essentially normal and indicated that he was conflict free about sexual adequacy and pleasure.

On a *deeper level*, Sheila had the more serious problems. These took the form of ambivalence about commitment to the marriage. The example of her housebound, phobic, panic-stricken mother, who depended on her husband (Sheila's father) for literally everything, had created ambivalence in Sheila about becoming close to and dependent on a man. On the one hand she wanted her independence; on the other she longed to be taken care of by her father. Unconsciously she used her husband's symptom as a rationalization for keeping her distance. Nevertheless, her history of excellent premarital sexual experience with men to whom she was not committed indicated that she did not have an intrinsic sexual conflict; rather, her conflict was in the area of commitment. It was hoped that this problem could be bypassed in sex therapy, at least to extent of enlisting her cooperation.

On this basis, the couple was accepted for sex therapy.

The start-stop exercises were modified to help Sy get "in touch with" or recognize his anxious as well as erotic sensations. He was instructed to come *rapidly*. This paradoxical strategy diminished Sy's obsessive concern about "lasting" which was interfering with his focus on pleasure. He had to learn to recognize and accept good feelings in a general sense before he could do the "pause" technique successfully. He learned to "scale" his levels of tension and excitement. Sy followed the directions, enjoyed the exercises, and rapidly increased his ejaculatory control. Sheila was exceedingly cooperative in the early phases of treatment, but as Sy improved she blossomed out with an array of hysterical resistances. She forgot to take her birth control pills, could not manage the female superior position (although she is an excellent athlete), splashed ice cold water on Sy's genitals, and dreamed of running off with other men and "moonlighting."

She accepted my confrontation about her sabotaging Sy's progress, and with the aid of active psychotherapeutic interventions, which included interpretations of her underlying conflicts, we worked on her ambivalence about commitment to Sy and marriage. She came to understand the destructive influence that her parents' problems and her unresolved attachment to her father still had on her own life. Her dreams started to include Sy and he acquired ejaculatory control.

Naturally, this couple's multiple problems were not cured by sex therapy, although they felt much better about their improved sexual relationship. They were referred for insight-oriented treatment at the conclusion of sex therapy.

For the purposes of the evaluation, it is useful to think of the deeper sexual anxieties as deriving from *negative sociocultural attitudes* about sex or from *neurotic processes*. Actually, this distinction is a blurry one, as neurotic persons tend to use moral and ethical guilt in the service of their intrapsychic sexual conflicts. However, in general, "cultural" anxieties are less resistant to treatment than those with "neurotic" roots.

Cultural Indoctrination

Our Judaeo-Christian heritage has equated sex with sin for two thousand years. A child in our culture is programmed with this equation. He is lovingly encouraged by his family to develop physically, intellectually, socially, and artistically. However, his budding sexual feelings are labeled as bad. Sexual curiosity, play, and masturbation are all discouraged. In very religious homes, masturbation and erotic fantasies are explicitly strictly forbidden, but in more liberal families, where the antisexual indoctrination is more subtle, children can hardly escape the feeling that sexual pleasure is somehow "not quite nice." Most of us experience a "guilty conscience" when we violate the old taboos later in life, and for some persons, the messages are so strong, that they inhibit the natural flow of sexual expression.

Neurotic Processes

According to psychoanalytic theories, psychosexual symptoms serve as defense mechanisms against unconscious emotional conflict. It is for this reason that the rapid improvement of sexual functioning that is often seen in sex therapy sometimes mobilizes anxiety and resistance to treatment. Many psychoanalytically oriented authorities believe that adult sexual disabilities occur only in persons who have had difficulties with their parents and siblings as children and have never managed to resolve these completely. These individuals make parents out of their current sexual partners, with whom they act out their infantile scenarios.

Specific symptoms are attributed to problems that occur at different stages of development. It is assumed that if psychosexual development is disturbed before the *oedipal period* (before the fourth year), the person will not learn to trust or develop the capacity to relate with the intimacy that it takes to form normal romantic attachments later in life (Erikson, 1956, 1959; Kernberg, 1972, 1976; Masterson, 1972). Individuals with *pre-oedipal* problems continue to be emotionally needy and unreasonable as though they were children; they avoid or destroy romantic relationships by transferring these inappropriate attitudes to their adult partners (Kernberg, 1976).

Individuals who have not resolved their oedipal problems may never be satisfied with any partner because they have not given up their wish for the parent. Also, unconsciously they may regard adult sexuality as incestuous, sinful, and dangerous and avoid these hazards by becoming impotent or anorgasmic (Bieber, 1967 a, b; Fenichel, 1945; Freud, 1905, 1925; Mack & Semrad, 1967; Stekel, 1926, 1927). More specifically, according to psychoanalytic theory, boys, if they are to become healthy, sexually functional adults, must resolve their longing for their mothers and their rage at not getting their wish and at the same time form a loving identification with their fathers. Girls face the same dilemma and in addition must give up their "disappointment" at not having a penis. If they do not, they remain pathologically competitive with men and never achieve mature female sexual gratification (Abraham, 1949; Deutsch, 1944, 1945; Freud, 1925).

The "penis envy" component of the psychoanalytic position on women has been widely criticized as erroneous and culturally biased (Sherfey, 1966). For the purpose of evaluating and treating women for psychosexual disorders, it can be unequivocably stated that the old psychoanalytic assertion that clitoral eroticism and female assertiveness are pathological manifestations of "penis envy" simply has no basis in reality. However, the anger that grows out of competitive feelings with males does in some cases interfere with a woman's capacity for love and sexual pleasure.

Some clinicians have discarded the entire psychoanalytic theory of neurosis and sexual pathology because it is quite clear, first of all, that not all patients with sexual symptoms have oedipal problems. Some have normal family histories and have simply "learned" their sexual anxiety in other contexts. Also, many persons with obvious oedipal problems enjoy excellent sexual functioning and find their erotic experiences gratifying. However, many concepts that derive from psychoanalytic theory are very useful in the diagnosis and treatment of psychosexual disorders. These should be kept in mind when trying to make sense out of some patients' excessive sexual anxiety and the tenaciousness of their symptoms. In treatment there are many instances where a patient must gain insight into the childhood origins of his problems before the sexual symptoms can be cured. Frequently, however, insight per se is not followed by remission of the sexual symptom, and behavioral interventions are needed to bring this about.

For these reasons, I have used some theoretical constructs that derive from psychoanalytic theory (e.g., unconscious mental processes, oedipal conflict, ego strength, transference) in the discussion of the evaluation of the deeper intrapsychic dynamics operative in psychosexual disorders, but only when these seem applicable and useful in specific instances.

The metaphors of *"messages"* and *"scripts"* (Berne, 1961), which are derived from psychoanalytic theory, are often helpful for conceptualizing the deeper psychological forces that cause and maintain a patient's sexual symptoms. This level of interpretation is especially useful in brief treatment, because it makes sense to patients and is seldom threatening.

According to this concept, the "messages" about sex we receive as children, as well as the "roles" we are assigned within our families, shape our adult sexual destinies, though we are seldom aware of their existence. Children who are encouraged to be "sexual winners" develop healthy sexual attitudes, but those receiving destructive sexual messages and "loser" roles end up with sexual problems. In the course of treatment, the patient who is repetitively acting out his script of sexual inadequacy may not be able to give up his impotence to behavioral tactics until the old sexual messages are brought into conscious awareness and replaced by the therapist's new permissive and encouraging ones.

Traumatic Sexual Experiences

In a small but significant number of cases the deeper currents of a sexual problem involve sexual trauma. Hetero- and homosexual incest and other forms of sexual abuse can, in some cases, lead to serious disturbances in a child's sexual development. Some children react with terror and/or rage when they are seduced or assaulted, and these emotions become associated with sex thereafter. Others actually enjoy the experience and later develop defenses against sexual feelings out of motives of shame and guilt. Nor is the potential damage of sexual trauma limited to childhood. Some adult victims of heterosexual and homosexual rape develop a traumatic anxiety reaction which impairs their subsequent sexual functioning.

The examiner should look out for a history of sexual abuse because some sexually traumatized patients will not improve unless this material is openly discussed and worked through during treatment.

7) HOW SEVERE ARE THE CAUSES?

Since the emotional conflicts of patients with psychosexual problems range from very minor anxieties to major neurotic processes, the *severity* of the patient's underlying sexual anxiety is another important dimension to be assessed during the evaluation. It should be remembered that identical symptoms can be caused by minor sexual concerns and by major neurotic conflicts and relationship difficulties. Thus, the *diagnosis* is not indicative of the severity of the psychological cause.

The *content* of the conflict also gives no information on this issue. Some persons have mild oedipal problems which merely cause them to be drawn to (or counterphobically avoid) "motherly" lovers. For other patients, the unresolved attachment to the parent is so strong and the conflict about this so severe that they cannot function sexually at all.

Some persons' religious scruples give them a little twinge when they have sex or masturbate. Others, with the same religious upbringing, engage in obsessive self-torture for each bit of erotic pleasure they allow themselves.

Sexually disruptive anxiety can be characterized as "minor" when it can be consciously perceived and recognized by the individual and when the sexual disability serves no unconscious psychological purpose or defensive function. Roseanne (Case 3), for example, had a sexual dysfunction caused by minor psychological problems. Patients like Roseanne may have no other emotional difficulties, may be happy and function well in other areas of life, and may enjoy excellent marital relationships. Minor anxieties about sex can be acquired anytime during life.

Common minor anxieties that are associated with sexual dysfunctions have been described elsewhere (Barbach, 1975; Kaplan, 1974, 1979; Masters & Johnson, 1970). They include anxiety about sexual performance based on lack of experience and unrealistic expectations, as well as mild insecurity about ones' sexual abilities and attractiveness; both result in "spectatoring" and prevent sexual enjoyment. Overconcern with pleasing a partner, insensitivity to the partner's needs, and poor communication about sex are also frequently seen in this population. Mild, socioculturally induced attitudes of guilt and feelings that sex is "dirty" or "wrong" may be added to this list.

Patients may be aware of their trivial sexual anxieties or readily recognize these when they are pointed out in the course of treatment. Such patients do not become anxious as they improve and have an excellent prognosis with brief, behaviorally oriented sex therapy.

At the other end of this continuum are patients like Jeff (Case 5), who may have the same sexual symptoms but suffer from serious underlying sexual and emotional conflicts. Severely disturbed patients usually have difficulty functioning in nonsexual areas of life as well, and their romantic relationships are often pathological. Their sexual problems stem from profound neurotic processes, into which they typically have no insight. In fact, they will often resist recognizing these when confronted with them in therapy.

Such patients are clearly more difficult to treat. They become anxious and resistant as they improve and do not have as favorable a prognosis as the emotionally healthy patient who suffers only from isolated sexual problems caused by minor performance anxiety.

8) WHAT ARE THE RELATIONSHIP FACTORS?

Traditional wisdom once had it that sexual problems were always caused by intrapsychic conflicts about sex; consequently, in the past only the symptomatic patient was treated. No attempt was made to intervene in the couple's relationship directly, and most often the analyst did not even meet his patient's spouse. However, some patients obviously function well with partners with whom they are comfortable, while their sexuality deteriorates with those who upset them. It makes simple common sense that when a person tries to have sex with a castrating, demanding, or withholding partner or with someone who intimidates him, his sexual reflexes may not operate smoothly, even if he has no intrinsic sexual problems. One of Masters and Johnson's greatest contributions was to call our attention to the fact that the critical cause of a couple's sexual difficulty can be found in their inadequate sexual interactions. They went so far as to claim, "The couple is always the patient," by which they meant that both partners are *always* involved in the problem and treatment is *always* conjoint and *always* aimed at improving the couple's faulty sexual system (Masters & Johnson, 1970).

However, treating every sexual dysfunction as a relationship problem does not make sense either. Some patients are premature or anorgasmic with all of their many partners; clearly, in these cases the symptom does not arise out of difficulty in the current relationship. In my experience some sexual problems are obviously partner specific, while others have clear intrapsychic origins. In most cases, intrapsychic and dyadic elements interact to produce the sexual problem. This is not surprising as neurotic persons often experience interpersonal difficulties, which then take on a "life of their own" to disturb the sexual process.

The analysis of the couple's relationship system and the role that this plays in the sexual problem completes the psychosexual evaluation. The examiner must determine whether the couple's interactions are causing the sexual difficulty so that treatment should focus on improving the system or the symptomatic patient has an intrinsic problem that needs to be resolved by individual therapy. Most frequently, both factors play a role and the therapist must be prepared to shift the therapeutic emphasis as resistances arise, sometimes confronting partners with their destructive interactions and at other times working with the intrinsic anxieties of one or the other.

It is not the objective of the evaluation of couples for brief treatment to precisely sort out the dyadic and intrapsychic causes; rather, the goal is to devise the most effective strategy to cure the problem. Sometimes it is more practical to soften the partner's attitude a little, than to try to change the symptomatic patient's 50-year-old neurosis.

Is the Problem Partner Specific?

The *nature of the symptom* will not indicate whether the problem is caused by intrapsychic conflict or by relationship problems, because the physical effects of sexually disruptive anxiety are identical, whether it is evoked by a demanding or hostile lover or by internally generated performance anxiety experienced with all partners, even the most attractive and loving ones. Therefore, it is always important to determine *partner specificity* when evaluating a sexual problem. When an anorgastic woman consults you to become orgastic with her husband whom she loves, and her history reveals that she has never been able to climax with her previous lovers either, it is fair to assume that the problem does not reside in her current relationship. On the other hand, if a man is currently impotent with his wife, but has previously enjoyed good sexual functioning with her, the examiner should explore the possibility that the marital relationship plays a role in his dysfunction.

The patient described in the following case history had a sexual problem which probably would have surfaced with any partner. However, he met his wife at the age of 17 and had never had sex with anyone else. That partner pressure was not an etiologic factor in this case had to be inferred from other data.

CASE 7: PREMATURE EJACULATION WITHIN A LOVING RELATIONSHIP

Mel was a 56-year-old businessman with a lifelong history of premature ejaculation (PE). He had almost no control and had always ejaculated after one or two intravaginal thrusts. His sexual interest was high and he had never had erectile problems.

One and a half years earlier, moderate hypertension was discovered on a routine physical examination. Since that time the patient had been taking hydrodiuril 50 mg. O.D.* He had no other illness and was taking no other medication. He did not smoke and was a light social drinker. Medical factors did not have to be explored further in this case because the patient had no erectile problem and longstanding, primary PE is almost always psychogenic.

Although Mel was free of major psychopathology, he was a tense, hyperactive man. His personality style could be described as obsessive-compulsive and overly achievement oriented. But he was kind and charitable and much beloved by his relatives and friends.

Mildred was a good match for Mel. An attractive woman, she was extremely loving and supportive. Mildred had centered her life around her husband and children. Their relationship was excellent; both were sensitive, caring and mutually supportive to one another. They shared values and many interests, such as music, political activities and a deep involvement with their family. She enjoyed excellent physical and emotional health.

Mildred was sexually responsive and enjoyed having orgasms by clitoral stimulation. The couple had worked out a routine: First they engaged in foreplay. Then he brought her to orgasm by manual or oral stimulation. After she climaxed, he entered and ejaculated rapidly. Often, she would have a second orgasm on manual stimulation after that. Mildred was completely satisfied with this arrangement. However, she was glad to cooperate in sex therapy because she could see that improved ejaculatory control would be very important to Mel. She committed herself to sex therapy with the same zeal with which she took up golf, which she thought would be good for Mel's health.

The immediate cause of this patient's PE was his failure to register and savor the pleasurable erotic sensations in his genitals when he was inside his wife's vagina. Entering her was his ultimate fantasy and he became lost in the excitement. On a deeper level, Mel's strict

---

*Thiazides may cause erection problems but do not affect ejaculation.

antisexual upbringing played a role in his sexual anxiety. Too guilty to focus on his own pleasure, he was preoccupied with pleasing Mildred. In addition, the symptom was consistent with his pressured, competitive, hyper-responsible personality style. Mel took care of everyone and did everything in a hurry.

Mel's father became ill while he was still a boy. The family had to apply for welfare, which was anathema to them. At the age of 12, Mel began working and bringing home money to his mother and caring for his younger siblings. At a very early age, he assumed the role of head of the household. His mother was a devoutly religious woman who instilled in him the feeling that sex was sinful and "nice" women were not to be "used" sexually.

The analysis of Mildred's current sexual functioning and a review of her psychosexual development indicated that she was essentially free of sexual conflict. She was raised in a liberal and loving family and was very close to her mother, who spoke about sex with pleasure and treated the father with love and respect. It seemed that Mel's sexual improvement would pose no threat to Mildred; in fact, she truly loved making him happy and would welcome his attaining ejaculatory control for this reason.

And, in fact, during treatment all the resistances came from him. He scheduled frantic and hectic social and business activities which interfered with his "sexual homework" assignments. Mildred, on the other hand, did not resist consciously or unconsciously. On the contrary, she proved an invaluable therapeutic ally, and without her gentle and tireless cooperation and encouragement this case might not have reached the successful conclusion that it did.

Sometimes a previously well functioning person gets involved with a hostile, demanding, or unsuitable partner and is surprised that he loses his erections or does not experience erotic feelings with her. Such cases are so obviously due to partner pressure that no great diagnostic skills are required to detect this. The next case history illustrates the significance of partner pressure in the genesis of a sexual dysfunction in a more complex context. This case is typical of the many in which the *partner has a stake in sabotaging the symptomatic patient's sexuality.*

CASE 8: IMPOTENCE TRIGGERED BY A PARTNER-SPECIFIC PROBLEM

Victor K was a successful 50-year-old orthopedic surgeon whose chief complaint was impotence. At the time of the evaluation he had been separated for one year from his wife of 23 years.

The patient's erectile difficulty began five years ago, when severe marital problems began to surface. Before that time he had functioned well with his wife; before his marriage, he had been sexually active with several partners and never experienced any problems. He had had no extramarital experiences since his marriage. Before his erectile problems, the couple enjoyed intercourse three to four times a week. At those times, he would erect spontaneously when he approached his wife and also as he fondled her breasts and kissed her. He did not require physical stimulation of his penis in order to attain an erection.

Apart from sex, the patient's marriage had never been entirely satisfactory. Victor described his former wife as a compulsive woman with a history of anxiety, recurrent depression, and very stormy interpersonal relationships since her adolescence. He claimed that she had always been withholding and critical, frequently screaming and carrying on when she did not get her way. However, she was Victor's sexual ideal and, finding her very attractive, he tried to overlook her emotional difficulties and did his best to appease her.

Five years ago, the marital relationship deteriorated when Mrs. K refused to use the diaphragm she had been using for many years, suddenly claiming it was "too messy," and insisted that Victor wear condoms. I do not believe that this was a deliberate and conscious attempt on Mrs. K's part to make Victor impotent. She was probably simply once again acting out her diffuse anger; however, this time she chose the wrong vehicle. Although Victor was enraged, he tried to comply, but his penis would not cooperate. He experienced increasing erectile difficulty. Moreover, Mrs. K refused to stimuate his genitals manually or orally, claiming that this disgusted her, but at the same time was vociferously critical when he could not attain a spontaneous erection.

With the breakdown of their sexual relationship, Victor faced the failure of his marriage and the couple separated. After the separation Victor tried to have sex with several partners and experienced performance anxiety and impotence with them all, despite their support and encouragement. When he failed to achieve an instant erection, he became upset and abruptly left the bed. He avoided women with whom he had failed sexually, and since he had been impotent with all partners since his separation a year previous, he found himself in quite a dilemma. He had become increasingly upset and preoccupied about his sexual problem.

Recently, Victor had met a woman to whom he was very attracted. So far, he had managed to avoid sex with her, but the anticipation of yet another failure had heightened his obsessive concerns. He was afraid that his impotence would interfere with this new relationship and that he would never find happiness with a woman again.

Medical factors were ruled out because the patient had morning erections of sufficient quality for penetration and good spontaneous erections when there was no demand for performance. He had no signs or symptoms of illness and was taking no medication with sexual side-effects.

His psychiatric history was negative for emotional or mental disorders. He was extremely successful and assertive in his practice, had many friends, enjoyed athletic and social activities, and led a well-rounded and pleasure-filled life. He had an excellent relationship with his sons, aged 18 and 20.

Victor admired his father who was also a doctor. However, he did not have a close relationship with him because of the father's intense involvement in his work. His mother was a critical person who was hypochondriacal and full of complaints, especially about the father. Although he was her favorite, Victor expressed "disgust" with his mother for never enjoying anything fully, even to this day.

The evaluation thus revealed that on an *immediate level* Victor's impotence was due to intense performance anxiety and sexual avoidance. In the past, he had functioned well as long as his partner was reasonably accepting and responsive. His inability to please his wife and her sexual rejection apparently tapped into latent sexual insecurities, which had their origins in his childhood relationship with a seductive and complaining mother and an emotionally unavailable father. This patient's history of excellent functioning with a variety of partners for many years and the fact that the problem only surfaced after years of serious provocations and marital hostilities were important diagnostic points. The underlying causes were *mild* in the sense that it would probably be possible to restore his previous level of functioning with brief sex therapy and that extensive psychotherapeutic reconstruction would not be necessary.

The following treatment strategy was formulated: First an attempt would be made to reduce Victor's acute sexual anxiety with behavioral measures; then, when he was functional again, he would be confronted with his vulnerability to hostile women. It was also planned to make him aware that his choice of a wife had been self-destructive, and that it was in his power never to get involved in such a "castrating" relationship again.

The initial aspects of treatment focused on interrupting the self-perpetuating cycle of performance anxiety and on repairing his damaged self-esteem. The behavioral work with his partner consisted of the standard, non-demanding sensate focus exercises. In the office sessions, Victor was reassured that his needs for a loving and supportive partner were legitimate and normal. He was confronted with his tendency to choose demanding women and to then "knock himself out" trying to please them. He gained insight into the genesis of this neurotic pattern and determined never to try to make love to a rejecting woman again. He learned to assess his self-worth more realistically and to assert himself appropriately with his current partner. He became aware of his anxiety and anger when he was not able to satisfy a woman and the origins of these problems in his relationship with his mother were briefly discussed.

Few resistances emerged during treatment and it was not surprising that this patient began to function rapidly and well with his new partner, who was highly motivated to please him. She transmitted the message to Victor that he was "great," that he made her happy, while playing down the importance of his sexual performance.

On follow-up two years later, Victor was married to a different woman. She was a warm and cheerful person who adored him and the couple enjoyed an excellent sexual relationship.

What Systems Problem is Causing the Sexual Difficulty?

The dynamics of romantic relationships have been conceptualized in various ways.* I have found the following theoretical constructs useful in evaluating the dyadic aspects of psychosexual disorders.

Specific Problems in the Sexual Interaction

1) Inadequate sexual techniques and poor communication. Some loving couples who have all the ingredients of a good relationship experience sexual difficulty simply because their sexual interactions are inadequate. They may be inexperienced and have misconceptions about sex. He may not know how much foreplay she needs to become aroused. He may not understand about the importance of clitoral stimulation to female orgasm. She may not realize he likes oral sex. She may not understand that he is anxious about his performance and be ignorant about the male refractory period.

---

*These have been described in detail in *The New Sex Therapy* (Kaplan, 1974).

The couple may overemphasize orgasm to the detriment of sexual pleasure.

Such simple technical problems can escalate into serious sexual disabilities if the partners lack the communication skills and sex information to help themselves out of the downwardly spiraling sexual dilemma. If neither partner has an investment in or receives secondary gain from the sexual problem, the prognosis with brief sex therapy is excellent in such cases.

But the evaluator must be alert to the possibility that what may appear to be a simple communication and technical difficulty may, in fact, express deeper hostilities and anxieties which must be resolved in the course of psychosexual therapy if outcome is to be successful.

2) Incompatible sexual fantasies. The sex therapist seldom sees couples whose sexual fantasies are in synchrony because partners who are each other's sexual fantasy are usually extremely satisfied with their sex lives. But if sexual fantasies are not complementary—if she and he both want to be dominated, if he craves anal sex and she finds this abhorrent, if she is fat while his sexual ideal is thin, if she adores an active male and he is passive, if she loves romantic monogamy and he needs sexual variety—the sexual aspect of the relationship is in trouble, even if in other respects the spouses have an excellent and caring association.

Therapy cannot change the basic sexual fit between two people, but it can sometimes help work out acceptable compromises if the motivation is there. If two people really care about each other, they will accept and accommodate to each other's sexual desires. Even though they do not turn her on, she will learn to tolerate erotic videotapes some of the time, while he will occasionally take the time and effort to gently, romantically and slowly caress her, even though this would not be his first choice for erotic fun. The examiner must gain a clear understanding of each spouse's sexual fantasy structure within their total relationship, in order to help them work out effective compromises when the sexual fantasies of an otherwise happy couple are not complementary.

However, problems that result from a *true lack of sexual attraction between two people* may preclude successful sex therapy. If he simply is not her sexual ideal, there is not much that a therapist can do to change this. The same is true if one partner is in love with someone else who really is his sexual fantasy. In such cases, it is up to the examiner to confront the issue honestly and spare the couple the frustration of sexual therapy which is doomed to failure.

Neurotic Interactions

Deeper problems are often acted out in the bedroom. These dynamics must be recognized during the evaluation so they can be confronted, by-passed or resolved. If they are not, partner resistance is likely to jeopardize the success of treatment.

1) Power struggles. When partners have not resolved issues of how power, privileges and dominance are to be distributed between them, their lives may be marred by constant jockeying over control. These power struggles may play a crucial role in a couple's sexual problem. A good lover takes pleasure from giving pleasure. But if his wish is seen as a command in the context of a struggle for dominance, she is likely to withhold a desired caress or to give it so begrudgingly that she might as well not have bothered at all.

Harry and Harriet's relationship was characterized by bitter power struggles. In fact, their failure to resolve their battle for control ruined their sexual relationship and finally destroyed their marriage.

CASE 9: UNRESOLVED POWER STRUGGLE — TREATMENT FAILURE

Harry, a 53-year-old highly competitive and succesful real estate man, became impotent and developed difficulty ejaculating after 24 years of marriage. An analysis of this couple's sexual interaction revealed that this sensitive man was responding to Harriet's angry depression and her withholding and unresponsive attitude in bed. She made him feel that making love to him was one of her more unpleasant household duties. This made it impossible for him to function. It turned out that she was punishing him for forcing her to move to New York, which she hated, from the West Coast, which she loved.

In treatment she was confronted with the fact that she was sabotaging Harry's sexuality and destroying her marriage, but she simply could not accept his "winning" this major victory over her. She was too angry, too ambivalent and too rigid to want to soften her hostile sexual behavior and attitude. This case was a failure. Harry divorced Harriet and is now functioning well with his new wife, who does not engage him in power struggles.

2) Contractual problems. Relationships may be conceptualized as being governed by "contracts" which are verbalized or unspoken, consciously recognized or outside either partner's awareness (Sager, Kaplan, Grundlach, Kramer, Lenz, & Royce, 1972). These contractual issues involve areas of privilege and responsibility. Problems arise when one partner feels that he or she has been "giving" but not "getting" his/her fair share. For example, an attractive, charming woman, whose earnings at a job she disliked had supplemented her husband's meager income for many years, was also an excellent cook and kept their house immaculate. She lost her sexual desire for her handsome, kind husband, who was an excellent lover but rather aimless and immature. She was totally puzzled by this. Exploration of her deeper feelings revealed that unconsciously she felt "gypped" because he had not been fulfilling his part of the (unconscious) contract between them, namely, that she would be loving and giving, take responsibility for the house, and be totally committed to him, while he was to be the successful provider of material comfort, status, and security, a role which her father had played for her mother. She had never admitted her disappointment in this sweet, gentle man to herself, because she did not want to think of herself as a materialistic person.

Couples may enter into a relationship unconsciously assuming that the contract that operated between their parents will also govern their own lives together. Unless the other operates by the same rules, bitter anger and outrage may result, when a woman gives as much as her mother did, but does not receive the same compensations.

Since the deeper contractual issues frequently operate outside either partner's conscious awareness, the patient may be puzzled and distressed by her chronic rages and irritability about apparently trivial issues, while her husband is equally mystified and hurt. Unless they gain insight into the dynamics of their contracts, couples remain stuck in their self-defeating behavior and sex therapy will fail because the angry partner does not *want* to give the other sexual pleasure.

In Case 8, Victor's (unconscious) contract with his first wife went something like this: "I will take care of you. I will do everything for you. I will provide for you. I will put up with all your difficulties, but in exchange you, who are my sexual fantasy, must always be available for me. You will reassure me that you love me." When his wife stopped using her diaphragm, she unknowingly violated her marriage contract.

3) Parental transferences. Sometimes a couple's apparently irrational problems can be understood by evoking the psychoanalytic construct of parental transference. According to this highly useful metaphor, a spouse unconsciously transfers to the partner childish and unreasonable attitudes originally felt in relationship to a parent. Not surprisingly, this is destructive to the current sexual relationship. An example of this was seen in the history of Jeff (Case 5), who inappropriately transferred to his current sexual partners the intense ambivalence and frustration he felt towards his mother when he was a child.

4) Ambivalence about intimacy, commitment and romantic success. Ambivalence has destroyed innumerable relationships. Patients who are governed by such unconscious conflicts function well in the initial stages of a romantic relationship but unconsciously sabotage their sexuality when it gets "too good" or "too intimate." When they marry, such individuals often act out their anxiety about closeness by withdrawing sexually. Desire phase problems are especially likely to be associated with these kinds of conflicts.

The diagnosis of an intimacy and commitment problem can often be made by pinpointing the onset of the difficulty precisely. Has the patient's dysfunction existed since the beginning of the relationship or did the trouble develop when he was faced with a deeper commitment or a demand for greater intimacy?

A review of the patient's romantic relationships may also reveal intimacy and commitment problems. A pattern of excellent brief romances terminating because the patient becomes critical and loses his sexual desire as soon as his partner demands exclusivity and more of a commitment suggests that he has a problem with intimacy and that the cause of his sexual difficulty is not specific to the current relationship. Sometimes an intimacy problem can be dealt with in brief sex therapy. An example of this was seen in the case of Sy and Sheila (Case 6). In many cases, however, these problems are tenacious and require lengthier treatment.

Psychopathology of the Spouse

The relationship between sexual difficulties and various forms of psychopathology has been discussed in the foregoing section. However, the sexual and marital difficulties that may grow out of a partner's mental or emotional illness merit special mention. Persons afflicted with a serious psychiatric disorder may not have the capacity for healthy sex or for making a normal romantic attachment to the spouse. The "healthy" partner is often very unhappy in his marriage and is having sexual problems, but may be totally unaware that the real source of his misery is the spouse's psychiatric disorder. While this is clearly evident to the examiner in the initial minutes of the interview, many individuals, even when they are highly intelligent and sophisticated, deny the spouse's illness, preferring to blame externals or even themselves for the problem. It is threatening to admit one has married an emotionally disturbed person and even more upsetting to face the possibility that the partner's mental health may never improve substantially.

Sometimes a partner can integrate the fact of his spouse's psychiatric disorder when he is confronted with this. At other times this insight frees him to leave the marriage. Some couples where one of the partners has a serious psychiatric diagnosis can be treated successfully for a sexual dysfunction but only if they are really committed, and only if the healthy partner truly accepts the spouse's pathology and the spouse's illness fits his own emotional needs. This was illustrated in Case 1 about Jack and Jill S, who had an excellent relationship because Jack felt gratified by playing a protective "doctor" role which Jill needed and appreciated.

The examiner may face a difficult dilemma when the evaluation reveals that one spouse is emotionally disturbed; a sensitive assessment of the significance of this in the context of the couple's marital/sexual system is crucial for humane and effective management in these complex cases.

Incompatible marriage

There are deep and irreconcilable marital incompatibilities that defy all therapeutic interventions. Neither spouse may be disturbed, and each may have the capacity to be a good sexual and marital partner to others, but the emotional and personality *fit* between the couple is too poor for a successful marriage. Attempts to improve the sexual aspects of such a relationship will not alter that reality, and it makes no sense to accept these couples for sex therapy.

The recognition that relationship problems are of importance in the etiology of a sexual disorder raises questions about what to do:

- Are the couple's marital problems amenable to treatment?
- Can these be circumvented in the course of improving their sexual interaction (can the problem be kept out of the bedroom)? Or will the relationship system have to be restructured in order to cure the sexual symptoms?
- Is this couple committed and loving enough for the emotionally difficult task of working on their relationship? Or are their difficulties so severe as to preclude brief sex therapy?
- Should they be referred for marital therapy or would it be in their best interests to help them separate?

In general, it is my bias to err on the side of giving the relationship every possible chance. If the partner is unwittingly undermining the symptomatic patient's sexual adequacy, I will confront him in the hope that the crisis created by facing an impending loss of the relationship will help the partner who is doing the sabotaging to decide that he really does not want to lose his marriage. This is an excellent diagnostic tactic if the evaluation leaves doubt about the person's basic desire for and commitment to the relationship. Fortunately, this maneuver (though very hard on the therapist) often works to resolve a spouse's ambivalence about committing him/herself to the other and to mobilize constructive forces in the relationship.

A case of this kind was described in *Disorders of Sexual Desire* (Kaplan, 1979, p 111). Donald, a 74-year-old man, became impotent with his second wife, in part because of her hostile attitude towards him in bed. Confronted with the risk she was taking of losing her husband, she first became extremely angry at the therapist but gradually came to understand that she really wanted this man. She did have some legitimate gripes about the relationship, but she realized that she was being infantile and self-destructive in sabotaging Don's sexuality. She resolved her ambivalence towards the marriage and found more effective ways to assert herself. As she became a sensitive and giving sexual partner, Don's potency improved.

It does not always turn out that way. I confronted Harriet with the fact that her hostile behavior was having the effect of "castrating" Harry and that she was risking her marriage, but she was too angry to accept him on his terms. Sometimes the sabotaging partner is simply too ambivalent, too discouraged, too sadistic, or too sick to make the changes it would take to restore the symptomatic partner's failing sexuality. Or he or she may be looking for a way to end the marriage for *legitimate* reasons.

All that can be done in such a case is to make sure that the person clearly understands what it would take to restore the symptomatic patient's sexuality, as well as the consequences of her behavior. I feel it is the examiner's responsibility to see to it that she realizes that she may really lose her husband if she does not cooperate. Then she can make a conscious decision in that matter and not act self-destructively without awareness.

9) EVALUATING THE SINGLE PATIENT

The single patient with a psychosexual dysfunction presents a problem. Even if the patient's sexual symptom is not related to difficulties in his relationship, a cooperative partner is usually necessary for sex therapy. With the exception of female anorgasmia and some cases of vaginismus, where the initial phases of treatment can be conducted with the patient alone, the therapeutic sexual assignments that are a crucial ingredient in sex therapy require two persons working together.

The evaluation of the patient without a partner has two objectives. First the sexual dysfunction must be assessed in the same manner as if the patient were involved in a relationship. This will entail the differential diagnosis between organic and psychogenic disorders, as well as an analysis of the immediate and deeper psychodynamic causes of the problem. In addition, it is greatly to the patient's interest to make a precise assessment of the reasons for his lonely state.

Roughly half of the people on this planet are males and the other half are females. The single person's complaint that there are simply no suitable partners available is (except in the case of elderly women, where this is a real problem) a defenseive rationalization designed to conceal his anxiety, conflict, and feelings of hopelessness about finding a mate. People are unsuccessful in their quest for a romantic relationship for reasons that vary from simple shyness and lack of confidence about their sexual adequacy to deep-seated emotional problems of neurotic and psychotic origin. This diversity mirrors the wide causal spectrum of the psychosexual disorders themselves.

Treatment Alternatives

A reasonable disposition for the patient who has no partner at the time of the evaluation, but who does not suffer from a significant block in this area, is to present him with an accurate picture of the dynamics of his sexual problem, explain the treatment process and his prognosis to him, and suggest that he return for sex therapy when he has found a suitable companion. As an alternative to deferring treatment, some single patients do very well in *sexually oriented individual psychotherapy* and/or *group therapy*. Like couples sex therapy, these modalities employ a combination of behavioral assignments and psychotherapeutic exploration of resistances, but are modified to accommodate the patient's single status. For patients who do not have someone to join them in therapy, erotic and social tasks are devised which they can do alone and which will facilitate their making contact with potential partners. For patients who are found on evaluation to have significant neurotic problems with romantic relationships, it makes more sense to recommend lengthier, *psychodynamically oriented psychotherapy*, with sex therapy being postponed until later, after the patient has overcome his conflicts about relationships.

Finally, some clinicians feel that the use of *surrogate sexual partners* has a place in selected cases (Masters & Johnson, 1970). There are potential risks as well as benefits to this treatment strategy. For one, in our society it is hard to find and train emotionally healthy and constructive women willing to do this work, who also possess the sexual attractiveness, ethical standards, and psychological sophistication entailed in helping a person overcome his sexual anxieties. Also, for the patient there is a risk of contracting a sexually transmitted disease and for the doctor the potential for legal problems. And, even if the patient learns to function with his surrogate, one cannot always be sure that he will then be able to transfer his newfound capability to another partner.

Nevertheless, certain patients derive considerable benefits from working with surrogates which would be difficult, if not impossible, to duplicate with less controversial modalities. In my experience the judicious use of surrogates can be extremely helpful in treating men who phobically avoid sex (and suffer from secondary emotional problems because of this), ego-dystonic homosexuals who are panicked by heterosexual situations, and extremely anxious and obsessive men with erectile and ejaculation problems who cannot be convinced to try to seek partners of their own until they have been reassured about their sexual adequacy by successful experiences.

It is my practice to limit surrogate therapy to patients who meet these criteria, and I see little value in this modality — and, indeed, potential hazards — unless it is used concomitantly with psychotherapy. Only this combination affords the patient the opportunity to integrate his new sexual experiences and to confront and resolve the psychological barriers he has erected against sexual gratification and adequacy.

CHAPTER

2

THE

METHOD

Helen S. Kaplan, M.D., Ph.D.

I have found it useful to organize the evaluation into seven segments:

1) The chief complaint
2) The sexual status examination
3) Assessment of the medical status
4) Assessment of the psychiatric status
5) Family and psychosexual history
6) Evaluation of the relationship
7) Summation and recommendations*

1) THE CHIEF COMPLAINT

The examiner who has a basic understanding of sexual medicine and sexual psychology can obtain a great deal of valuable information about the medical and psychological aspects of the problem from a clear and detailed description of the patient's symptoms and of their onset and progression.

This portion of the evaluation will provide answers to the first two ques-

---

*Masters and Johnson have called the summation portion of their evaluation method the "round table discussion" (Masters & Johnson, 1970).

tions outlined in the preceding chapter: Does the patient's complaint represent a real sexual disorder? If so, what kind is it?

It is not always easy to obtain a clear picture of complaints in the area of sexuality. Persons who can describe their gastric or muscular symptoms precisely may not be able to muster equal clarity about their sexual experience. To the evaluator's question, "What's the problem?" an embarrassed patient may answer in generalities or explain his ideas of the causes of the problem instead of describing his symptoms clearly. This will not provide sufficient information for making a diagnosis. The evaluator needs to know precisely what the patient means by his complaint. When a patient complains that he is *impotent* does he mean that he cannot attain an erection, or that he loses it too easily? Or does he mean that his penis becomes only semi-hard, or is he really implying that he has lost his interest in sex?

The examiner must pursue this inquiry until he has defined the *physical parameters* of his patient's complaint, which provides the criteria for the correct diagnosis.

John is a 42-year-old businessman who has been married to Mary, age 35, for three years. John's first marriage lasted ten years and ended in divorce five years ago. This is Mary's first marriage.

The patient complains that he is impotent. He is embarrassed and vague about his symptom, stating, "I have a sexual problem — I am not functioning — "

What he means is that he often has difficulty attaining an erection when he tries to make love to Mary. On the occasions when he does get hard, he becomes flaccid as soon as he tries to penetrate. Further questioning reveals that his erections are not entirely firm, except for just a few seconds prior to ejaculation.

John's desire for sex is high and his orgastic sensations are normal. The quantity and quality of his ejaculations have not changed.

Now we know exactly what the physical aspects of the problem are. We have established for one that the complaint is a genuine sexual one. We also know that the diagnosis is impotence and that only the excitement phase of John's sexual response is impaired. In addition, we have learned the important fact that John sometimes has erections, which immediately suggests psychogenicity.

The History of the Chief Complaint

The history of the complaint refers to the onset of the symptom and its course and progression. A carefully done history of the sexual complaint can help with the differential diagnosis between organicity and psychogenicity and also narrow down the kind of disease or drug which may be causing the problem. Also, if the symptom is psychogenic, a detailed analysis of the emotional circumstances under which it first appeared can reveal specific psychological causes that would otherwise elude us. The details of the physical and emotional circumstances surrounding the onset of a difficulty are important for the assessment of both physical and psychological causes. The examiner must actively elicit these if they are not spontaneously offered.

Examiner: Was there ever a time when you had no problem with your erection?

John: Oh, sure'. Everything was okay until five years ago.

Examiner: Tell me exactly what happened the first time when you couldn't have an erection. When did it happen? How did it happen?

John: Before I was married, I never had any problem and I slept with two other girls. It never happened to me while I was married to my first wife, except once in a blue moon when I had a little too much to drink. After I was separated, I was at a party. This girl, this real beautiful girl, came on to me. We went to bed. I just couldn't do it. It really bugged me.

Examiner: Was that the first sexual experience you had after you moved out of your house?

John: Yes.

Examiner: How long had you been separated from your wife?

John: About three months.

Examiner: I would like to hear more about this. Were you drinking? How were you feeling? How did you feel when you both got undressed? What happened exactly? What were the physical conditions? Did you have privacy? How did she react? What was going on in your head? Did you feel guilty?

The history of the chief complaint has provided us with the following information: John's impotence was secondary. On the occasion of his first episode of erectile failure, he was in the midst of a major trauma. He had been depressed, moderately inebriated and afraid of being discovered, as the bedroom in which he attempted to have sex was in a strange house and did not have a lock. He was repelled by the woman's unpleasant odor, and for all these reasons, was highly ambivalent about wanting to have sex. But he felt it unmanly to refuse and tried to force himself to perform. When he failed, he became obsessive about his performance. (As it later turned out, obsessiveness is a characteristic of John's performance-oriented and perfectionistic personality style and is not confined to his sexuality.)

Since that time, he has had episodic and progressive problems with several partners. When he first met Mary, he functioned well with her. After they became engaged, he began to experience potency problems which have become progressively worse, to a point where successful intercourse is rare. Anticipating failure, the couple has developed an avoidance problem and attempt sex only once every two months or so. We also know that John's deeper psychological problems are not very profound, since he functioned well for over 20 years. It is hardly likely that a person will develop major psychological problems about sex after functioning well for a substantial period of time. Major sexual conflicts that have originated in childhood usually manifest themselves earlier, when a person first tries to become sexually active or committed to a serious relationship. Minor sexual problems and performance anxiety can, of course, also cause sexual inadequacies and these may be acquired at any time during life. For these reasons sexual problems that emerge late in life are usually organic or due to relatively minor psychological causes.

In sum, exploration of the chief complaint and its history has yielded some important pieces of information: 1) The onset was sudden; 2) it occurred within an emotionally traumatic setting; 3) the symptom is situational, which suggests but does not establish psychogenicity; 4) since he functioned well with many partners prior to the onset of his problem, we assume that he does not have profound sexual conflicts. However, the traumatic incident somehow tapped into old vulnerabilities which we do not understand. We also do not know at this point about Mary and her contribution to this problem.

2) THE SEXUAL STATUS EXAMINATION

The next step in the information-gathering process is to obtain a highly detailed description of the couple's current sexual experience. We have called this part of the interview the *sexual status examination*.* The sexual status examination is the closest we can get to actually observing the

---

*Sharon Nathan, Ph.D., suggested this term.

couple's sexual interaction and, in a sense, has an advantage over physical observation because it also gives us information about subjective experiences and mental processes.

Traditional psychiatric and psychoanalytically oriented evaluations do not pursue the patient's sexual experience in such fine detail. These diagnostic techniques focus more on illuminating the deeper psychological structure and the origin of such problems, which are inferred from historic material. The sexual status examination is essentially an analysis of the patient's current sexual behavior and entails a precise description of the antecedents and contingencies of his or her sexual symptom. This approach is similar to the behavioral analysis that is used by behavior therapists to assess their patient's symptoms and to plan treatment. However, the sexual status examination goes beyond analysis of behavior, because inferences regarding unconscious emotional conflict and hidden transactions between the partners are also made on the basis of the examination of the patient's current sexual functioning. This information is also essential for the medical evaluation of the sexual problem.

The sexual status examination serves to verify or to correct the diagnostic impression gained from the description and history of the chief complaint; in addition, it advances the exploration of the medical and psychological causes of the problem.

A detailed description of the patient's current sexual experience and an analysis of his sexual behavior and of the couple's erotic interaction is the best method for ruling out organic causes and for identifying the immediate and currently operating psychological antecedents of the sexual disorder. The sexual status examination is, therefore, the single most important diagnostic tool at the clinician's disposal.

> *Examiner:* When was the last time you two made love? Was it typical? Can you describe this to me in detail? I would like to have a "video" picture of what goes on when you two make love. I am interested in the experiences of both of you.
>
> *John:* We tried to make love last Saturday night. It was pretty typical. We got home from a party and went to bed. I kissed her and touched her and felt excited and started to get an erection. But I couldn't enter; I got soft.
>
> *Examiner:* Then what happened?
>
> *John:* Nothing. Mary got upset. We went to sleep.
>
> *Mary:* That's just what's been happening, doctor. He just doesn't function anymore. I can't stand it any longer.

The sexual examination is the equivalent of the physical examination in medicine. When trying to diagnose a medical illness, the examiner inspects and palpates and auscultates the patient's body until he has a mental image of the patient's internal physical anatomy and pathology. He notes irregularities such as rash, swollen lymph nodes, a tense abdomen, painful areas, a rapid pulse, and a solid sound where there should be a hollow one, which are all clues to underlying pathology. This information enables the physician to make inferences about the nature of the illness which underlies the patient's complaint. These impressions are confirmed and augmented by data from the medical history, the review of systems, and laboratory tests.

Similarly, in assessing a sexual problem, one tries to get a "feel" of the couple's experience until one has a mental image of their behavior and interactions, as well as of each lover's underlying emotional and mental experiences. All three phases of the sexual response — desire, excitement, and orgasm — are specifically "palpated." Inferences about the etiology of the disorder are based on this information and may then be augmented, tested, and confirmed by the patient's psychosexual history and by the special laboratory tests used in sexual medicine.

Few patients give the necessary details spontaneously. The examiner should be sensitive to the fact that in our society we are encouraged to maintain privacy about our sexual lives and few people are open about revealing their vulnerabilities in front of their mates. Therefore, patients need support and encouragement to get them to describe their sexual experiences in the detail which is needed for the evaluation. At the same time, the examiner must maintain control of the interview and must actively pursue relevant questions and confront patients whose embarrassment prevents them from giving sufficient information.

The evaluator should not move away from the examination of the sexual status until he has a sharply focused and highly detailed image of the couple's current sexual experience. This will include:

- their behavior as well as their feelings and thoughts;
- their interactions as well as their physical responses;
- what they do, how each one feels, how they react;
- how sensitive and responsive they are, how well they "read" each other, how well they communicate;
- at what point anxiety is evoked (if, in fact, anxiety is experienced), how they deal with this anxiety;
- what their fantasies are, how open or defensive they are about their fantasies, what evokes desire in him and in her;

- whether there are disappointments or anger, whether they are too performance-oriented;
- whether all physical intimacies lead to intercourse;
- whether they engage in self-defeating or sexually sabotaging behaviors;
- what their expectations are, whether they are realistic;
- how they deal with their sexual problems.

If there are any obscure areas, any "fuzziness," if the examiner does not have a crystal clear mental image of what goes on when this couple makes love, which phase of the sexual response cycle is impaired, and to what extent and under what circumstances this occurs, the sexual status examination should not be considered finished. More questions should be asked to bring the couple's physical responses and emotional experiences into clear focus.

John tells me that he frequently loses his erection just when he tries to penetrate.

Examiner: Does this always happen? What goes on in your head when it happens? Tell me about the last time you were successful. How was that different? What were you thinking about that time? Did you always worry about your performance? When did you start to observe yourself like that?

John starts to worry about losing his erection as soon as he thinks about making love. He experiences an additional "jolt" of fear when he knows that it is time to penetrate. He is apprehensive about Mary's angry disappointment if he should become flaccid or come too rapidly. He is overly concerned with pleasing her. When he ejaculates he feels intense physical pleasure, but is then immediately plagued by fears and doubts about whether Mary has enjoyed it. Mary does not reassure him. She is cold and withholding. When he fails to penetrate, she is silent and turns away.

Mary can masturbate to orgasm. She has enjoyed making love to John in the past, but she has lost her desire for him. She can no longer abandon herself to erotic pleasure and does not become aroused when he tries to kiss or caress her. She claims that this happens because she is afraid that he will lose or not attain an erection. She feels that he does not really enjoy making love to her and is doing this only out of a sense of duty. She claims that only coitus gratifies her and she no longer enjoys oral sex. When he loses his erection she feels anger and impatience. She does not want to stimulate his penis. Although she thinks that John is physically attractive, she is filled with angry and critical thoughts about him when he tries to make love to her.

They tell me that on a recent vacation they were successful twice. A detailed analysis of this experience revealed that at that time Mary felt much more loving and far less critical toward John than usual. The couple made love spontaneously in the afternoon. He came rapidly but she did not seem to mind and allowed him to give her an orgasm manually after he ejaculated. She felt more desire, less avoidance, less anger than she had for a long time.

She told me that she loved the luxurious resort where they went and, for once, their vacation was without his daughter. He was not preoccupied with his work. She felt that during this holiday he was more intimate and closer to her, and she definitely saw him as more attractive in this setting.

John seems to be very sensitive to Mary's responses and is deeply affected thereby. It appears that if he does not feel welcomed and accepted, he simply cannot function sexually. But I am not clear about the deeper dynamics of their system. Why is Mary so withholding? Is he setting her up? I continue questioning Mary.

Examiner: When did you last feel desire for John? Do you ever make love without feeling desire? Why do you think you feel less desire? Is he a good lover? Is there enough foreplay to arouse you? Do you like the way he approaches you? Do you lubricate? What annoys you about him? What used to arouse you? How long does it take you to become aroused? Do you think he can tell how excited you are? Do you tell him when there isn't enough foreplay, when you want more caressing? How do you feel when he loses his erections? Did you always get angry? Tell me about the thoughts that enter your head.

These detailed questions yield valuable information about the immediate causes of the problem and suggest possible points of intervention. There is nothing technically wrong with their lovemaking. True, he is somewhat too performance-oriented, but when she is in a giving mood he functions well. He is a considerate lover and likes to stimulate her to orgasm. But she has recently lost her desire for sex; she feels nothing but irritation and annoyance when she senses he wants to make love to her. She thinks he won't get hard, she anticipates that she will be called upon to make a tedious effort to stimulate him, that he is an anxious jerk.

John is extremely tense about making love to Mary. *If she does begin to get excited, he panics,* fearing that he will come too rapidly. *If she does not become excited*, he panics, fearing he is not pleasing her and he will lose his erection or will not be able to get an erection when it is time to penetrate.

Mary withholds encouragement and insists on having coital orgasms. She claims that she is not comfortable with clitoral stimulation, although in the past she had accepted this. John feels that a "real man" gives his wife an orgasm with his penis. Mary agrees. Clitoral stimulation is "second best." He likes erotic magazines and videotapes and uses these to masturbate, but he is guilty about using fantasy or erotica when he is with Mary. Mary taps into his guilt. She tells him using fantasy is "sick." She reveals that she feels anxious and annoyed when a man does not immediately become erect when he gets into bed with her, or if he loses his erection while he stimulates her. She is insecure, jealous of other women, jealous of erotica, angry at John. She is very sensitive to rejection. She thinks that if he "has to" use fantasy he is not attracted to her.

The process of obtaining descriptions of the couple's sexual interactions may also serve to begin the therapeutic process. Mary feels rejected. She really fears that John would be more potent with another woman. He is surprised to hear that. She is a beautiful woman and it has never occurred to him that she might feel rejected by him. They have never communicated about this issue. He immediately tries to reassure her. He is moved by her discomfort.

The process of improving communication between this couple has begun. She had no insight into his anxiety and his fears that he was not pleasing her. She is amazed to hear how tense and insecure he is. She wants to think of him as a strong, adequate male. As he describes his experience of doubt about his sexual adequacy, his eagerness to please her, she begins to glimpse his vulnerabilities and expresses compassion for him.

I briefly step into the therapist role and encourage their growing empathy and understanding, and giving to each other, even as I assess their responses and their capacity for insight and change.

I now have a clear picture of this couple's current pathological sexual interactions and of the immediate, currently operating psychological causes of the problem. *John suffers from sexual perform-*

ance anxiety which is heightened by Mary's demands for coitus and her passive-aggressive withholding of support.

John loses his erection if lovemaking is not rapid. At those times, he experiences obsessive fears of losing his erection; once he loses his erection, he considers lovemaking finished. He is too upset to try to relax and see if his erection will return. Mary's fantasy is for a sexually secure and strong man. She is turned off by his anxiety. She does not help him out. She withholds encouragement and also considers lovemaking finished if he loses his erection.

John is so agonized by his sexual insecurity that he is unable to focus on Mary's state of arousal and on her sexual needs. However, her desire is inhibited and she requires long foreplay in order to be receptive. He is plagued with fears of failure. Both need a great deal of reassurance. Both feel that he must keep his erection without losing it throughout the whole foreplay period, no matter how long this is. Both think that the use of fantasy is "wrong." If he should become flaccid, he feels like a failure and she feels rejected and angry and punishes him. The self-imposed pressure is terrific.

By now, he enters the sexual situation in a very tense state, anticipating failure, fearing that he will not please Mary. This sets her up. She enters the sexual situation in an angry state, hating his anxiety, anticipating frustration, anticipating that she will have to make love without pleasure. They do not reassure each other. They cannot. Each is too involved in his/her own pain and uncertainty to be generous to the other.

The analysis of John and Mary's sexual behavior has also revealed that John's impotence is situational. This establishes that the problem contains significant elements of psychogenicity and indicates that at least a piece of the problem is amenable to sexual therapy. Apparently, when he is in a low pressure situation, when Mary is more accepting and supportive, when he is allowed to come quickly, he has erections which are firm enough for penetration. Perhaps the sexual interaction can be restructured to allow him to function — but only if this also meets Mary's needs, only if she can get over her anger. I am a little concerned about the fact that he has *partial* erections which may (but not always) indicate that there are physical problems as well.

The *sexual status examination* is the best means of ascertaining if a sexual symptom fluctuates; it is, therefore, invaluable in differentiating organic from psychogenic problems. It is also the best and possibly only way in which to obtain information about the immediately operating psychological mechanisms that are impairing the patient's sexual reflexes. In addition, when the problem is psychogenic, inferences about the deeper underlying psychodynamic issues can also be drawn. In fact, in simpler cases, an experienced examiner has a fairly good concept of the etiology of the problem when he has completed the sexual status examination.

However, more data are needed. Even though I now have a clear "video picture" of this couple's sexual interaction and understand the immediate causes of John's impotence, I still do not understand the deeper roots of Mary's anger or of John's anxiety with women. I do not understand what psychopathological processes were set in motion by his traumatic rejection by his first wife five years earlier, which obviously precipitated his impotence. Nor do I know if John or Mary have other psychiatric problems.

The *chief complaint*, the *history of the chief complaint* and the *sexual status examination* must be pursued in detail for all patients. The next two parts of the evaluation, the *assessment of the medical status* and the *assessment of the psychiatric status*, should be administered, at least in their brief screening form, to all patients and their partners who are being evaluated for sexual difficulties. However, they do not need to be pursued in depth unless there is evidence of a significant medical or emotional disorder in either partner.

3) ASSESSMENT OF THE MEDICAL STATUS

Does the patient have an illness or is he taking a drug that could be causing the symptom? When the patient's sexual symptom is clearly situational or when a healthy young person is complaining of a sexual problem which carries a low medical risk, a brief review of the patient's health and drug use will serve to screen out possible organic factors. However, when the risks of organicity are substantial, the investigation of medical causes must be meticulously pursued. The information yielded by the first portions of the diagnostic interview provides the basis for substantial inferences regarding the differential diagnosis between organicity and psychogenicity. By the time we reach this stage, we have established whether the symptom fluctuates with emotional stress, and uncovered its onset and clinical course. We also know the diagnosis, which tells us whether there is a high

TABLE 5
Laboratory Tests and Examinations Used for Screening Medical Causes of Sexual Symptoms

FOR IMPOTENCE

1) nocturnal penile tumescence (NPT) monitor (global pattern of impotence)
2) serum testosterone (testosterone deficiency)
3) serum prolactin, LH, FSH (pituitary problems)
4) penile hemodynamics studies: penile blood pressure and penile blood flow (penile circulatory problems)*
5) two hour glucose tolerance test (diabetes)

FOR LOW LIBIDO

1) serum testosterone (testosterone deficiency)
2) serum prolactin, LH, FSH (pituitary problems)

FOR VAGINAL DRYNESS

1) estrogen level (estrogen deficiency)
2) microscopic study of vaginal smears (estrogen deficiency)

FOR:
COMPLAINTS ABOUT ABNORMAL GENITALIA,
INABILITY TO CONSUMMATE MARRIAGE (BOTH PARTNERS),
SEXUAL PAIN,
PRIMARY ANORGASMIA OF FEMALES, AND
PRIMARY IMPOTENCE

1) physical examination of the genitals (anatomical abnormalities, reproducible pain, pathological conditions of the genitalia)

---

*Normal results on these blood flow tests do not rule out arteriosclerotic changes in the small vessels of the penis.

or low risk of organicity. In other words, we have a good idea of what the probability is that the patient's sexual symptom is being caused by a drug or an illness. All patients, even those with a low risk of organicity, should be asked the following questions in order not to miss an unsuspected organic problem:

1) When did you have your last medical examination?
2) Do you have any illness or are you taking any drug at the present time?
3) Have you ever had any serious illnesses or surgical procedures in the past?
4) Do you smoke, use alcohol or any other substances?

5) For women: Are your menses normal, regular? Have you had any children? Were any problems associated with pregnancy, delivery, breast-feeding?
6) For men: Do you notice morning or nocturnal erections? Are they firm enough for penetration?
7) What sort of birth control methods do you use?

If the answers to these screening questions indicate that the patient has no illness and is not taking a drug with sexual side effects, further investigation of medical factors need not be pursued and the examiner can go on to investigate the psychological causes of the problem in greater detail. But patients do not pass through the medical screen if:

1) the patient's answers to the questions on the medical survey indicate he has an illness or is taking a drug with sexual side-effects;
2) the patient's symptom is not clearly situational; and/or
3) he has a high risk symptom.

In all of the above cases, the presence of a diagnosed illness or the signs and symptoms of a possible illness or the use of a drug that could be causing sexual difficulties is not ruled out, and questions about the patient's medical problems must, of course, be pursued in greater detail. If the patient reports that he has had any significant diseases or surgical procedures, their nature and extent and the kind of treatment he or she is receiving must be explored. If he is taking any drugs, the examiner inquires about doses. Since when have the drugs been taken? For what indications? Are there side-effects? If the patient answers in the affirmative about a history of illness or surgical procedure, these are likewise investigated in enough detail to make sure that they do not entail a type of disability or disease state which could be causing sexual problems. If signs of a possible medical problem such as diabetes or circulatory or endocrine disorders are revealed, these are pursued in greater detail. If the patient smokes tobacco, it is important to ascertain how much he smokes and whether his smoking is associated with circulatory problems. Similar considerations apply to the use of alcohol, cocaine, narcotics, or any other substances. The examiner must inquire how much of the substance is ingested and whether the patient notices any effects on his sexual response.

Sexual disorders have different sets of causes; therefore, the medical and drug history emphasizes different problems according to the diagnosis. The specific symptoms of different disease states and drugs are discussed in Section II on The Medical Aspects of Evaluation and also in

Chapter 10, which summarizes the medical and psychological evaluation of each psychosexual dysfunction.

The diagnostic interview serves as an effective screen which can rule out physical causes in many cases, for it makes no sense to subject all patients with sexual problems to the expense and stress of medical examinations. In most cases, the differential diagnosis is clear-cut, but if there is even the slightest question of an organic cause, the patient's medical status must be evaluated further.

For example, a 22-year-old college student who had recently become engaged presented himself with the complaint of impotence. His sexual functioning had been excellent until three months previously and he had been able to enjoy sex with several different partners. Occasionally he experienced impotence in a new relationship, but this was usually resolved rapidly, as soon as he became comfortable with his new partner. He had excellent morning erections which were undiminished in frequency and were sufficiently rigid for penetration. He also stated that, on the rare occasions when he masturbated, he experienced no difficulty with his erection. His appearance was fit and strong, and the medical screen revealed that he had no illness and was taking no drugs except marijuana on an occasional, recreational basis. A recent medical examination which he took as part of being admitted to the college lacrosse team revealed that he was in excellent health. Clearly, in this case, no further investigation of physical problems was necessary.

In contrast, a 54-year-old man complained of impotence of one year's duration. His history revealed that he had had temporary bouts of erectile dysfunction throughout his life, when he was with a new partner or when he was under stress in relation to his business. These episodes never lasted for more than two or three weeks. The analysis of his current sexual functioning revealed that he had stopped having morning erections about a year and a half previously. He had tried to masturbate and was able to ejaculate but only with a flaccid penis. His libido was unimpaired, and he continued to have pleasurable orgasms. The patient said he had been feeling somewhat tired, which he attributed to stress, but the annual physical examination that his company required was entirely normal. His medical survey did not reveal the presence of any known illness. He was taking no drugs and showed no signs and symptoms of any known illness. However, the global nature of his erectile problem, occurring in a setting of emotional stability with the same partner after a long period of good functioning, raised the suspicion that an organic process might be involved. Before he could be considered for psychological treatment, this patient had to undergo nocturnal penile tumescence monitoring to rule out an occult physical problem.

Or, we might consider the case of the 28-year-old, recently divorced woman, who presented herself with a complaint of never having had an orgasm in her life. The sexual history revealed that she had a very stormy relationship with her husband and that sex was never pleasant with him. She had never tried to masturbate and came from a strict Irish Catholic background in which she was taught that it was wrong and sinful to have "impure" thoughts or to engage in sex for other than procreational purposes. The patient's menses were normal. She suffered from no known illnesses and had no signs and symptoms of a physical disorder. Her routine gynecological checkup one year earlier was reported as normal. She did not drink excessively and did not smoke. In this case, a trial of sex therapy was considered a legitimate diagnostic procedure because the risk of missing organic causes in an otherwise healthy, young anorgasmic woman is exceedingly low.

However, another 28-year-old patient who was married for one year presented with a similar complaint of anorgasmia and sexual avoidance. An analysis of her sexual functioning revealed that she always experienced pain on intercourse. She did not use tampons, nor has she ever had a gynecological evaluation because she avoids these with a phobic intensity. This patient could not be treated until she was examined in order to rule out a painful gynecological condition or a physical obstruction of her vagina (e.g., an imperforate hymen), which could certainly be causing sexual avoidance and contributing to her anorgasmia.

A Situational Pattern

It has already been stated that the most important piece of information in differentiating organic from psychogenic disorders is whether the patient experiences the difficulty at all times or only under certain circumstances. When a sexual symptom has a psychological cause, it is apt to show a situational or fluctuating pattern of impairment and the patient will have trouble only in emotionally threatening situations. Patients whose impairment is caused by organic factors, on the other hand, will experience their disability each time they try to have sex, irrespective of the emotional meaning of the situation. The detailed analysis of the couple's or patient's current sexual experience, which was described in the previous section, is the most effective means of ascertaining whether the patient's sexual functioning fluctuates. However, the interview is not foolproof in this respect because the patient does not always know whether his or her sexual symptom is situational or global. He may fail to notice the circumstances under which he is unable to function, or he may suppress this knowledge because it is too threatening.

In some cases, the sexual partner can supply vital information on this point. The wife may know whether her husband, who is impotent when he tries to make love to her, has erections while he is asleep, and the existence of good nocturnal erections confirms a physically intact erectile apparatus and obviates the necessity for more elaborate diagnostic procedures. But when the patient's description of his symptom is equivocal, behavioral and physiological techniques are available which will augment the diagnostic interview.

Tests of Function

Diagnostic behavioral assignments can be devised in some clinical situations which create erotic situations that are less emotionally stressful to a patient than the typical lovemaking experience in which he has difficulty. We have called these "probe sigs."

For impotent patients, a test of masturbation, which often does not entail as much performance anxiety as sex with a partner does, can be helpful. Naturally, this is not a practical measure if masturbation is anathema to him; nor is it foolproof. Very anxious patients may have performance anxiety even when they masturbate. For anorgastic women, self-stimulation with a vibrator, when they are alone and without an "audience," can sometimes be used for this purpose. Again, only positive results are definitive.

Patients whose libido is inhibited with their partner may be able to feel erotic sensations when they fantasize, view or read erotic material. Patients with retarded ejaculation may be able to ejaculate while they are distracted from their customary "orgasm watching" by erotic visual material. Severely retarded ejaculators are advised to sleep with condoms which will catch their nocturnal emissions. And, for those patients where this is appropriate, a change to a different, more skillful, reassuring or desirable partner, or one with whom the patient feels less conflict or ambivalence, may establish the differential diagnosis between organic and psychogenic sexual disabilities.

It has already been mentioned that in some cases it makes sense to use a trial of sex therapy as a diagnostic procedure. This is appropriate only when there is virtually no risk of missing an underlying illness requiring prompt medical attention.

Physical Assessment Procedures

Some special diagnostic procedures are available which can be used to determine whether impotence, female dyspareunia, and vaginal obstructions are situational or global. Unfortunately, no comparable physiological tests have been developed to document the situational pattern of orgasm and desire phase disorders.

Nocturnal Penile Tumescence Monitoring

For *impotent patients* who recall no spontaneous AM, nocturnal or masturbatory erections, the NPT (nocturnal penile tumescence) monitor is an ingenious diagnostic device which can often settle the question of whether the erectile problem is situational. As in all tests of functioning, normal findings are the most valuable and *a normal sleep record rules out organic causes.* An *abnormal sleep record* indicates only that there is a *likelihood* that the patient's difficulty has an organic cause, but gives no information about the nature of this. NPT monitoring is discussed by Melman and Leiter in Chapter 8 and also in Chapter 10.

Physical Examination of the Genitalia

Some sex therapists conduct a physical examination of all patients for research and medical information and also as an opportunity for sex education and therapy. Masters and Johnson always examine both partners in their efforts to collect research data. Hartman and Fithian (1972) and Zussman and Zussman (1976) have described conjoint examinations where both partners are examined in each other's presence. The examining doctor takes the opportunity to show them each other's genital organs and discusses their functioning in a nonthreatening, matter-of-fact, supportive manner.

Undoubtedly, there are benefits to be gained from such procedures in some clinical situations, but in my experience the physical examination of the genitals and reproductive organs is necessary or useful only for patients who have specific complaints that can be clarified by such an inspection.

The physical examination of the genital and reproductive organs is essential in the differential diagnosis of complaints about sexual pain (dyspareunia), vaginal dryness, unconsummated marriage and vaginismus. Examinations are especially revealing, of course, when the patient *always* experiences these symptoms. If the examiner can penetrate the vagina with the speculum or palpate the genitals without evoking pain, the situational nature of the complaint is thereby rapidly established. The physical inspection of the genitalia of totally anorgasmic women who have never had a gynecologic exam is also indicated.

There are some special situations where a *conjoint examination* may be useful. For example, in one case it was a relief for the husband to see that his "failure" to penetrate his wife was caused by the spastic closing of her vagina and there was nothing wrong with his penis. The examination was also helpful in overcoming his fears of injuring a woman, as he could see the examiner's finger enter his wife's vagina without doing any damage. The emotions and thoughts evoked by these procedures were immediately available for therapeutic intervention.

The conjoint examination of the genitals of an anxious male who is obsessed with doubts about their size may reassure both him and his wife about their normalcy. Also, an examination by an encouraging physician in the presence of her husband can help a woman work through her fears that her genitals are unattractive.

Nevertheless, such procedures are not necessary for the accurate evaluation or effective treatment of most patients with psychosexual complaints and we do them only when there are specific reasons (Kaplan & Moodie, in press). It is my practice to conduct a physical examination when there is a question about the anatomy or the functioning of a patient's genitals that could rapidly be resolved by a physical examination. Without such an inspection, it may not be possible to tell whether a patient is merely obsessed or delusional or whether, in fact, there is a real physical abnormality. Most men who are concerned about the size or shape of their genitals turn out on examination to be anatomically normal. However, there are some men with the same complaints who are found to suffer from micropenis, chordee, hypospadias, or another of the rare physical abnormalities of the penis.

I have examined a woman who claimed that she did not have a clitoris — I was surprised to find that she really did not have one.* But most of the women I have examined because they complained about abnormal genitals were perfectly normal anatomically. Reassurance has, of course, much more validity when it comes after a proper physical examination.

---

*She had a congenital abnormality which involved an incomplete fusion of the midline structures with consequent failure of the anlagen of the clitoris to fuse.

Laboratory Tests

Some examiners make it a practice to order certain laboratory tests to narrow down possible organic causes and screen out those patients who will need more intensive medical, gynecological, and urological evaluations. Thus, for example, it is my practice to order screening testosterone LH, FSH and prolactin levels for patients who complain of (globally) low sexual desire. Penile circulation using a Doppler device and penile blood pressure studies are ordered for patients where subtle circulatory problems are suspected from the diagnostic interview. Table 5 summarizes the tests that can be used for screening and also lists the complaints which can be screened by a simple examination of the genital organs. The indications for these procedures and the information they yield are discussed in Chapter 10.

Mary has no physical problems and is taking no medication which could account for her complaints. Her menses are normal and she uses an IUD for contraception. In her case, the brief medical review is all that is necessary to rule out medical problems.

But John is diabetic. His illness was diagnosed 10 years ago. For the past year, he has been in the care of an excellent physician who has seen to it that John's glucose level is kept under tight control and that his nutrition is good. Before that John had neglected his health and had sustained some diabetic damage in the form of eye problems and some peripheral neuropathy evidenced by numbness in his legs. This, together with some doubts left by the interview about the short duration of John's erections and their partial rigidity, suggests the advisability of NPT monitoring to insure that we are not missing an organic element in his impotence.

The results of the NPT studies (which were conducted with a portable monitor) demonstrate that John's diabetes has not damaged his erectile mechanism, at least to the extent of precluding normal intercourse. During NPT monitoring his erections were within normal limits in architecture, amplitude, and duration.*

The NPT monitor yielded the following important information:

---

*John had three erections on the first night and four on the second. They lasted from ten to 18 minutes. The average increase in circumference at the tip was 2.0 cm, at the base 2.8 cm. The increases during sleep were *greater* than those attained during a masturbatory baseline which John reported as only "7" on a scale of 0–10, sufficient for penetration.

1) It established that John's erectile problem was situational and that he had erections sufficient for normal sexual intercourse.
2) No further medical tests or examinations had to be conducted in this case.
3) The symptom could be accounted for by psychological factors.
4) The goals for sex therapy could be set high, i.e., the restoration of his previous level of potency.

These excellent results were shared with the couple, who were much encouraged by this. It was now appropriate to proceed with the investigation of the psychological causes in greater detail.

4) ASSESSMENT OF THE PSYCHIATRIC STATUS

The examiner needs to determine if the sexual symptom is secondary to a psychiatric problem. It is not practical or necessary to conduct a complete psychiatric evaluation on all patients who seek help for their sexual problems. The skillful and experienced examiner can often make astute judgments about a patient's or a couple's psychiatric status on the basis of his observations of and interactions with them. He can infer whether there is any underlying thinking disorder by observing their appearance, speech, and demeanor, and by listening with his "third ear" to their descriptions of their sexual problem. He can learn a great deal about them by the way they relate to the examiner and each other and the feelings they evoke in him are the most sensitive diagnostic sensors at his disposal. By the time the patient and his partner have described their chief complaint and their current sexual interactions, the examiner often has a very good notion about whether either has an emotional or mental disorder severe enough to preclude sexual therapy and/or require psychiatric treatment, and it will usually be clear by this time whether the patient's sexual symptom is secondary to another psychiatric diagnosis.

For example, the *compulsive* patient will answer questions in such minute detail that the examiner begins to feel impatient. He may come in with a written list of complaints or have previously prepared a letter detailing historical information. Moreover, the examiner experiences firsthand the compulsive's need to control, his rigidity, lack of sensitivity, and tightly reined hostility, which may have repelled his sexual partner.

The *obsessive* questions the doctor anxiously, is overly concerned about his symptom and worries about the examiner's credentials. He is likely to drive the receptionist to distraction with anxious queries. He has read everything there is to read about his problem and may have tried a whole gamut of treatments, ranging from psychoanalysis to hypnosis. He fears that his problems are unique and that the prognosis is hopeless. He is in desperate need of reassurance. At the end of the interview, he will find yet another question: "If we have just one more minute, doctor, I would like to ask . . . " When the examiner finds himself being excessively reassuring and fighting a feeling of running over the scheduled time, chances are that he is dealing with an obsessive patient and that the very obsessiveness is creating the sexual difficulty for the patient.

Passive-aggressive patients are lovely, compliant and pseudo-cooperative. They answer all questions and assume complete responsibility and blame for the sexual problem. "It's all my fault. She's a perfectly wonderful woman." They are ready to do "anything" to keep the partner from leaving and to improve their sex life. But their hostility emerges in subtle ways. They withhold a comforting hand or gesture when the partner sobs out her story in despair. They "forget" to bring the money for your fee. They simply cannot arrange a suitable hour for the subsequent visit. They subtly undermine the examiner and the partner — and their own sexual happiness as well.

Some clinicians have an almost uncanny ability to draw correct inferences about a person's psychiatric status on the basis of a brief contact, without a formal diagnostic psychiatric interview, but even the most gifted examiner can be wrong. The patient with a latent psychiatric problem can sometimes appear very normal and can fool even the most astute clinician. Therefore, even when a patient and his partner seem to be mentally healthy, the following questions should be asked of all potential participants in sex therapy to screen out those with significant psychopathology:

1) Have you ever suffered from an emotional or mental illness or from substance abuse?
2) Have you ever had psychiatric or psychological treatment?
3) Have you ever been hospitalized for an emotional or mental disorder? Have you ever taken psychoactive drugs (tranquilizers, antidepressants or sleeping pills)?

Also, since undiagnosed depression and panic disorder are often associated with sexual complaints, all patients are specifically asked:

4) Have you ever been depressed?
5) Do you have any phobias? Have you ever had a panic attack?

A brief review of each partner's functioning in the work, social and family areas will also yield a measure of mental and emotional status.

If the patient relates to you in a pleasant, sensitive manner, if his story makes sense, if he is gentle and appropriate with his partner, if he tells you that he enjoys his work and has a successful position and good friends, and if his answers to the questions about his mental health indicate that he has never had a psychiatric symptom or treatment, the psychiatric status need not be pursued further and serious psychopathology has been ruled out. But if any of the questions are answered affirmatively or if the examiner senses that the patient may be suffering from an undiagnosed or unsuspected mental or emotional disorder, a complete mental status examination should be conducted.*

If the patient has been in psychotherapy, I always ask him why he sought treatment and what he learned from this. Answers are often revealing about the patient's degree of insight and his capacity to benefit from treatment. If the patient is currently in treatment, it should be determined whether he is seeking sex therapy for constructive motives, which is often the case, or as a resistance to his ongoing therapy, for it is not uncommon for patients who are confronting painful issues in their analysis to try to avoid these by seeking a "quick sex therapy cure."

Sometimes, valuable information about a patient's deeper sexual conflict can be gained by asking him or the couple directly what they think the meaning of their sexual symptom is or what psychic function it might serve. However, these tend to operate beyond a person's awareness and often, of course, the patients are mystified or have erroneous notions about their problem. But sometimes, especially if the patient has previously been in psychotherapy or if he is particularly insightful he can give quite an accurate diagnosis and explanation of the genesis and the dynamics of the problem.

The question arose during the evaluation of whether John's impotence could be secondary to depression, since he seemed mildly depressed during the interview and had been depressed at the time of his divorce when he initially experienced erectile problems. This raised the question, which to treat first? Should I prescribe antidepressants

---

*It is beyond the scope of this volume to describe the mental status examination. The reader is referred to psychiatric texts for information on this topic (Mackinnon & Michels, 1971; Kaplan, Freedman, & Sadock, 1980; Strayhorn, 1982).

and see if his impotence improves or recommend sex therapy and re-evaluate his mood after he functions better?

This question was resolved by a more detailed examination of the pattern of John's affective status. It turned out that he did not experience mood swings or spontaneous depressions. There was no family history of depressions. He did tend to react with a mild depressive mood to frustration, but these depressive reactions had *not* interfered with his sexual response before his divorce. This information, together with the clear evidence of performance anxiety and partner demand to account for his potency problem, suggested that John's psychogenic impotence was primary and that his depressed mood was a *reaction to* his sexual problem and to the danger this posed to his valued relationship with Mary.

I decided not to treat John's depression but to reevaluate his mood at a later point in treatment.

Sexual phobia had to be ruled out because Mary had developed a pattern of sexual avoidance. A brief psychiatric history was obtained, during which she was questioned closely about and denied any phobias or panic attacks. There was no family history of phobic anxiety or conditions which sometimes mask this disorder, such as alcoholism, agoraphobia, and an isolated life pattern. It was speculated that Mary's avoidance of sex was motivated by her anger at John and her disappointment in their sex life, rather than by irrational fears of sex.

5) FAMILY AND PSYCHOSEXUAL HISTORY

- What are the deeper psychological causes?
- What are their origins?

A psychosexual and family history provides insight into the deeper causes of the patient's problem and may reveal their cultural and/or neurotic origins. This portion of the interview will indicate whether the patient's problem is simply due to performance anxiety or has deeper emotional roots. For patients with simple psychosexual dysfunctions, this consists of a brief "thumbnail" sketch of his family background and of the landmarks of his sexual development. In more complex cases, where significant intrapsychic and relationship problems are suspected, this area is investigated more extensively.

I ask all patients:

- What was the composition of your family?
- What were your parents' occupations?
- How did they get along?
- How did you get along with your father (your mother, your siblings)?
- Were you a "good" boy/girl?
- What kind of person is your mother (your father, your siblings)?
- What was your family's attitude toward sex?

A patient's relationships with his parents and siblings and the role he played in the family are important determinants of his adult sexuality and play a crucial part in the psychodynamics and origins of many sexual problems. The key to a patient's sexual anxiety may be a destructive relationship with his parents and siblings and the conflict-laden role he played within his family.

For example, many women with orgasm and arousal difficulty have a history of having had a covertly competitive relationship with their mother. A little girl needs her mother to be conflict free about her daughter's becoming an attractive and sexually successful woman. If mother is threatened, her daughter's sexual development may become stunted. The same is true for males. A warm, emotionally available, encouraging father is extremely rare in the history of homosexual men and men with severe sexual anxieties and conflicts. Seductive parents can also distort a child's sexual development, by placing her into a conflict she does not have the maturity to handle. The little girl who adores the excessive attentions of her flirtatious father is placed into an unfair competition with her mother, whom she also loves and needs.

A pathological attachment to the parent of the opposite gender and negative feelings for the other may reveal unresolved "oedipal" problems. Was the male patient overly involved with his mother? Was she intrusive and controlling? Was his father competitive with him? Does he still have problems with authority figures?

Similarly, understanding the female patient's relationship with her father and mother may provide the key to her sexual problem. Is she too close to her father? Does she overidealize him? Or is she too critical of him? Is she jealous of mother? Did her mother get in the way of her closeness with father? Did mother flirt with her dates?

The family of origin's cultural and religious attitudes are probed to detect culturally determined sexual guilt and conflicts. Highly religious families and deeply conservative families may place a heavy emphasis on controlling a child's emerging sexuality. This can be a factor in later sexual problems. However, there are sexually normal individuals in all segments of society and the examiner really needs to understand how the patient has been *affected* by any early antisexual conditioning he may have received. The family attitudes about masturbation and premarital sex are good indicators of the "message," and the patient's reaction to this is a clue to its impact. Did he masturbate despite dire warnings? Was he able to enjoy this? Was he guilty? Did he abstain altogether? Did he have sex before marriage?

Sexually destructive messages frequently found among patients with sexual problems include: "Sex is not nice." "It is wrong." "It is sinful." "Your genitals, body, feelings, erections, secretions, etc. are disgusting." "Masturbation is dangerous to your health." "It will drain you." "It will make you impotent." "Sexual thoughts are wrong, sinful, and you will be punished for them." "Nice girls don't." "Don't do that to a nice girl." "Men are only after one thing." "You are not attractive." "No one will want you."

A family silence about sex can also be a powerful message which may translate into: "S-e-x is so bad we don't even talk about it."

I always ask straight out: "What sort of sexual message did you receive when you were growing up?" Patients invariably understand what I mean.

The construct of "sexual messages" is so important in understanding the psychopathology of sexual disorders and so useful in their treatment that the evaluation of a psychosexual problem should not be considered complete until the examiner understands the sexual programming of each partner.

If the messages the patient received were constructive and healthy, the examiner need not probe further into this area. However, if the message was destructive and if it appears that it is still operative, this issue must be explored further.

Next, all patients are briefly queried about the landmarks of their sexual development to insure that no sexual events of significance, such as incest or rape, are missed. And the age at which the patient's sexual development began to deviate from its normal course provides a clue as to the severity of the emotional problem. The patient whose psychosexual development was normal until adult life has a better prognosis than a patient who already showed signs of sexual difficulty and conflict during childhood. Thus, for example, the woman who felt normal erotic curiosity as a child, masturbated to orgasm when she was a teenager, became aroused on foreplay during her dating years, but developed sexual avoidance after her marriage when she began to have coitus has a far better prognosis in treatment than the woman with the same symptom who never masturbated as a child, does not remember having erotic feeling, and never experienced arousal and pleasure with men during her adolescence.

I ask all patients: Tell me about your sexual development:

1) Did you ever have sexual feelings as a child?
2) When did you start to masturbate? How do you masturbate? What were your fantasies?
3) What happened in adolescence? Did you feel attractive? Were you popular? Did you have any sexual feelings? Did you kiss? Did you pet? When did you first have intercourse? What was it like?
4) What was your sex life before marriage? During marriage? Between marriages? At menopause?
5) Did you ever experience a sexual trauma, such as rape or incest?

Only when it seems appropriate from the answers to the foregoing questions is the sexual history pursued in greater depth during the initial interview.

Finally, the examiner tries to get a sense about the pattern and quality of the patient's romantic relationships. Important issues for planning treatment and predicting outcome involve: whether he has the capacity for normal love, whether he can handle love or if he becomes obsessive, whether he masochistically and repetitively becomes involved with destructive partners, and whether he keeps setting himself up for rejection.

The examiner asks: I'd like to know about your romantic relationships:

- Were you ever in love?
- What happened?
- What usually happens to your love relationships?
- What kinds of persons do you become involved with?
- Do you get rejected or do you usually do the rejecting?
- How do you handle this?
- Is there a pattern?

It is not necessary or appropriate to do an exhaustive sexual and family history during every evaluation. The investigation of these important issues should be selective so that the diagnostic interview does not become unnecessarily lengthy. If the questions reveal that the patient came from a normal, nurturing family and that his psychosexual history was essentially normal, and if he seems to have a normal capacity for love, then his sexual problems probably have their roots in minor anxieties. In such cases, these issues need not be probed further during the initial interview, as they are probably not important in the etiology of the problem and are not likely to emerge during treatment.

However, the inquiry into development must be comprehensive enough to detect crucial developmental issues. If the patient received destructive messages and if his role in his family was pathological, these factors are likely to be important in the dynamics of his sexual problem, and this is noted for more detailed exploration in future therapy sessions.

Both John and Mary underwent an essentially normal sexual development. John masturbated as a youngster, using fantasies about girls who had aroused him in real life. He was attractive, athletic and popular as an adolescent. He dated extensively and became aroused by petting. He had his first intercourse at the age of 18 on the girl's initiative. He had successful sexual experiences with several partners before his first marriage. He had no sexual difficulty and no extramarital sex during his first marriage. His unfortunate sexual experience right after his separation ushered in a period of impotence with several partners. With Mary, who was then extremely seductive and supportive, John had his first successful postmarital sexual experience.

Mary remembered feeling somewhat guilty about her sexual curiosity and sensations as a youngster. She started to masturbate to orgasm when she was 20, after she stopped attending church. As an adolescent she was not popular and felt unattractive. She hardly dated in high school. In college, she began to attract men and became aroused on kissing and petting. She had several successful sexual relationships before her marriage to John at the age of 27.

John's family never discussed sex, but nonverbally transmitted a traditional American upper-middle-class sexual message: "The man is in charge, and sex is his responsibility. A real man produces and performs." For John, sex has many elements of an athletic competition: "You score, you win, you lose." He was very attracted to women and, although charming and easy with them in the social situations, was ambivalent underneath and did not trust them. He saw them as demanding and destructively critical. Later on in therapy, when John's mistrust of Mary and his overconcern about "performing" for her was dealt with, it emerged that these attitudes derived from John's relationship with his mother.

John was raised in an affluent, socially prominent family. His father was distant and preoccupied. His mother was described as cold, perfectionistic, demanding, very beautiful, and accomplished. She was an elitist and had very high expectations of herself and her family, and was extremely critical of John and his father as well. John adored his mother. To this day he carries her picture in his wallet, which he showed to me during our initial interview. He had tried very hard to please her, getting good grades in school, attending an ivy league college, joining a top fraternity, excelling in athletic competitions, taking pains with his appearance, espousing all the values which he thought would please her. But he felt that he had never been able to meet her high standards or win her approval. He still feels that his mother preferred his sisters. In his family men were second-rate citizens. She died of cancer when he was 19.

Mary was raised in a poor family, dominated by her ambitious mother. Her father, who had been a clerk, was pressured by the mother to open his own drugstore. Both parents worked very hard in the family business throughout the patient's developing years. The family was religious and Mary attended parochial schools.

In Mary's family also, women were the dominant force. The mother taught her two daughters that their mission in life was to marry "winners" — strong, ambitious, successful men who would raise their station in life. She gave the impression that she had married beneath her, but was obsessed with the wish that her daughters do better than she did. Mary's older sister, who was extremely beautiful, took her mother's message to heart and married a successful junk dealer who was extremely generous to her. She was considered the family star. Mary was encouraged to take care of her appearance, develop her female charms, but to keep herself "pure," all in the service of finding a rich, successful husband. Mary was very close to her mother and also close to, but highly competitive with, her more attractive sister. Her father was totally absorbed with and controlled by the mother and the children played secondary roles in his life.

The family attitudes about sex were nonchalant and practical. Mary's message about sex from her church was "Don't do it," and from her mother, "Use it to get a successful man. Sex is a tool, not a pleasure."

The family and psychosexual histories of John and Mary have given us the following information: We know that neither partner has a very *severe* intrinsic sexual problem, because they both functioned well with other partners under the right circumstances. Also, their early sexual developments were essentially normal and their problems surfaced later on in life.

But this was not a case of simple performance anxiety on John's part. Clearly there were some elements of a "mother transference" in John's reactions towards Mary. That was why her sexual demands held such terror for him. Also, rejection by his first wife tapped into some latent problems and vulnerabilities which are somehow related to his mother, but this is not yet entirely clear. However, I had enough information for the purposes of the evaluation and the detailed exploration of these issues could be deferred until later.

Similar considerations apply to the assessment of the deeper roots of Mary's sexual avoidance. There certainly was a reality basis for her anger at John. She was truly disappointed because he was detached, not intimate, anxious and insecure as a lover — not at all the skillful and romantic man of her dreams. But there was more to it than that. Clearly, Mary was overreacting and this was somehow connected with her mother's messages to her and with her competition with her sister. However, I had enough information about her to make a treatment decision; it was all right to wait for the details of Mary's psychodynamics and their origins to emerge later on during the treatment process.

6) EVALUATION OF THE RELATIONSHIP

Is the couple's faulty system causing the problem? The examiner has obtained a clear view of the couple's sexual interactions from the sexual status part of the examination. This part of the interview is designed to detect and analyze deeper difficulties in the couple's relationship system and to determine what part, if any, these play in the symptomatic patient's sexual problem.

The examiner can surmise a great deal about the partners' relationship, their feelings for each other, their degree of intimacy, and their hidden struggles and ambivalences by *observing* their interplay during the initial part of the interview and by noting the *feelings they evoke in the examiner*.

It feels good to be in the presence of a loving, mutually supportive, caring couple and the examiner can sense that no serious problems exist between them, while disharmonious spouses transmit their tensions. When one is dominant or excessively critical of the other, when one tries to draw the examiner into his or her side in the struggle against the other, the examiner sometimes feels a little internal signal of discomfort. Sometimes one evokes sympathy or annoyance. The husband's manipulations may shift the examiner's feelings towards the wife, or her carping, complaining, demanding attitude may evoke protective feelings for him. The examiner must, of course, guard against "taking sides," but he should not try to suppress these evoked feelings. They are the most sensitive diagnostic tools at his disposal, often far more valuable than the direct questions. The skilled clinician is open to these evoked sensations and feelings, treasures them, and learns to make good use of them in the diagnostic and the thera-peutic process.

The *observation* of the partners' interaction can also provide important clues about the dynamics of their relationship. Some are sensitive, consid-erate, and supportive and show this by their eye contact, body movement, and the way they talk to and about each other. If one becomes anxious dur-ing the interview, the other is quick to reassure and support and the exam-iner can surmise that this couple will cooperate and help each other in therapy. Others will reveal their *ambivalences, anger and power strug-gles* by the bitter way they describe their difficulties. They may stalk by each other as they enter the room, sit facing away from each other, inter-rupt each other, try to gain the examiner's attention, dominate the inter-view, criticize, attack, diminish, threaten. When one gets anxious, the other will sit there and let the other "stew," coldly withholding reassurance.

The quality of the couple's *communication*, an important diagnostic is-sue, should be apparent from observing and talking with them. Inade-quate communication in the sexual area is often an immediate cause of sexual failure and can often be improved rapidly in sex therapy. But even when the examiner observes that the partners communicate sensitively and beautifully in the office about the nonsexual aspects of life, they may still be completely dumb, deaf, and blind to each other in the area of sexu-ality.

Intimacy is another important but sometimes elusive quality in a rela-tionship which may have important implications for the sexual problem. Many women "turn off" if the only time the husband is interested in their feelings is as a prelude to intercourse. This, too, can best be assessed by observing and noting the couple's sensitivity and empathy with each other and with the examiner.

Their manner of presenting the complaint may reveal a great deal about the couple's underlying dynamics. For example, the husband takes all the blame: "All your problems are *my fault*. I was very immature, chauvinistic and selfish, but I'm really trying to improve. I will do anything." His wife nods in cold agreement, withholding any encouragement or support. This may be a sample of the couple's sadomasochistic interactions, which could be an etiologic factor in their sexual problem. If he is as anxious, obses-sive, and self-demeaning and she is as withholding and cold in bed as in your office, it is not surprising if he develops a sexual dysfunction.

Another husband makes a frontal assault: "Our problem is all her fault. I had to drag her in here. She never would do anything about it if I didn't push her. She doesn't care how sexually frustrated I am and she never lets anything go. She won't admit anything. I tried my best. I do everything for her. I even support my mother-in-law but she is so damned stubborn and critical. Maybe *you* can do something with her, doctor." The wife agrees in silent misery or returns with a volley of counteraccusations. Is it any wonder that she has lost her desire for him?

Thus, the examiner is witness to power struggles and evidences of contractual disappointment and mutual transferences which may be acted out in the bedroom as well as in the office.

The following questions can help rule out or detect the presence of etiologically important problems in the couple's system:

1) What are the reality circumstances of the relationship? Are you married, divorced, separated, single, living together, dating, seeing each other exclusively? How long have you known each other? How did you meet?
2) Do you love each other?

The second question sometimes startles them and may create a mini crisis, but that's not bad. It sets the stage for the serious work of therapy, transmitting the message that this is not a social hour. Patients must be prepared to deal with highly charged and sometimes painful emotional material.

In addition to confronting the couple, the question about love is very important for planning treatment and estimating prognosis. Patients do not have to be in love to benefit from sex therapy, but it certainly helps. Love is a powerful therapeutic ally. Sexual dysfunctions that can be cured in the context of a loving relationship might not be helped in an ambivalent one. The quality of the touch, the kiss, the lover's subtle attitude — all are important ingredients in a couple's sexual interaction and also influence the outcome of sex therapy. The totally committed, loving partner identifies with the therapist's efforts to enhance the symptomatic patient's sexuality and often proves helpful far beyond following the specific directions. Case 7 about Mel and Mildred illustrates such partner support. However, an ambivalent partner tends to sabotage sex therapy. He may not follow the directions or, if he does, manage to do them in a destructive manner. His ambivalence, as well as his tendency to sabotage treatment, are heightened as the partner improves. Case 6 about Sy and Sheila illustrates such partner resistance.

The examiner continues with questions about the relationship:

3) How committed are you to this relationship? How would you characterize your relationship? Are you committed to improving your sex lives?

4) How much do you fight? What about? How do you handle your arguments?
5) How good is the fit between the couple?

The area of complementarity or fit between two people is difficult to assess with specific questions. In a good relationship, there is a good deal of complementarity in the personal and sexual proclivities of both partners. He is dominant in the area where she is passive. When she takes the lead, he follows happily. They share and identify with each other's interests.

When nothing in the couple's system suggests that relationship difficulties contribute to the sexual symptom and when they can clearly cooperate with one another in therapy, the examiner has all the information he needs about their relationship for the purpose of planning treatment. However, when the interactions between them seem to contain the seeds of the sexual difficulty, the system must be explored in greater detail, as this is often the critical factor in the cause and the cure of a sexual problem.

Sometimes, when I am still unclear about a couple's relationship after questions and observations, I will arrange a "viewing" of a typical interaction between them:

Examiner: I'd like to know just what happens when John gets home at night.

Mary: Well, I hear the key in the door and I get very excited and happy that he's coming home. But by the time I get to the front door, his nose is deeply buried in the mail, he brushes me off with a kiss on my forehead, goes upstairs and takes a shower, gets into his jeans, and disappears. He hides out in the garden or in the basement to work. I really don't see him until dinner, in about an hour and a half. By that time, I've had two drinks and I'm good and angry at him.

John: When I drive home, I'm already nervous. I'm afraid she's going to want sex. I'm afraid I'm not going to be able to perform and that she will have a fit. When I open the door, I feel her overwhelm me, rushing over to me, demanding sexually. I feel like splitting.

The interaction between them has become crystal clear. John has intense performance anxiety and withdraws. She is "turned off" by his anxiety, feels rejected by his withdrawal and becomes angry and demanding. She becomes the "critical mother" and this intensifies his problem. It is a vicious cycle.

John loves Mary. She is his sexual fantasy and he really wants to make their marriage work, but he is closed off and cannot express his angry nor his loving feelings. Mary is more ambivalent about her commitment to John and their marriage, but it is quite clear that on balance she has no intention of losing her handsome, rich husband.

John cannot tell Mary that she intimidates him by her demanding and critical attitude, that he is anxious about performing, that he needs her to be more supportive, welcoming, and accepting, that he is embarrassed about asking her to stimulate him. She cannot admit that she is disappointed by his anxiety and insecurity, that she no longer sees him as a strong and adequate man but as a nervous weakling. This is too threatening to face. Nor can she acknowledge her infantile jealousy of his business and of his child by his first marriage. She focuses instead on his poor sexual performance, which she considers a "legitimate" complaint.

John's performance anxiety had an element of reality in that Mary really was sexually demanding and excessively critical, but there was also a transferential element. Mary became the cold, beautiful mother whom he could never satisfy. This intensified his anxiety and he lapsed into his old defenses of detachment and withdrawal.

Mary's anger and sexual avoidance were also partially based on real disappointment with her marriage. Who could fault her for wanting a sensitive husband and an intimate connection with him? Of course she wanted her husband to be an ardent and passionate lover. But her anger was intensified because she felt "gypped." She had met her contractual "obligations." She had made the effort to become an attractive, charming woman and centered her life around her marriage as her mother had taught her. But he was not fulfilling his end of the bargain.

 On a still deeper level, Mary was repelled by John's anxiety and overreacted to his impotence because this made her feel that she had "lost once again." She became once again the unattractive adolescent. Her man was not a "winner" like the "star" her beautiful sister had managed to marry. The best she had been able to do was an anxious, impotent "loser."

I now have enough information to know that this is a suitable case for a trial of psychosexual therapy. John's impotence, if not entirely psychogenic, has a significant and critical *psychogenic element*. The *immediate cause* is *performance anxiety*, which is aggravated by *partner pressure*; usually both these causes are very responsive to the behavioral aspects of sex therapy. It is also evident that some *deeper psychodynamic conflicts* about sex are operative in John's impotence, but since he has functioned well in the past it may be speculated that these are only of moderate intensity and can probably be bypassed in sexual therapy.

Mary's destructive behavior is more serious. She avoids sex and withholds support from John because she is angry. The causes of her anger are in part realistic and in part neurotic. However, since she is deeply committed to maintaining the marriage, her anger is probably not severe enough to preclude success in brief psychosexual therapy.

On the basis of all this information the following rather simple treatment strategy was formulated:

1) Behavioral tasks would be prescribed to diminish John's performance anxiety. These would consist of standard sensate focus exercises (Masters & Johnson, 1970), to be supplemented by openly using and sharing erotic fantasy.
2) The destructive effects Mary's sexual demands and lack of support were having on John's functioning would be confronted and explored during the therapy sessions.
3) If resistances arose, John's deeper problems with women and the roots of Mary's unhappiness and anger would be explored in greater depth during the therapy sessions.*

7) SUMMATION AND RECOMMENDATIONS

A skilled and experienced clinician can do a valid evaluation in a single 45-minute session when the problem is relatively simple. In more complex cases, up to four sessions may be needed to complete the evaluation. When the diagnostic interview does not clearly indicate that the patient's sexual symptom is psychogenic and when physical examinations and/or

---

*Ultimately this case was successfully concluded but with some difficulty. A great deal of resistance emerged from Mary. This took the form of her strenuous objections to John's use of fantasy or erotica. Mary's resistance could not be bypassed with confrontation and support or behavioral measures. I saw her alone and we explored the early origins of her ambivalence and insecurity. She gained considerable insight into the dynamics of her anger and disappointment. Most important, she got in touch with her genuine feelings of love for John. Only then was she able to become the supportive partner that he needed to function. On his part, John gained sexual confidence. He began to understand the genesis of his immature and hostile reactions to Mary and became a more intimate and sensitive husband and lover. The couple was seen for a total of 32 sessions.

tests are required to evaluate the medical aspects of the problem, the patient or couple should be seen again after the test results are in.

A single diagnostic session may not be sufficient for patients who have severe communication difficulties and in highly complex and bilateral cases, where the problems of both spouses must be evaluated in depth. When it appears that one spouse has a "secret" from the other — for example, if one has not admitted that he finds his spouse physically unattractive, or that he has decided to leave, or that he is having an affair, or that he is homosexual — he will want to speak to the examiner alone. When a single visit does not give me the information I need, I will make an appointment with each spouse separately and see them again together to discuss my findings and recommèndations.

The final feedback is the most important part of the evaluation from the patient's point of view. Patients are usually very concerned about their sexuality and urgently want to hear the examiner's conclusions and recommendations. The manner in which the summation is handled is very important in making the evaluation a constructive experience for the patient and the partner, as well as for engaging them in the treatment process.

Some clinicians prefer to wait until the end of the evaluation session to discuss their conclusions and recommendations. However, since patients are very anxious and worried and eager to know what is wrong, I like to express interim conclusions, especially when these are encouraging, throughout the interview.

Thus, for example, when the sexual status examination has revealed that a patient's impotence is clearly situational, I might say right at that point, "Good, now we know the problem is not physical and we won't have to pursue special medical examinations and tests." If the patient does not understand the basis for this inference, I clarify the point: "There can't be anything physically wrong with your penis if you have good erections when you masturbate. Now we will have to find out what psychological factors are causing you to lose your erections when you are with a woman."

Sharing my thought processes throughout the interview accomplishes several things. It is more gratifying, bringing me closer to the patient and his/her spouse and involving them actively in the data-gathering and decision-making process. Reassuring them about an issue that has worried them as soon as I have the needed information demonstrates my sensitivity to and caring about their anxiety and communicates to them my feeling that their urgent need to receive an answer is legitimate. *I* feel better this way and patients are liable to trust a person who understands and cares about their feelings.

During the summation, I might say to Mary: "We know that your lack of sexual desire for John is not due to physical problems or to a deep psychological one. It isn't physical because you still have erotic feelings when you fantasize. Your lack of desire only occurs in John's presence. We also know you don't have profound sexual conflicts because you've had several successful relationships before you met him. A person with serious sexual problems has usually not had any good sexual relationships."

At a point when I need further information or tests, I might explain my thoughts to John: "We know that you are not basically a neurotic person with major sex conflicts because you have no difficulty in other areas, and you've only had this problem since your divorce. You functioned very well before this traumatic episode for many years. It is clear that the problem is specific to this relationship. But your interactions are very complex and I do not have enough information yet to be able to tell exactly what is wrong between you and Mary or how it can be resolved. We'll have to have another session to try to find answers to these questions."

And, "From the evaluation it looks like your problem is psychological. I say that because you made love during your vacation and do report some morning erections, but I'm not quite clear and neither is Mary if there has been any change in their quality. Since you've had diabetes, which sometimes causes an erectile problem, I think we should check out your erections with a sleep test. If the sleep record is normal, we'll know for sure that your erectile difficulty is being caused only by performance anxiety. That has a very good prognosis with sex therapy."

The summation should be sensitive to and take into account the anxiety of the patient and his partner and be as reassuring to them as is possible within the limits of accuracy and honesty.

"John certainly does not have erection problems because he doesn't love you or no longer finds you attractive. To the contrary, he is probably trying too hard to please you."

Or, to another patient, "Premature ejaculation is not a form of hostility. It does not mean he wants to frustrate you. Some very loving, caring men have never learned voluntary control over their ejaculation. It is more of a learning problem. It has an excellent prognosis with treatment."

Or, "You are not 'frigid.' Many women have trouble reaching orgasm. You are perfectly normal physically. You merely do not get enough stimulation during lovemaking and you have not learned to 'let go' when you are with a partner. But there is nothing basically wrong with your sexuality."

Sometimes the summation includes very difficult material. A problem is organic and irreversible. A spouse has a major mental illness. The marriage is in serious trouble. Such findings must be conveyed with great sensitivity and the examiner may have to offer the patient and the partner help with integrating this threatening material.

The very last thing I tell the patient is what to expect from treatment:

"You will have to come in once a week and meet together with the therapist. You must also be prepared to put aside two or three evenings a week to be alone with your partner for your assigned sexual interactions. Probably the treatment will take from 10 to 14 sessions. We will reevaluate your situation after a few sessions when we can tell better how you are proceeding. Sex therapy is not magic. You *both* have to be prepared to change and you may have to work very hard to accomplish your goals."

If a patient or couple is accepted for treatment, but this cannot commence at the end of the first interview for reasons of time and scheduling, a "holding sig" might be offered. This is a suggestion designed to interrupt the cycle of sexual frustration, pressure and defeat which is so common in these situations. The exact nature of the sig will depend on the findings of the evaluation.

Often it is useful to "prescribe the symptom":

"I'd like to make a few suggestions until our appointment. You two can make love if you are moved to, but *I do not want you to try to have an orgasm, Cleo.* You have never climaxed and this is highly unlikely to happen even if Tony holds out longer. Just try to enjoy the feelings and don't think about an orgasm. We'll work on that when you start therapy next month."

REFERENCES FOR SECTION I

Abraham, K. Ejaculation praecox. In *Selected papers on psychoanalysis*. London: Hogarth Press, 1949, 280–310.

Ayd, F. J. Introduction: New antidepressant drugs. *Psychiatric Annals*, 1981, *II*, 11.

Barbach, L. G. *For yourself*. New York: Doubleday, 1975.

Benedek, T. The functions of the sexual apparatus and their disturbances. In *Psychosomatic medicine*. F. Alexander (Ed.) New York: W. W. Norton, 1950.

Berne, E. *Transactional analysis in psychotherapy*. New York: Grove Press, 1961.

Bieber, I. Sexual deviations I: Introduction. In *Comprehensive textbook of psychiatry*, 1st Ed. A. M. Freedman & H. L. Kaplan (Eds.) Baltimore: Williams & Wilkins, 1967(a), 959–962.

Bieber, I. Sexual deviations II: Homosexuality. In *Comprehensive textbook of psychiatry*, 1st Ed. A. M. Freedman & H. L. Kaplan (Eds.) Baltimore: Williams & Wilkins, 1967(b), 963–976.

Deutsch, H. *Psychology of women: A psychoanalytic interpretation*. New York: Grune & Stratton, 1944 (Vol. I), 1945 (Vol. II).

Erikson, E. H. The problem of ego identity. *Journal of American Psychoanalytical Association*, 1956, *4*, 56–121.

Erikson, E. H. *Identity and the life cycle, psychological issues*. New York: International Universities Press, 1959.

Fenichel, O. *The psychoanalytic theory of neurosis*. New York: Norton, 1945.

Freud, S. Three essays on the theory of sexuality (1905). In *The complete psychological works of Sigmund Freud, Vol. VII*. London: Hogarth Press, 1953, 125.

Freud, S. Some psychical consequences of the anatomical distinction between the sexes (1925). In *The complete psychological works of Sigmund Freud, Vol. XIX*. London: Hogarth Press, 1953, 243.

Friedman, M. *Overcoming the fear of success*. New York: Warner, 1981.

Gorman, J. M., Fyer, A. J., Glicklich, T., King, D., & Klein, D. F. Effects of sodium lactate on panic disorder patients with mitral valve prolapse. *American Journal Psychiatry*, 1981, *138*, 247–249.

Gräfenberg, E. The role of the urethra in female orgasm. *International Journal of Sexology*, 1950, *3*, 145–148.

Hartman, W. E., & Fithian, M. *The treatment of the sexual dysfunctions*. Long Beach: Center for Marital and Sexual Studies, 1972.

Kaplan, H. I., Freedman, A. M., & Sadock, B. (Eds): *The comprehensive textbook of psychiatry* 3rd Ed. Baltimore: Williams and Wilkins, 1980.

Kaplan, H. S. *The new sex therapy, vol. I*. New York: Brunner/Mazel, 1974.

Kaplan, H. S. *The illustrated manual of sex therapy*. New York: Quadrangle, 1975.

Kaplan, H. S. *Disorders of sexual desire: The new sex therapy vol. II*. New York: Brunner/ Mazel, 1979.

Kaplan, H. S., & Moodie, J. L. The treatment of psychosexual dysfunctions. For the *APA Commission on Psychiatric Therapies*. T. B. Karasu (Ed.) In Press.

Kaplan, H. S., Schwartz, S., Kaye, A., & Glass, J. B. J. Post gastrectomy pain and schizophrenia. *Psychosomatics*, 1970, *II*.

Kernberg, O. F. Early ego integration and object relations. *Annual New York Academy of Science*, 1972, *193*, 233–247.

Kernberg, O. F. Boundaries and structure of love relationships. *Journal of American Psychoanalytic Association*, 1976, *25:1*, 81–114.

Klein, D. F. Delineation of two drug responsive anxiety syndromes. *Psychopharmacology*, 1964, *5*, 397–408.

Klein, D. F. Anxiety reconceptualized. In D. F. Klein, & J. G. Rabkin (Eds.), *Anxiety: New research and changing concepts*. New York: Raven Press, 1980, 235–241.

Kolb, L. C. *Modern clinical psychiatry*. Philadelphia: Saunders, 1973.

Kolodny, R. C., Jacobs, L. S., Masters, W. H., Toro, G., & Daughady, W. H. Plasma gonadotrophins and prolactin in male homosexuals. *Lancet*, 1972, *2*, 18–20.

Ladas, A. K., Whipple, B., & Perry, J. D. *The G spot and other recent discoveries about human sexuality*. New York: Holt, Rinehart & Winston, 1982.

Lief, H. I. What's new in sex research? Inhibited sexual desire. *Medical Aspects of Human Sexuality*, 1977, *11:7*, 94–95.

Lief, H. I. *Sexual problems in medical practice*. Monroe, Wis: American Medical Association, 1981.

Lief, H. I. Medical aspects of sexuality. In *Cecil textbook of medicine, 16th edition*. J. B. Wyngaarden, L. H. Smith, & F. Plum (Eds.) Philadelphia: Saunders, 1982, 1998–2004.

Mack, J. E., & Semrad, E. V. Classical psychoanalysis. In *Comprehensive textbook of psychiatry*. 1st ed. A. M. Freedman, & H. L. Kaplan (Eds.) Baltimore: Williams & Wilkins, 1967, 269–320.

MacKinnon, R. A., & Michels, R. *The psychiatric interview*. Philadelphia: Saunders, 1971.

Masters, W. H., & Johnson, V. *The human sexual response*. Boston: Little Brown, 1966.

Masters, W. H., & Johnson, V. *Human sexual inadequacy*. Boston: Little Brown, 1970.

Masterson, J. *Treatment of the borderline adolescent. A developmental approach*. New York: Wiley-Interscience, 1972.

Money, J., Hampson, J. G., & Hamson, J. L. Hermaphrodism: recommendations concerning assignment of sex, change of sex, and psychological management. *Bulletin Johns Hopkins Hospital*, 1955, 97:284–300.

Perls, F. S. *Gestalt therapy*. New York: Grove Press, 1961.

Sager, C. J., Kaplan, H. S., Grundlach, R. H., Kramer, M., Lenz, R., & Royce, J. R. The marriage contract. In *Progress in group and family therapy*. C. J. Sager, & H. S. Kaplan (Eds.) New York: Brunner/Mazel, 1972.

Sheenan, D. V. Panic attacks and phobias. *New England Journal of Medicine*, 1982, *307:3*, 156–158.

Sherfey, M. A. *The nature and evolution of human sexuality*. New York: Random House, 1966.

Spark, R. F., White, R. A., & Connolly, P. B. Impotence is not always psychogenic: Hypothalamic-pituitary gonadal dysfunction. *Journal of the American Medical Association*, 1980, *243*, 750–755.

Stekel, W. *Frigidity in women in relation to their love life.* New York: Boni & Liveright, 1926.

Stekel, W. *Impotence in the male.* New York: Boni & Liveright, 1927.

Strayhorn, J. M., Jr. *Foundations of clinical psychiatry.* Chicago: Year Book Medical Publishers, Inc., 1982.

Wagner, G., & Green, R. *Impotence.* New York: Plenum Press, 1982.

Wasserman, M. D. The differential diagnosis of impotence: The measurement of nocturnal penile tumescence. *Journal of the American Medical Association,* 1980, *243,* 203–242.

Witkin, M., & Kaplan, H. S. Sex therapy and penectomy. *Journal of Sex and Marital Therapy,* Fall, 1982, *18*:3, 209–221.

Wolpe, J.: The experimental foundations of some new psychotherapeutic methods. In *Experimental foundations of clinical psychology.* A. J. Bachrach (Ed.). New York: Basic Books, 1962.

Zorgniotti, A. W., & Rossi, G. *Vasculogenic impotence.* Springfield, Il: Charles C Thomas, 1980.

Zussman, L., & Zussman, S. The conjoint physical examination. In *Clinical management of sexual disorders.* John K. Meyer (Ed.) Baltimore: Williams and Wilkins, 1976.

SECTION II
THE MEDICAL ASPECTS OF EVALUATION

A comprehensive specialty of sexual medicine, integrating the psychiatric with the medical, urologic, and gynecologic components of this field, does not exist yet. (In this respect the genitals have not quite caught up with the rest of the body.) Therefore, the medical aspects of the evaluation of sexual disorders are described by specialists in gynecology, urology, and endocrinology, from the perspectives of their area of expertise.

CHAPTER 3

THE GYNECOLOGIC EVALUATION OF FEMALE ORGASM DISORDERS

Sherwin A. Kaufman, M.D.

ANATOMY AND PHYSIOLOGY

The physiology of female orgasm is complex. Like excitement, orgasm is a genital reflex controlled by spinal neural centers. The sensory impulses which set off female orgasm enter the spinal cord in the pudendal nerve at the sacral level, while the efferent nerves emerge from T11 to L2. However, unlike excitement, orgasm does not involve a vascular reflex; rather, there are reflex contractions of certain genital muscles (the ischio and bulbocavernosi) located around the vaginal introitus. Since the spinal reflex centers for orgasm are anatomically close to those governing bladder and rectal control, injuries to the lower cord can result in impairment to all three: urination, defecation, and orgasm.

It is rare to find organic orgasm disorders in healthy women. However, certain illnesses, injuries, or drugs may cause either partial or total impairment of orgasm, depending upon the severity of the illness, extent of the injury, or dosage of the drug.

As in all sexual disorders, a clear and detailed description of the complaint and its history and a medical history are important in diagnosis. These are described in Section I of this volume. All patients should have a gynecological examination to rule out adhesions or phimosis of the clitoris (rare) or weakness of the pubococcygeal muscles, which may interfere with orgasm. In addition, a thorough general physical examination may reveal a systemic disorder, in which case appropriate laboratory studies should be done to help confirm the diagnosis. A detailed description of many of the medical and neurological disorders mentioned is beyond the scope of this book, and the reader is directed to standard texts for reference.

PATHOLOGY: DISEASE STATES AND DRUGS THAT CAN IMPAIR FEMALE ORGASM

Neurologic Disorders

Neurologic Disorders Affecting the Spinal Cord

Conditions such as *multiple sclerosis* and *alcoholic neuropathy* frequently interfere with female orgasm, which may become diminished or entirely absent. The mechanism of impairment is by irregular lesions in the spinal cord. In fact, sexual difficulties are often among the first manifestations of multiple sclerosis, a disease of unknown etiology characterized by patches of demyelinization in the cord and brain. Other neurologic conditions which may, less frequently, be responsible for decreased or absent female orgasm include *tabes dorsalis* (locomotor ataxia; a form of neurosyphilis), *syringomyelia* (cause unknown), *amyotrophic lateral sclerosis* (Lou Gehrig disease), *myelitis* (e.g., polio), and *severe malnutrition with vitimin deficiencies*. The mechanism of impairment of female orgasm is similar in each, namely, irregular lesions in the spinal cord.

Neurologic Disorders Causing Injury to Peripheral Nerves

Female orgasm rarely may be impaired by disorders such as: *alcoholic neuropathy, herniated lumbar disc*, or *lumbar canal stenosis*. The mechanism of impairment is injury to the somatic and autonomic nerves controlling orgasm, the spinal reflex centers in the lower cord.

Diabetes mellitus may result in decreased or absent female orgasm because of severe neuropathy of the sensory nerves of the clitoris. The gynecologic examination may be normal, although diabetic women are subject to vaginal infections. In addition, the physical examination may appear normal unless the diabetes is prolonged or uncontrolled. Eyegrounds may reveal so-called "diabetic retinopathy," microaneurysms, and punctate hemorrhages and white exudates in the macular area. Paresthesias, ulcerations, and skin infections are common. In severe cases, Achilles and patellar reflexes are diminished or absent, as well as vibration sense. The laboratory findings may reveal repeated elevated fasting blood sugar, glycosuria, and "diabetic" curve on glucose tolerance test, and, with uncontrolled diabetes, elevation of blood ketones (acidosis). Renal involvement may eventually produce albuminuria, fixed urinary specific gravity, lowered serum albumin, and a rising BUN.

Surgical Injuries to the Spinal Cord
and Peripheral Nerves Involved in Orgasm

Surgical *thoraco-lumbar or lumbar sympathectomy* may result in impairment of female orgasm if the operation interferes with or disrupts the sympathetic pathways. Similarly, *retroperitoneal lymphadenectomy* can impair orgasm because of interference or disruption of sacral somatic nerves due to paralysis of the perineal muscles. *Aorto-iliac* surgery may have the same consequences with the same mechanism. In addition, radical pelvic surgery (sacral resections and operations for rectal, cervical, or bladder cancer) can cause diminished or absent orgasm phase by disrupting the parasympathetic, sympathetic and sensory fibers which are essential for orgasm.

Traumatic Injuries to the Spinal Cord
and Peripheral Nerves Associated with Orgasm

Paraplegia involving a low lesion transection of the spinal cord will preclude orgasmic sensation due to interruption of the sensory pathways. The same orgasmic impairment results from a high lesion, due to disruption of the sympathetic pathways. A similar orgastic problem results from *posterior urethral rupture*, due to injury to sympathetic fibers as well as vascular injury. The gynecologic examination is usually normal in neurological diseases. The physical examination may reveal motor and sensory loss below the level of the lesion as the chief neurogenic deficits. Laboratory findings are not pertinent in chronic cases.

Vascular Causes of Female Orgasm Disorders

Vascular disorders do not affect orgasm. However, the quality of orgasm may be diminished due to anxiety about sudden death in the post-coronary or post-stroke syndrome, or in patients suffering from severe hypertension.

The gynecologic examination is usually normal in vascular diseases. In the case of hypertension, the important signs in the physical examination are elevated systolic and diastolic pressure. Fundoscopic examination may reveal arterio-venous compression, hemorrhages, exudates or papilledema. Cardiac hypertrophy may be found on percussion.

Laboratory findings may reveal cardiac hypertrophy which may be confirmed on x-ray. ECG may show evidence of left ventricular strain—left axis deviation. Diminished ability of the kidneys to concentrate results in proteinuria, hematuria, cylinduria, and eventually nitrogen retention.

Endocrine and Metabolic Disorders Interfering with Orgasm

Diabetes mellitus has been mentioned. *Testosterone deficiency states* such as would result from removal of the adrenals and ovaries in certain breast cancers may result in retardation of orgasm. This is because the sex centers require testosterone. In addition, there may be impairment of neural transmission and cellular response of the genitals. Female orgasm may also be retarded (by unknown mechanism) in *thyroid deficiency states*, whether from surgery, trauma, infection or iodine deficiency. Other endocrine disorders, such as Addison's disease, Cushing's disease, acromegaly, and hypopituitarism, may also retard orgasmic response, since these disorders produce various glandular deficiencies which can affect the neural pathways of the brain and/or cellular response of the genitals.

The gynecologic examination is usually normal except for diminished pubic hair in some endocrine disorders. The clinical manifestations of overt hypothyroidism seen during the physical examination include diminution of cephalic, pubic, axillary, and eyebrow (lateral aspect) hair, dry skin, and delayed return of deep tendon reflexes. Common *laboratory findings* are that T3 and T4 (RIA) are low, as is the free thyroid index (T7).

The other endocrine disorders are less common. Further information on the evaluation of such specific disorders may be found in standard medical texts.

Other Medical Disorders Which May Affect Orgasm

Liver disease (hepatitis, hepatic failure from alcoholic cirrhosis, post-mononucleosus hepatitis) may retard female orgasm, since such liver disorders cannot conjugate estrogen sufficiently, with the result that androgens are neutralized. Obviously, with cirrhosis associated with ascites and peripheral edema, general sexual discomfort also plays a role. *Renal disease* (nephritis, renal failure, dialysis) can similarly retard female orgasm because of premature arteriosclerotic changes in the pelvis, as well as debility and depression. Other *debilitating diseases* (degenerative disorders, pulmonary diseases, malignancies) exert a negative effect upon orgasm due to declining health and depression.

Drugs That May Impair Female Orgasm

Drugs Which Affect the Brain (Central Nervous System)

Sedatives and hypnotics such as alcohol, barbiturates, chloral hydrate, etc., taken in high doses, usually retard orgasm. Possible mechanisms of action include general CNS depression. The effects are dose-related. Thus, small doses of alcohol may reduce inhibitions and enhance sexual response, while larger doses inhibit those same responses, including orgasm.

Tranquilizers such as meprobamate, chlordiazepoxide, and diazepam do not affect orgasm in usual doses, but may retard orgasm with very high dosage. The action appears to be on the limbic system, and on internuncial neurons in the spinal cord.

Narcotics such as codeine and morphine inhibit orgasm in high doses, due to general depression of the central nervous system and possibly by direct depression of the sex centers. An alteration of the normal balance of biogenic amines in the CNS may also play a role.

Antidepressants: Tricyclics such as Elavil and Tofranil may delay orgasm in some women. The mechanism of this effect is not clear. MAO inhibitors such as Nardil have an even greater tendency to retard orgasm. In contrast, lithium does not affect the female orgasm phase.

Stimulants such as cocaine or amphetamines have been anecdotally reported to enhance orgasm, but in high doses they tend to interfere with orgasm. Such drugs are CNS stimulants, and augment sympathetic nervous system function. Marijuana (a hallucinogen) may produce mixed, unpredictable effects (enhanced orgasm?) by mechanisms poorly understood.

Antihypertensives which act centrally, such as alpha-methyldopa, may inhibit female orgasm, depending upon the dosage. The mechanism is unclear, but probably related both to catecholamine depletion in the central nervous system and a production of neurotransmitters directly affecting the peripheral nerves associated with the vaginal blood supply. Diuretics do not affect female orgasm, but ganglionic blockers such as ammonium compounds may inhibit orgasm by blocking post-ganglionic nerves, the same holding true for general antiadrenogenic drugs such as phentolamine, phenoxybenzamine, and ergot alkaloids. Orgasm may also be inhibited by sympathoplegic drugs, such as Guanethidine, which block the release of norepinephrine from sympathetic nerve endings.

Beta adrenergic blockers may delay orgasm as part of a general depression of libido.

CHAPTER 4

THE GYNECOLOGIC EVALUATION OF FEMALE EXCITEMENT DISORDERS

Sherwin A. Kaufman, M.D.

ANATOMY AND PHYSIOLOGY

The excitement phase in females is accompanied by reflex vasodilation with generalized swelling of the labia and the tissues surrounding the vagina, resulting in heightened labial coloring and increased lubrication or wetness, the latter a transudate from the vessels in the vaginal barrel. Arteriolar dilation is caused by activation of two centers in the spinal cord, one at S2, S3, and S4, and the other at T11, L1, and L2. As with the male, excitement can be enhanced or inhibited by signals from the brain, which are in turn influenced by previous experiences.

Estrogen plays the dominant role in vaginal lubrication. Its physiologic, cyclic effect upon cervical secretions is well known, that is, increased wetness during the midcyclic ovulatory phase and diminished secretions postovulatory, coincident with progesterone (anti-estrogen) release and diminished estrogen production.

Estrogen also affects vaginal lubrication directly by enhancing the vascular bed beneath the epithelium, which results in improved lubrication. This effect upon the vaginal mucosa is not dependent upon ovulation and continues as long as sufficient estrogen is produced by the ovaries. Although estrogen production by the ovaries diminishes and eventually ceases beyond the menopause, estrogen levels in postmenopausal women can continue to be substantial, due primarily to the peripheral conversion of adrenal androstenedione to estrone and, to a much lesser extent, of testosterone to estradiol. However, with increasing age such adrenal contribution to estrogen production becomes inadequate to sustain secondary sex tissues such as the vaginal mucosa and, indeed, even adjacent tissues such as the urethra and trigone.

Although excitement phase dysfunction in females can exist as a separate syndrome, the discomfort of intercourse with a dry vagina can easily lead to secondary inhibition of sexual desire, if not complete avoidance. In essence, then, female excitement phase disorders are due chiefly to impairment of the vasocongestive excitement phase response, associated primarily with diminished or inhibited estrogen production. It should be emphasized that in the premenopausal woman such disorders are relatively uncommon.

PATHOLOGY: DISEASE STATES AND DRUGS THAT CAN IMPAIR THE FEMALE EXCITEMENT PHASE

Estrogen Deficiency States

Atrophic vulvo-vaginitis. This condition is by far the most common *gynecological* cause of excitement phase dysfunction (see Chapter 5 for further discussion).

Gynecological examination reveals that the introitus is dry and often reddened. There may be less muscle tone and fascial strength (inelasticity) of introital and vaginal supports. The vaginal mucous membrane exhibits various degrees of dryness and thinning, sometimes to the point of minute mucosal hemorrhages.

Laboratory findings will usually show the following: In the absence of other causes of vaginitis, the wet smear of vaginal secretions shows mainly parabasal cells. Blood levels of estrogen are low, while FSH and LH are typically elevated.

Aside from physiological postmenopausal estrogen deficiency, other conditions which would produce atrophic vulvo-vaginitis include:

Oophorectomy, particularly in younger women whose ovaries are still producing significant amounts of estrogen. The mechanism is, of course, by removal of the chief source of estrogen supply ("surgical menopause").

Radical pelvic surgery (as for cervical cancer), since it includes oophorectomy and also interferes with the parasympathetic and sympathetic sensory pathways.

(The emotional components of surgery and illness are discussed elsewhere).

To a lesser but sometimes significant degree, vaginal dryness may be induced by *progesterone* compounds such as medroxyprogesterone, which act as anti-estrogens (less lubrication) and also anti-androgens (diminished excitement). This would include certain oral contraceptives containing a high progestin ratio (hypoestrogenic). In such instances the gynecological examination reveals a noticeable vaginal dryness but no thinning of the mucosa or petechial spots, as in atrophic states. The vaginal smear reveals a preponderance of intermediate cells, rather than cornified or parabasal.

Medical Disorders

Although the following theoretically can interfere with the female excitement phase by causing a longer arousal time and, in some instances, by decreasing vaginal lubrication, it should be noted that they are, with rare exception, *not* associated with the primary clinical complaint of excitement phase disturbance.

Neurogenic disorders: Disorders affecting the sex centers of the brain include *head trauma* or *CVA*. This may decrease excitement phase by direct injury to the sex centers and/or injury to the limbic system or parietal lobe. *Hypothalamic lesions* or chraniopharyngioma results in the same from pressure on cerebral structures, while *chromophobe adenoma* (pituitary tumor) decreases excitement not only by pressure on the sex center and limbic system, but also by elevating the prolactin level. *Psychomotor epilepsy* may diminish female excitement phase by disturbance of the limbic system.

Disorders affecting the *lower neural structures* associated with genital reflexes include the following: Neurological conditions may cause diminished or even absent excitement phase due to patchy lesions in the spinal cord which interfere with genital reflexes. Those which are most frequently responsible for such sexual difficulties are *multiple sclerosis* and *alcoholic neuropathy.* In fact, sexual difficulties are sometimes among the first manifestations of multiple sclerosis, with variable complaints such as diminished lubrication, diminished or absent clitoral sensitivity, and dyspareunia, all of which interfere with arousal. Patches of demyelinization in the spinal cord are responsible. Other disorders affecting the spinal cord, and possibly associated with decreased or absent arousal phase, are *tabes dorsalis, amyotrophic lateral sclerosis, syringomyelia, myelitis,* and *severe malnutrition and vitamin deficiencies.*

Alcoholic neuropathy and *herniated lumbar disc* lead to diminished or absent excitement phase by virtue of injury to somatic and autonomic nerves concerned with genital reflexes, as does *primary autonomic degeneration* (Shay-Drager syndrome).

Traumatic injuries to the spinal cord resulting in *paraplegia* preclude sexual excitement since no sensations are perceived. The sensory pathways are interrupted and sympathetic fibers may also be disrupted.

Vascular problems may result in diminished or absent excitement phase because of thrombotic injury and occlusion of pelvic blood vessels. The arousal phase is diminished in many patients suffering from *coronary disease* or *severe hypertension*. The reasons are probably predominantly psychological — including depression and anxiety about sudden death. Antihypertensive and beta adrenergic blocking drugs or possibly diseased pelvic blood vessels may contribute to diminished excitement on an organic basis.

Endocrine and metabolic disorders: The following are more likely to impair the orgasm and desire phases rather than excitement; the effect on excitement is secondary. *Diabetes mellitus* may be associated with diminished or absent excitement due to neuropathy of the sensory nerves of the clitoris. *Testosterone deficiency* states in females (such as after surgical removal of the adrenals, ovaries, or pituitary for treatment of breast cancer) result in diminished lubrication and interference with the functioning of the sex centers, which require testosterone. In addition, neural transmission and cellular response of the genitals may be impaired. *Thyroid deficiency* states may interfere with arousal by mechanisms not clearly understood. Other endocrine disorders, such as *Addison's disease, Cushing's syndrome, acromegaly* and *hypopituitarism* may all diminish excitement because of various endocrine deficiencies which affect the sexual circuits of the brain or the cellular response of the genitals.*

Detailing the clinical evaluation and laboratory findings of these many disorders is beyond the scope of this book, and the reader is referred to the standard medical texts listed in the Bibliography at the end of this chapter for more detailed information.

It is also recognized that in many of the aforementioned medical disorders the patient is seriously ill; therefore, the sexual evaluation must be viewed with a sense of proportion, within the entire clinical syndrome. This is particularly true of the additional medical disorders discussed below.

Other medical disorders which may diminish female excitement include *liver disease* (hepatitis, alcoholic cirrhosis, and postmononucleosis hepa-

---

*The endocrine causes of diminished libido are also discussed in Chapter 9.

titis), due to insufficient conjugation of estrogen and resulting neutralization of androgens. Such sexual dysfunction may also result from *kidney disease* (nephritis, chronic renal failure, dialysis). Diminished lubrication and dyspareunia are the chief causes of interference with arousal, though obviously depression plays a dominant role, as with other debilitating diseases. Responsible factors are premature arteriosclerotic changes in the pelvis and uremic neuropathy affecting the pelvic autonomic system. Anemia and electrolyte imbalance may contribute to the weakness and impaired neuromuscular function. Other debilitating diseases such as *malignancies, degenerative diseases,* and *pulmonary disorders* affect the sexual arousal phase because of general poor health and depression. In this connection, it should be noted that *any* physical or emotional preoccupation, from whatever cause, can interfere with female (or male) arousal and orgasm; the effect on the excitement phase is secondary.

Drugs

Theoretically, the following substances *may* cause vaginal dryness, but in clinical practice they are rarely associated with disturbance of the excitement phase.

Antihistamines and *ephedrine* may cause lessened lubrication. Antihistamines may also interfere with sexual arousal by their sedative effects.

Anticholinergic drugs, such as Banthine, Probanthine and atropine, may occasionally diminish lubrication. The mechanism is inhibition of acetylcholine leading to an inhibition of the parasympathetic nervous system which, in turn, causes impairment of reflex vasocongestion, resulting in diminished lubrication and interference with female arousal.

Antihypertensive agents, such as alpha-methyldopa (centrally acting), may impair female excitement; this is apparently dose-related. The mechanism is not clear, but it may be associated with depletion of catecholamine in the central nervous system, as well as with the drug's effect on peripheral nerves relating to vaginal congestion. Other agents, such as reserpine and clonidine, may also interfere with female excitement due to depletion of catecholamines.

Psychotropic drugs: The antihistamine action of some phenothiazines may lead to decreased vaginal lubrication. Tricyclic antidepressants may, in some, cause arousal disturbances from atropine-like drying effects.

BIBLIOGRAPHY

Adams, R. D., & Victor, M. *Principles of neurology,* 2nd ed. New York: McGraw-Hill, 1981.
Beeson, P., MacDermott, W., & Wyngaarden, J. (Eds.) *Cecil textbook of medicine,* 15th ed. Philadelphia: Saunders, 1979.

Harvey, A. M., et al. *The principles and practice of medicine*, 20th ed. New York: Appleton, 1980.

Isselbacher, K. J., et al. (Eds.) *Harrison's principles of internal medicine*, 9th ed. New York: McGraw-Hill, 1980.

Kaplan, H. S. *The new sex therapy*. New York: Brunner/Mazel, 1974.

Kaplan, H. S. *Disorders of sexual desire*. New York: Brunner/Mazel, 1979.

5

THE GYNECOLOGIC EVALUATION OF FEMALE DYSPAREUNIA AND UNCONSUMMATED MARRIAGE

Sherwin A. Kaufman, M.D.

The complaint of pain on coitus is always a matter of urgency for the woman and her partner. The physician must take the responsibility for determining the etiology and correcting the problem, since chronic dyspareunia precludes sexual enjoyment and can pose a serious threat to the marital relationship (Kaufman, 1981).

Frequently, the patient will not complain of coital pain even though it is present. Therefore, a simple question such as, "Do you have any discomfort during sex?" is a useful opening gambit for the discussion of *any* sexual problems the patient may have. Indeed, the importance of a detailed history cannot be overemphasized, since key questions will provide clues as to where the woman feels pain (e.g., superficial or deep) and under what circumstances (e.g., occasionally or with each encounter). Other questions of importance are whether the pain is mild or severe and whether the pain is aggravated or minimized by coital positions. Finally, duplication of the pain upon pelvic examination, or failure to do so, not only provides another clue but is, in fact, the essence of the physical examination. This topic is also discussed in Chapter 10.

It should be kept in mind that, although there are many physical causes for coital pain, chronic dyspareunia will understandably have a significant emotional overlay (Kaplan, 1979).

PATHOLOGIC STATES THAT CAN
RESULT IN COITAL PAIN

On Entry

1) Vaginismus

Vaginismus is the contraction of the paravaginal and perineal muscles, making attempts at intromission impossible due to pain or spasm. It is usually evident at the start of a marriage, precluding consummation (Kaplan, 1974).

Vaginismus may stem from emotional inhibitions, misinformation, or traumatic sexual experiences. It may also be a protective reflex to avoid pain due to pelvic pathology. Since vaginismus is a conditioned response, and since the woman associates intercourse with fear or pain, even the elimination of existing local pathology may fail to alleviate the disorder.

Pelvic examination is not possible due to spasm at the introitus (and often the adductor thigh muscles as well). The patient cannot tolerate penetration of even one finger.

2) Intact or Rigid Hymen

The gradual hymenal stretch from the use of menstrual tampons has considerably diminished the incidence of anatomic "virginity." If the hymen is intact, however, or partially stretched but still rigid, attempts at coitus will be painful. Occasionally discomfort is due to tenderness of irritated hymenal remnants.

The pelvic examination will reveal whether this is the anatomic condition responsible.

3) Clitoral Problems

Irritation of the clitoris may result from smegma, tight jeans, or trauma from overzealous use of a vibrator. Another common cause is chemical irritation or "allergy" from so-called deodorant sprays, perfumed soaps, or detergents.

Clitoral phimosis is rarely found in clinical practice, and is even more rarely a cause of dyspareunia. So-called clitoral adhesions are clinically indistinguishable from phimosis, except in women who have undergone a surgical procedure in or near that area. On the other hand, a very common cause of clitoral "tenderness" results from unintentionally rough manipulation by the male; the discomfort may be confined to high levels of female arousal, not a result of pathology but merely extreme sensitivity.

Pathologic lesions involving the clitoris (e.g., herpes, monilia) can occur as part of a generalized vulvitis. Herpes is usually distinguished by small blisters or punched-out red areas, often appearing in clusters. The extreme pain is out of proportion to the size or appearance of the lesions. Monilia and trichomonas infection rarely involve the clitoris alone, but present rather as a diffuse vulvitis (see #4 below). The same is true of atrophic vulvitis, except for the much less commonly encountered leukoplakia or kraurosis, wherein the thickening and whitening may single out the area in and around the clitoris.

A careful history will clarify the possible causes of clitorial irritation, while examination of the vulva will disclose its extent, as well as the nature of any pathologic conditions.

4) Vulvitis (Vulvo-vaginitis)

Two common causes are monilia and trichomonas, which usually also cause contiguous vaginitis. Besides dyspareunia, vaginal discharge, itching, and irritation are frequent complaints. Another increasingly common cause is herpes genitalis, type 2. Hemophilus bacteria may produce discharge and odor, but this source is typically non-irritating and hence not a cause of dyspareunia.

Monilia: This infection is more prevalent in diabetics, pregnancy, and while taking oral contraceptives. The discharge is often cheesy in appearance and both the vulva and vagina show varying degrees of inflammation. Laboratory findings: A simple wet smear of the vaginal secretions, aided by a drop of 10 percent potassium hydroxide, generally reveals the typical spores or filaments of candida albicans. If not, the yeast will readily grow on special media such as Nickerson's.

Trichomonas: Local signs often resemble those of monilia and, indeed, the two infections may co-exist. With trichomonas, odor is often the predominant complaint. Laboratory findings: Motile trichomonas parasites are seen on wet smear if the patient has not recently douched or used vaginal medications.

Herpes genitalis type 2 is a viral disease which may be so painful that intercourse is not even attempted. The typical clusters of tiny vesicles may sometimes ulcerate to form oval lesions surrounded by diffuse erythema. Fever and inguinal lymphadenopathy may accompany the infection during its acute stage. In perhaps less than 10 percent of cases, herpetic lesions of the labia, vulva and vagina may be caused by herpes simplex type 1, probably following oral-genital contact. In any event, the first (primary) infection is usually the most severe. Unfortunately, recurrent lesions are common, even without further sexual exposure, since the virus apparently lies dormant in underlying nerves.

Gynecologic evaluation: Although herpetic lesions may be atypical, depending upon the duration of the disorder, during the acute stage there are usually characteristic small blisters or ulcerated lesions with red borders. As mentioned, inguinal adenopathy may occur in more severe cases.

Laboratory findings: Culturing virus isolates on special media can be done but is cumbersome and present techniques have given a generally low yield of positive isolations. Smears from the lesions (or if the virus is present in the cervix) using Pap stain will sometimes demonstrate suggestive nuclear changes.

Atrophic vulvo-vaginitis is by far the most common cause of genital discomfort during the postmenopausal years. Upon gynecologic examination it is seen that the introitus and vaginal mucosa are thin, dry, and frequently inflamed, so that taking an ordinary Pap smear may cause a slight blood stain on the vaginal swab. Much less frequently, one finds thickening or whitening of the epitheleal layer with shrinkage (leukoplakia and kraurosis), which can cause intense itching and irritation.

Laboratory findings: Diagnosis of atrophic vaginitis is confirmed by wet smear of the vaginal secretions, which reveals mainly parabasal cells (in the absence of other causes of vaginitis). For kraurosis or leukoplakia, biopsy may be warranted to rule out neoplasia.

Chemical irritation or sensitivities ("allergies") may result from contraceptive spermicides, scented douches, perfumed sprays, new soaps or detergents. The combination of nylon underwear with tight-fitting slacks can be either a predisposing or causative factor. Often overlooked as a common cause of vulvo-vaginitis is the persistent use of one or more prescribed medications. Allergy to semen is very rare, but has been reported.

It is apparent that a detailed history is essential to clarify the cause of vaginitis. There is an absence of pathogens on the wet smear and/or culture media.

5) Dermatologic Conditions

The vulva may be involved in dermatologic disorders and a variety of such conditions may affect this area, but may also be manifested in other areas of the body as well. *Folliculitis* consists of pustular inflammation around hair follicles caused by staphylococci or other organisms. Poor genital hygiene and tight underclothing may be contributing factors. *Intertrigo* is a superficial inflammation caused by moisture and friction from two opposing skin surfaces. In the genital area it may occur in the interlabial sulci and the furrows between the vulva and thighs, particularly in obese women. Burning and itching are common complaints and a dermatophytosis is often superimposed. *Tinea cruris* may be caused by a variety of ringworm organisms, usually Epidermophyton floccosum. Typically, ringed lesions or patches may cover the vulva, groins and inner thighs. Culture on Sabouraud's medium may corroborate the diagnosis. *Psoriasis*, a chronic, relapsing skin disease, may occur also on the vulva. However, the reddened, slightly elevated dry patches characteristically involve the scalp, the extensor surfaces of the extremities, the back, and the buttocks. *Lichen sclerosis et atrophicus* is a secondary skin change usually caused by prolonged scratching from chronic pruritis vulvae. The skin appears thick and leathery, with normal markings markedly accentuated. *Pediculosis pubis* is caused by the crab louse, and may cause intense itching in the pubic and vulvar areas since the lice attach to the base of the hairs.

Among the less common veneral diseases that may involve the vulva and cause pain are: *chancroid*, "soft chancre" ulcerations caused by the Ducrey bacillus, often accompanied by suppurative inguinal nodes or "buboes"; and *granuloma inguinale*, usually localized to the genitals, anus, or perineal area, and characterized by chronic ulcerations. Diagnosis is by demonstration of Donovan bodies in spreads or when biopsy reveals the pathognomonic large histiocyte cells. *Lymphogranuloma venereum* is caused by a virus which causes extensive suppuration of inguinal nodes, and may lead to abscesses, and even elephantiasis. The intradermal Frei test is specific.

6) Bartholin and Skene Glands

Gynecologic evaluation will readily reveal the presence of a Bartholin gland cyst which, if large or infected (abscess), can cause dyspareunia. In addition, milking the paraurethral (Skene's) ducts will disclose if they are inflamed.

Laboratory findings: Culture for gonorrhea may be indicated from these locations if there is any purulent drainage; the cervix and urethra should be included in such cultures.

7) Inadequate Lubrication

Poor lubrication is a frequent cause of coital discomfort upon entry and thrusting and should be suspected. Some of the many possible causes are insufficient foreplay, estrogen deficiency states, other atrophic conditions, some medical disorders (e.g., multiple sclerosis), and certain drugs (e.g., antihistamines) (see Chapter 4).

Although dryness may be noted on pelvic examination, the history is of special importance. This is because insufficient vaginal lubrication might not be evident until after thrusting has begun. With atrophic states, the finding of predominantly parabasal cells on wet smear is characteristic, as previously mentioned.

8) Operative Scarring

Coital pain on entry may result from: poorly healed obstetrical episiotomy; tightness from a snug perineorrhaphy; and vaginal irradiation. Pain at mid-level or on deep thrusting may be due to an unyielding scar at the vault after vaginal hysterectomy (infrequently after abdominal hysterectomy unless a large vaginal cuff is purposely taken) or to adhesions from other pelvic surgery.

The various conditions mentioned will be demonstrable on pelvic examination.

Mid-Vaginal Pain

1) Urethritis, Trigonitis, Cystitis

These conditions usually cause mid-vaginal (rather than deep) pain during coital entry and thrusting, particularly when the woman is in the supine position. So-called "honeymoon cystitis" is a mechanical rather than bacterial irritation from unaccustomed pressure during intercourse. The use of a diaphragm, particularly if too snug or left in for prolonged intervals, may add to the discomfort of trigonitis.

Bacterial cystitis usually causes urinary frequency, urgency, dysuria, nocturia, and occasionally hematuria. Sources of infection are variable, including disease of the kidneys, bladder, and urethra. However, the common finding of E. Coli on culture suggests the introduction of such bacteria if a woman wipes herself from back to front after defecating or urinating. The relationship between intercourse and cystitis is not definitely established and remains controversial. In favor of a causal relationship is the premise that sexual activity results in the introduction of bacteria from the urethra into the bladder, by the penis or tongue; in the absence of voiding, the bacteria tend to grow overnight. However, it is possible that sexual activity is not the cause but rather the aggravating factor in a preexisting infection.

Digital pressure on the urethra, bladder base, and suprapubically will usually elicit discomfort. On inspection, a urethral caruncle may be discovered as the cause of the problem. (Other urethral pathology, such as ure-throcele or diverticulum are usually painless.)

In addition to a urinalysis on a "clean catch" specimen (including a micro-scopic examination for red and white cells), a urine culture should be done, including sensitivity tests. Cervical and urethral cultures for gonorrhea may also be indicated, according to the individual history.

2) *Congenital Shortened Vagina*

In the absence of previous pelvic surgery, a shortened vagina (sufficient to cause dyspareunia) may be seen in such congenital anomalies as Turner's syndrome and testicular feminization.

Obvious endocrinopathy will be evident on general physical examina-tion. The gynecologic examination may reveal immature genitals or may be normal.

Pain on Deep Thrusting

Unlike superficial coital pain, which is often transient during entry or can be minimized with medications or lubricants, pain on deep vaginal pene-tration can be a formidable obstacle to sexual pleasure. It is frequently intol-erable. There are several common causes (Barber, Fields, & Kaufman, 1979).

1) *Pelvic Inflammatory Disease (PID) (acute or chronic)*

There is usually a history of pelvic pain with fever during the first epi-sode; subsequent exacerbations are often postmenstrual. With PID the pain on deep thrusting is in *any* coital position.

Gynecologic evaluation will reveal tender adnexal masses, usually bilat-eral, but typically unilateral when caused by infection from an intrauterine device. Chronic PID is often confused with endometriosis. Recto-vaginal examination, sonography, and endoscopy are helpful in the differential diagnosis.

Laboratory findings: A markedly elevated sedimentation rate is expected during the acute phase of pelvic inflammatory disease, as well as a high white count. Cervical cultures may reveal gonococci or other pathogens.

2) *Endometriosis*

A history of increasing dysmenorrhea, infertility, and irregular menses is common. Coital pain is often cyclic, being worse premenstrually or during a period. The discomfort can often be modified according to coital position; for example, with the female above there is less pressure on the utero-sacral ligaments. There is often low back pain as well.

There is tenderness on pelvic and recto-vaginal examination, depending upon the extent and location of endometrial implants and time of the menstrual cycle. However, a definitive diagnosis cannot be made without direct visualization by endoscopy or laparotomy, the latter for gross pathology (e.g., endometrial cysts).

Laboratory findings show signs of inflammation, such as an elevated sedimentation rate, but not as high as with PID.

3) Fixed Uterine Retroversion

A movable uterine retroversion is common and does not cause coital pain. A fixed retroversion, however, causes discomfort from the underlying disorder causing the fixation, notably PID or endometriosis, less commonly postoperative adhesions.

Upon gynecologic evaluation the uterus cannot be moved from its fixed position in the cul-de-sac and is usually boggy and tender to manipulation.

4) Endometritis

The endometrium is normally quite resistant to infection, but inflammation may arise postabortally or due to an IUD. The history will clarify.

In this case manipulation of the uterus and movement of the cervix causes pain, and there may be a foul discharge.

Laboratory findings show signs of inflammation, such as in PID (which may co-exist), with elevated white count and sedimentation rate. Cervical cultures will usually reveal pathogens.

5) Ovarian Pathology

Ovarian tumors and cysts do not generally cause coital pain unless very large or fixed. However, a prolapsed ovary may cause severe pain during intercourse if caught between the penis and lateral pelvic wall. Not to be overlooked as a very common source of dyspareunia is mid-month ovulatory discomfort or its occasional aftermath, hemorrhage into a corpus luteum cyst.

Pelvic examination will usually reveal the ovarian pathology. In obscure cases, sonography is helpful. Prolapsed ovary is sometimes confused with another, infrequent source of dyspareunia, broad ligament varicosities.

6) Pelvic Congestion

Chronic sexual stimulation, unrelieved by orgasm, may result in enough congestion to cause pelvic discomfort. A detailed history of sexual habits is necessary to elicit this syndrome.

On pelvic examination there may be some diffuse discomfort of a non-specific nature.

7) Ectopic Pregnancy

This dangerous condition is diagnosed by an adnexal mass or tenderness on pelvic examination, together with a positive pregnancy test. Endoscopy is often needed to confirm.

8) Lower Bowel Disease

Painful hemorrhoids, fissures or inflammatory bowel disease may cause dyspareunia because of their location.

There is no gynecological pathology, but the presence of hemorrhoids or fissures will be evident on rectal examination.

X-rays of the gastrointestinal tract and sigmoidoscopy are important diagnostic aids.

9) Parapelvic Dyspareunia

Not all coital discomforts have a pelvic origin. Orthopedic disorders such as arthritis (especially the hips) can limit motion and cause distressing pain. The same applies to lumbosacral strains and intervertebral disc (Comfort, 1978).

10) Psychogenic Dyspareunia

(See Chapter 10.)

11) Dyspareunia from Disparate Size or Shape of Penis

Although the average normal vagina will readily distend to comfortably accommodate an erect penis, there are some uncommon exceptions. Vaginas vary in depth, and gynecologists always have an extra-long speculum on hand to visualize the cervix of a woman with an unusually deep canal. Similarly, some normal vaginas are relatively short and it is possible that such a woman, paired with a man whose erect penis is longer than average, may find full penetration uncomfortable. Under such circumstances, and in the absence of other possible causes of dyspareunia, a change in coital position to one in which the woman controls the degree of penetration may offer a solution.

An unusual disorder that causes a peculiar distortion in penile shape is Peyronie's disease. In this disorder there is a formation of plaques in the penis that distort its shape into a downward bend. During erection, the penile curvature becomes pronounced, often making vaginal penetration painful if not impossible, for both partners (Kolodny, Masters, & Johnson, 1979).

Pain on Orgasm

Under certain circumstances, orgasm may elicit uterine spasms which may be experienced as painful.

Postmenopausal women may complain of painful orgasm apparently associated with constriction of the vessels during uterine muscle contractions. Such tonic contractions may last for a minute or more, and are experienced as lower abdominal pain, sometimes radiating to the vagina or the legs. (Frictional discomfort usually coincides with and contributes to the pain.) This type of painful orgasm, which is due to a hypoestrogenic state, is both preventable and reversible by the administration of estrogen.

During pregnancy, orgasms are occasionally associated with spastic uterine contractions, presumably due to the increased contractility and responsiveness of the pregnant uterus. It is not certain whether this is due to the release of prostaglandin locally or of oxytocin centrally.

Patients with primary or secondary dysmenorrhea sometimes complain of pain with orgasmic uterine contractions, particularly when associated with adenomyosis.

Some women will note pain during orgasm after an IUD insertion, presumably due to heightened uterine contractility.

A hypersensitive clitoris may signal painful, rather than pleasurable, stimuli at orgasm if it is inflamed or, in the absence of pathology, if it is rubbed too harshly.

As mentioned, phimosis or adhesions of the clitoris are rarely seen in clinical practice, and not an expected cause of orgasmic pain.

Occasionally a woman's abdominal muscles may go into a brief but painful spasm coincident with a particularly frenzied orgasmic response.

Post orgasmic headaches may be associated with temporary dilation of the cerebral vessels.

REFERENCES

Barber, H. R. K., Fields, D. H., & Kaufman, S. A. *Quick reference to ob-gyn procedures*, 2nd ed., Philadelphia: Lippincott Co., 1979.

Comfort, A. (Ed.) *Sexual consequences of disability*. Philadelphia: George F. Stickley Co., 1978.

Kaplan, H. S. *The new sex therapy*. New York: Brunner/Mazel, 1974.

Kaplan, H. S. *Disorders of sexual desire*. New York: Brunner/Mazel, 1979.

Kaufman, S. A. *Sexual sabotage*. New York: Macmillan, 1981.

Kolodny, R. C., Masters, W. H., & Johnson, V. E. *Textbook of sexual medicine*. Boston: Little Brown, 1979.

6

THE UROLOGIC EVALUATION OF EJACULATORY DISORDERS (MALE ORGASM DISORDERS, RE AND PE)

Jon M. Reckler, M.D.

ANATOMY AND PHYSIOLOGY

Orgasm is the final component of the biphasic sexual response. In the male this phase is the manifestation of two integrated events: emission and ejaculation. These reflex events have been shown by physiologic study to be dependent on the autonomic nervous system. The role of the peripheral sympathetic nervous system is rather well understood; less well delineated is the interaction of higher centers within the CNS. Areas of the cerebral cortex, hypothalamus, and brainstem are known to play a role in normal ejaculatory function. The reflexes involved in emission and ejaculation are subject to degrees of voluntary inhibtion and facilitation by centers within the CNS and psychological factors may block or delay orgasm or release it from voluntary control (Kaplan, 1974).

Emission results from contraction of the smooth musculature of the walls of the structures comprising the internal genitalia: vasa deferentia, seminal vesicles, prostate, and accessory glands. Emitted secretions are thusly propelled into the posterior urethra through the prostatic and ejaculatory ducts (Krane, Siroky, 1979).

Ejaculation of the seminal fluid is provided by contraction of skeletal musculature of the ischiocavernosus and bulbocavernosus muscles (Siroky, Sax, & Krane, 1979). In the physiologic state during sexual activity, wherein the bladder neck or internal sphincter is tightly closed, the seminal fluid bolus is ejaculated in an antegrade fashion along the urethra and out through the meatus.

The orgasm phase may occur totally distinct from the erection phase. Both are dependent on the autonomic nervous system, but erection mainly on the parasympathetic, and orgasm entirely on the sympathetic component. Afferent impulses from the glans penis are transmitted via the internal prudential nerves to the spinal cord. Efferent impulses leave the upper lumbar cord over lumbar rami communicantes and hypogastric nerves through the hypogastric plexus. Stimulation of the structures in turn stimulates the smooth musculature of the internal genitalia and results in emission and closure of the bladder neck (internal urinary sphincter) (Furlow, 1981).

Neurotransmitters, biochemical compounds within the CNS, play an important role in control of the autonomic nervous system. Acetylcholine is the transmitter at sympathetic ganglia. Ganglionic blockade is effected by various drugs competing with acetylcholine at the receptor-site of the target structure. In effect, the blocking agent keeps acetylcholine from reaching the receptor and stimulating it to function. Noradrenaline (norepinephrine) is the neurotransmitter synthesized, stored, and released by the nerve terminal of the postganglionic sympathetic nerves. It is classified as an alpha sympathometic or alpha adrenergic agent. Noradrenaline stimulates the alpha adrenergic receptors of the musculature of the internal genitalia to bring about emission and ejaculation. Drugs which interfere with synthesis, storage, and release of noradrenaline, or which compete with it and block receptor sites, will alter what may be the desired action of this component of the sympathetic nervous system.

Ejaculation results from a complex neurologic integration of smooth and striated perineal musculature. With stimulation of the alpha adrenergic lumbar hypogastric nerves there is contraction of the posterior urethra and muscles of the bladder neck, which prevents backflow of semen (retrograde ejaculation) or passage of urine. Contraction of the striated perineal muscles providing for the forceful ejaculation of seminal fluid is dependent on clonic contraction of the bulbocavernosus and ischiocavernosus muscles. Innervation of these muscles is by internal pudendal nerves, the somatic fibers of which originate from the 3rd and 4th sacral nerves (Sjostrand, 1965). Acetylcholine is the neurotransmitter substance of the involved myoneural junctions.

The neurophysiology of the role and interaction of the CNS in the orgasm phase is far less well understood than that of the autonomic nervous system. Electrostimulation studies in animals have shown areas which may result in emission or ejaculation. The spinothalamic tract, areas of the thalamus, and the median foregrain bundle (a major outflow from the hypothalamus) are related to emission. Orgasm is dependent on intact spinothalamic tracts, although usually only one tract need be functioning properly for orgasm to occur (Johnson & Spalding, 1974). Ejaculation may result from stimulation of the preoptic area. Presumably there are inhibitory as well as facilitative centers in communication with the reflex centers in the lumbosacral cord. It is believed that the cord center is proximate to centers governing micturition and defecation and that the cortical centers are near both the pleasure and erection areas (Kaplan, 1974).

PATHOLOGY: DISEASE STATES AND DRUGS THAT CAN IMPAIR EJACULATION

Disturbance of the orgasm phase as the sole manifestation of a physical disease is rare indeed. Based on an understanding of the normal physiology of emission and ejaculation, one can extrapolate from any particular neurologic disorder to its potential effect on male orgasm phenomena.

Neurological Disorders

Interruption of afferent sensory pathways from the glans via pudendal nerves will preclude emission. Alteration of the integration center in the cord or of sympathetic efferent nerves may also preclude emission and closure of the internal sphincter requisite to antegrade ejaculation of seminal fluid, and lastly, dysfunction of the pudendal nerves will preclude forceful ejaculation as the ischiocavernosus and bulbocavernosus muscles cannot be stimulated to clonic contraction. *Lesions of the spinal cord* caused by *trauma, syringomyelia, tumor or demyelinating diseases* such as *multiple sclerosis* are among the most common examples of primary neurologic problems. *Parkinson's disease*, acute and chronic *polyneuropathy* should be considered among these.

Diabetes mellitus, amyloidosis, bronchogenic carcinoma or other *carcinomas, porphyria, chronic alcoholism*, the occasional *medication*, and *uremia* represent the most frequent causes of autonomic polyneuropathies causing ejaculatory problems.

Rare neurologic syndromes exist wherein there is either primary or secondary disruption of functions of the *autonomic nervous system*. In CNS or end lesions, the severity of autonomic abnormalities will depend on the extent of involvement of the autonomic pathways. Expulsion of semen into the urethra is rare in patients with complete upper motor neuron lesions. It is more common among patients with complete lower motor neuron lesions whose erections persist, as the sympathetic nerve supply is more likely to be preserved (Johnson & Spaulding, 1974).

Endocrine and Muscle Disease

The effects of primary degenerative muscular diseases or endocrinological disorders on the physiology of ejaculation and in causing ejaculatory disorders are unknown. The subspecialist physician concentrating on diagnosis and treatment of the patient with the endocrinopathy or myopathy quite understandably focuses on the disease state. Consideration of sexual dysfunction as a ramification of physical diseases is a relatively new concept.

Among patients with diabetes mellitus, erectile impotence is well recognized as a most common sequela. However, in this specific population, ejaculatory disorders do not seem to be associated with the endocrinopathy and its effect on the vascular and nervous systems. Men with testosterone deficiency may experience a delay or diminution of ejaculation, along with loss of libido.

Urological Disorders

Complaints of *pain on ejaculation* are not uncommon among patients with the irritative symptom complexes frequently diagnosed as prostatitis —bacterial or nonbacterial (Harrison, Gittes, Perlmutter, Stamey, & Walsh, 1979). Occasional comments regarding changes in the volume and color of ejaculate, what the patient usually describes as texture, viscosity, or consistency, are made by patients with irritative symptoms. Diagnosis in these cases is difficult. Except for the relatively few patients with what is an easily recognized infectious process, the overwhelming majority of patients who complain about ejaculatory pain have *no demonstrable organic basis for their symptoms* and are not relieved by physical therapeutic efforts. The patients tend to consult a number of different urologists and all parties are frustrated by the unsuccessful efforts at treatment. The urologic community is all too aware of the problem and looking for its solution, but at present is largely dependent upon empirical treatment in an effort to alleviate symptoms.

The lower urinary tract obstructive symptom complexes, most commonly caused by benign prostatic hyperplasia, less frequently secondary to prostatic carcinoma, and least often associated with stricture disease, seem to have *little association* with ejaculatory dysfunction. Patients with symptoms secondary to these diseases may occasionally comment on a decrease in force and or volume of ejaculate, and also occasionally of a diminution in the sensation of orgasm. As regards the obstructive lower tract disease processes, it should be stressed that the patients in question are of relatively advanced age and thus tend to have multisystem disease, are being treated with various medications, have greatly varying degrees of sexual activity, and appear to be more aware of and concerned about erectile than ejaculatory disturbances.

Surgical Procedures

An area in which there is a rather good understanding of causes of ejaculatory inadequacy does exist. Over the years it was observed that various *operative procedures* appeared to be directly associated with changes in ejaculatory function. Once attention was directed to the study of the apparent causes and their effects, the neurophysiologic basis was established.

As discussed earlier, the sympathetic nervous system is integral to proper functioning of the emission and ejaculatory components of the orgasm phase. Many somewhat common surgical procedures may involve transection of the sympathetic nerves upon which normal functioning is dependent. The effects of a given operation upon a particular patient cannot be specifically predetermined. Each operative procedure and the exact anatomic course of the nerves in each patient will vary somewhat. At best, we can predict the probable effect of a given type of operation upon a population of patients.

In essence, almost all of the various operations effect a localized sympathectomy, as the lumbar sympathetic nerves, ganglia, the hypogastric plexus, or hypogastric nerves are transected surgically as a proper component of the operative procedure. This iatrogenic disruption of the sympathetic nervous system may be reflected by variable changes in ejaculation (Whitelaw & Smithwick, 1951).

Retrograde ejaculation results if the sympathetic nerves necessary for reflex closure of the bladder neck are transected. With an open bladder neck but otherwise normal emission and ejaculation, the seminal fluid bolus will preferentially follow the path of least resistance into the bladder rather than distally against a narrower, longer urethral passage with its greater resistance to the flow of fluid. This is a harmless process; the patient's only perception of it is the absence of the appearance of seminal fluid upon ejaculation. The seminal fluid is passed out of the bladder along with the urine as soon as the patient voids.

Transurethral, suprapubic, and retropubic prostatectomies for benign prostatic hyperplasia represent the most common operations which mechanically remove the internal sphincter and result in retrograde ejaculation (Harrison et al., 1979). Transurethral resection of the prostate, often done for relief of bladder outlet obstruction in patients with carcinoma of the prostate, similarly results in retrograde ejaculation. Y-V Plasty of the bladder neck in association with anti-reflex surgery and incision of a hypertrophied bladder neck, often seen with urethral valves, was, until recently, a common operative procedure. It is to be expected that some of the boys who had these operations will manifest retrograde ejaculation.

Anejaculatory orgasm will result from transection of the nerves, by which emission of secretions from the vasa, seminal vesicles, and prostate are effected. Again, the patient has no perception of a change in ejaculation aside from not seeing any seminal fluid expelled. The phenomena of retrograde ejaculation and anejaculatory orgasm may be somewhat variable in degree, depending on the nerves which are transected with a particular patient and a given operation. On occasion, there may be some reversal in the ejaculatory defect, presumably due to spontaneous regeneration or reanastomosis of the sympathetic nerves.

Surgical transection or resection of the sympathetic nerves and ganglia occurs to a variable degree with lumbar sympathectomy, a previously common but now relatively rare procedure for treatment of hypertension or peripheral vascular disease.

The anatomic proximity of the sympathetic nerves and ganglia with retroperitoneal and pelvic lymph nodes, as well as the aorta and its major distal branches, accounts for the effects of a variety of vascular and cancer operations upon ejaculatory function (Leiter & Brendler, 1967). Among the vascular procedures are those for aneurysmal and atherosclerotic disease of the aorta (May et al., 1969; Weinstein et al., 1975), internal and external iliac arteries. Common cancer operations are the abdominal-perineal resection and low anterior resection of the sigmoid for colorectal cancers. The lymph node dissections done in association with a radical nephrectomy for cancer of the kidney, operations for prostatic or bladder carcinoma, and the staging node sampling of lymphomatous disease may well result in trauma to the sympathetic nerves and ganglia. The retroperitoneal lymph node dissection which is currently a standard part of the treatment of non-seminomatous germ cell tumors of the testes will most frequently result in anejaculatory orgasm. Most patients are thusly informed in advance of this procedure and semen banking is to be recommended.

Drugs

As with so much of the information regarding the effects of illness on orgasm phase disorders, reports of the effects of various drugs and chemical substances are largely based on impressions, anecdotes, and theoretical speculation. The first adage of pharmacology — no drug has a single effect — must be kept in mind.

In theory a number of drugs can impair ejaculation on a pharmacologic basis. Those drugs which interfere with proper neurotransmission of impulses in the sympathetic nervous system may be associated with ejaculatory dysfunction by altering the secretory and/or expulsion components.

The sedatives, drugs which may impair orgasm, are those which act centrally on the brain with a depressant effect. Alcohol, the barbiturates, and the narcotics represent classes of such agents. Taking large doses of these drugs may cause an adverse effect on ejaculation.

Alteration of the sympathetic nervous system integral to normal emission and ejaculation by drugs which decrease sympathetic activity does occur. Clinical manifestations of the various drug effects are variable; the spectrum includes retrograde ejaculation, retarded ejaculation, and anejaculatory orgasm. There is no good evidence of drugs causing premature ejaculation, though the monoamine oxidase inhibitors, which slow metabolic degradation of norepinephrine, could theoretically have this effect.

Many drugs have well documented *alpha adrenergic sympatholytic effects*. Sites of action may be single or multiple, including the central nervous system, the ganglia, and nerve terminals peripherally, and, since emission is dependent on an alpha adrenergic response, these drugs can theoretically impair ejaculation.

Antipsychotic drugs, the phenothiazines — e.g., Thorazine, Trilafon, Stelazine, Mellaril — in theory interfere with dopamine as a neurotransmitter in the CNS. Haldol is thought to act similarly. These drugs may also cause peripheral cholinergic blockade and peripheral alpha adrenergic blockade.

Ganglionic blockers impair ejaculation by disrupting the transmission of impulses at their stated sites. Common offenders are hexamethonium, pentolinium, mecamylamine, and trimethaphan.

Peripheral interruption of alpha sympathetic impulses occurs at the nerve terminal. Drugs may interfere with synthesis, storage, release, transport, or uptake of the neurotransmitter norepinephrine. Mood regulators, the tricyclic antidepressants, e.g., Elavil, Tofranil, block uptake of norepinephrine at the nerve terminal. Lithium can be shown to inhibit release of norepinephrine. Cocaine effects peripheral alpha blockade.

Many other non-psychotropic drugs may cause ejaculatory dysfunction by effecting alpha adrenergic blockade. Reserpine, guanethidine, bretylium, and methyldopa, used as antihypertensive agents, have potent sympatholytic effects. The ergot alkaloids have a similar action but are of lesser potency (Goodman & Gilman, 1979).

A few drugs are in common usage specifically as alpha adrenergic blocking agents and these frequently impair ejaculation. Phenoxybenzamine (Dibenzyline), phentolamine (Regitine) and prazosin (Minipress) are those used most frequently. Appropriate questioning of patients taking these drugs will often elicit the presence of ejaculatory dysfunction. Most patients will report retarded ejaculation or "dry ejaculation." Whether the latter phenomenen represents retrograde or anejaculatory orgasm is unknown because of lack of investigation.

Drugs which may enhance libido may be perceived by the patient as having a beneficial effect on ejaculation and orgasm. Whether or not there is actually any physiologic effect of such agents is unknown. Androgens, the neurotransmitter L-Dopa, stimulants such as the amphetamines and cocaine, hallucinogens, and amyl nitrite have attributed enhancement effects. The beneficial effects of the psychotropic drugs are in all probability indirect and efficacious only because of their favorable effects on the psychic state. (Also see Table 11.)

EVALUATION

History

Urologic evaluation of orgasm phase disorders is best begun by clarification of the problem as perceived by the patient. In medical parlance, there may be retarded or partially retarded ejaculation, premature ejaculation, retrograde ejaculation, or anejaculatory orgasm. Orgasm may be totally absent or painful. Changes in volume, color, or viscosity of seminal fluid may be noted.

Since other sexual phase disorders may impact on the orgasm phase, problems in these areas should be elicited. From the outset of the interview attention must be given to the personality of the patient, his "sexual vocabulary," and the effect of both on his ability to express himself. Determination and the establishment of a common language are important. It is important to evaluate the patient's personality and its potential as the cause or role as a modifier of the disorder.

Once a statement and understanding of the problem are established, the current status is determined. In sequence, information is then elicited regarding the date of onset, as well as potentially associated factors at that time, and the subsequent sexual history, arriving back at the current state. In addition to evaluating the patient's personality throughout the course of history-taking and physical examination, the examiner formulates an idea about how the patient views his problem and its importance in his life. In addition, he needs to consider the patient's perception and assessment of his sexual partner's overt and covert responses to the problem. The diagnostic interview is discussed more fully in Section I of this volume.

A detailed *genitourinary history* is then obtained. A chronologic history of any urologic diseases, modalities of diagnosis, treatments and responses, with evaluation of the patient's recollection of associated symptoms, is undertaken. Any ongoing problems are elicited.

A more general medical history follows with a catalogue of medications being taken, why, and when begun. Alcoholic beverage intake, smoking habits, and drug usage are established. Next a list is made of any past and/or ongoing medical problems and dates of onset; where relevant, an internal check is made of the actualities of these by evaluation of symptoms, means of diagnosis, and response to treatment. A brief family history and record of any allergies complete this portion of the evaluation.

Physical Examination

The urologic physical examination concentrates on notation of blood pressure, the location of any surgical incisions, and examination of the abdomen, inguinal areas, external genitalia, and digital rectal examination with attention to the anal sphincter tone and prostate gland — its size, shape symmetry, texture, mobility, and sensitivity to examination. Normal seminal vesicles are not palpable. Neurological evaluation is performed where applicable, checking reflexes, cutaneous sensation, and motor strength. Peripheral pulses and cutaneous effects of peripheral vascular disease are noted. Most patients with ejaculatory complaints have a normal physical and urologic examination.

Laboratory Studies

Laboratory studies are limited. Of interest may be an urinalysis, including a check for glucose and the microscopic sediment. Prostatic secretions may be examined. Appropriate cultures are obtained. Microscopic examination of urine voided after ejaculation for the presence of spermatozoa will distinguish between retrograde ejaculation and anejaculatory orgasm.

If the problems of libido or impotence are present, endocrinologic evaluation may include blood studies for testosterone, prolactin, and LH levels. Consideration of associated or concurrent pathologic urologic conditions might indicate the need for cystoscopic examination, intravenous urography, or other radiologic studies of the urinary tract.

Semen Analysis

Regardless of the alleged problem for which the patient seeks consultation, it is not uncommon for the occasional individual to ask, usually as an aside, "How can I tell if I'm fertile?" While at times this question may be taken at face value, I suspect that the majority of the time the patient has concerns regarding potency, knows of the semen analysis study, and is looking for the reassurance which may derive from knowing the results of a normal semen analysis with its implication of fertility. In actuality, in a physical sense, there is no association between fertility and potency. Fertility derives only from the presence of fertile sperm and these cells play no part in physiologic potency.

Semen analysis is a study performed by specialized laboratories wherein ejaculate produced by masturbation is evaluated for various parameters. Evaluation of the data permits an estimate of the probability of the individual having average or less than average fertility. There is a great range in "normal values." "Normal" or "below normal" are probably poor terms and it would be more desirable to speak in terms of averages.

Semen analysis is diagnostic of infertility only if there are no sperm cells present. Pregnancy, the end product of fertility, requires two individuals, each of whom contributes to the overall fertility of the couple. One "very

TABLE 6
Normal Semen

	(Minimal Standards)	Morphology	(Minimal Standards) ($\geq 60\%$)
Ejaculate Volume _____	(2.0–2.5 ml.)	Ovals	
Sperm count (million/ml) _____	(≥ 20 million)	Large	_____
Total count (millions) _____	(≥ 40 million)	Small	_____
Motility at _____ hours after ejaculation		Tapering	_____
Quality of activity _____	(3 −)	Bicephalic	_____
Percent mobile _____	($\geq 40\%$)	Amorphous	_____
		Immature	_____

fertile" partner may well make up for below average fertility of the other partner, whereas a couple with low average fertility of each partner may never achieve conception and a successful pregnancy. Thus, the azospermic male can be said to be sterile, whereas the man with subaverage parameters by semen analysis may father many children if paired with an appropriate partner.

The physician specializing in fertility will usually require two or three semen analyses before formulating an impression regarding an individual. For the purposes other than a fertility workup, only one semen analysis is appropriate, assuming parameters fall within average ranges.

REFERENCES

Furlow, W. L. (Ed.) Male sexual dysfunction. *Urol. Clin. N.A.*, 1981, *8:1*.

Goodman, L. S., & Gilman, A. (Eds.) *The pharmacological basis of therapeutics*. New York: Macmillan, 1979.

Harrison, J. H., Gittes, R. F., Perlmutter, A. D., Stamey, T. A., & Walsh, P. C. (Eds.) *Urology*. Philadelphia: W. B. Saunders, 1979.

Johnson, R. H., & Spalding, J. M. D. *Disorders of the autonomic nervous system*. Philadelphia: Davis, 1974.

Kaplan, H. S. *The new sex therapy*. New York: Brunner/Mazel, 1974.

Krane, R. J., & Siroky, M. B. (Eds.) *Clinical neurourology*. Boston: Little, Brown & Co., 1979.

Leiter, E., & Brendler, H. Loss of ejaculation following bilateral retroperitoneal lymphadenectomy. *Journal of Urology*, 1967, *98*, 375.

May, A. G., DeWeese, J. A., & Rob, C. G. Changes in sexual function following operation on the abdominal aorta. *Surgery*, 1969, *65*, 41.

Siroky, M. B., Sax, G., & Krane, R. J. Sacral signal tracing: The electrophysiology of the Bulbocavernosus reflex. *Journal of Urology*, 1979, *122*, 661.

Sjostrand, N. O. The adrenergic innervation of the vas deferens and the accessory male genital glands. An experimental and comparative study of its anatomical and functional organization in some mamals, including the presence of adrenaline and chromaffin cells in these organs. *Acta Physiol. Scand.* (Supp. 257), 1965, *65*, 1.

Weinstein, M. H., & Machleder, H. I. Sexual function after aorto-iliac surgery. *Ann. Surg.*, 1975, *181*, 787.

Whitelaw, G. P., & Smithwick, R. H. Some secondary effects of sympathectomy. *New England Journal of Medicine*, 1951, *245*, 121.

7

THE UROLOGIC EVALUATION OF MALE DYSPAREUNIA

Jon M. Reckler, M.D.

Cases of male dyspareunia may be categorized on the basis of the point in the sexual act at which pain occurs. This facilitates diagnosis and successful treatment of the individual patient. Conceptually, male dyspareunia is classified as pain on erection, pain on intromission, or pain accompanying ejaculation.

PATHOLOGY OF DYSPAREUNIA

Pathology of Pain on Ejaculation

The diagnosis and treatment of patients with pain on ejaculation can be extraordinarily difficult. The perception of pain may be localized to the glans, shaft or base of the phallus, the suprapubic area, the perineum, the groin, or the testes. Discomfort may be present in a combination of sites. Pain is usually reported as occurring with ejaculation and lasting for variable periods of time thereafter.

Prostatitis and urethritis are the most common pathologic conditions found on evaluation of the patient with painful ejaculation. Only the occasional patient with benign prostatic hyperplasia or carcinoma of the prostate will have discomfort on ejaculation and this symptom may or may not be affected by treatment of the prostatic disease. Intraurethral lesions, such as strictures, condyloma acuminata, carcinoma, and scarring of the ejaculatory ducts, are rarely found on evaluation. Seminal vesiculitis may be present in association with primary prostatitis, but as an isolated disease is most uncommon. Infrequent causes of groin or testicular pain on ejaculation are inguinal hernias, vasitis, and epididymitis. Seemingly there is a syndrome of painful retraction of the testes with ejaculation; this is thought to result from forceful contraction of the cremaster muscles in conjunction with clonic contraction of the ischiocavernosus and bulbocavernosus muscles which effect ejaculation of the seminal fluid bolus from the posterior urethra. The actual cause of cremaster spasm is unknown.

All too often no physical pathologic entity can be demonstrated. In most of the patients where this is the case, other signs and symptoms suggest the presence of nonbacterial or congestive prostatitis. There is much speculation as to the etiology of this process. The most common factor seems to be a recent change in the pattern of sexual activity — more often a reduction rather than an increase in frequency — but whether this is cause or effect of painful ejaculation is unclear. Alcoholic and caffeine beverages, nicotine, and spices have also been implicated. Functional painful spasm of the cremasteric and perineal muscles has been reported (Kaplan, 1979). Many patients report a temporal relationship between symptoms and "stress" at home or at work.

Treatment of the specific identifiable pathologic condition can be expected to eliminate both the disease state and the secondary symptom of painful ejaculation. When no disease process can be identified, treatment must consist of empiric remedies and reassurance as to anatomic normalcy and the absence of potentially harmful underlying pathologic processes. A psychogenic basis for the symptom must then be considered (Kaplan, 1979; Melman, 1982).

Pathology of Erectile Dyspareunia

Phimosis, balanitis, balanoposthitis, and *frenular tethering* are among the most common causes of painful erection (Ansell, 1982). These entities are all very much interrelated. Phimosis is narrowing of the opening of the foreskin which restricts its being retracted over the glans. This may be either congenital or acquired subsequent to traumatic retraction and/or infection. Balanitis is defined as inflammation of the foreskin. Balanoposthitis is inflammation of both the prepuce and glans. Frenular tethering results from scarring of the frenulum. The loss of elasticity may create pain on erection, with the "too short" frenulum acting as a tight bowstring on the ventral aspect of the phallus. Trauma and infection are very much a part of all of the above processes. Trauma causes tearing of the skin; inflammation with fibrosis is part of the normal healing phenomenen; and loss of elasticity results in the predisposition to recurrent trauma. *Infection of the foreskin* has exactly the same course of events. Infection of the prepuce most frequently results from the fungus Candida; underlying *diabetes mellitus* is common in the adult, though the organism is often seen at any age and in the absence of diabetes. In general, trauma and infection go together. With tearing of the skin, mild secondary infection usually occurs; then healing with fibrosis results.

Paraphimosis is constriction of the glans penis by a foreskin with a narrow opening, which when retracted behind the glans is sufficiently tight to constrict the phallus, a most painful condition.

Peyronie's disease is an illness of unknown etiology often associated with Dupuytren's contractures. Peyronie's plaques of dense fibrous tissue arise in the dorsal midline of the phallus. The clinical presentation is virtually always painful erections. Fibrosis may progress to cause a localized restriction of erection resulting in chordee — curvature of the erect phallus. A Peyronie's plaque is usually easily felt on palpation of the phallus.

Trauma to the phallus with injury of the investing tunics or erectile bodies may result in formation of scar tissue which will have the same effect as the ideopathic Peyronie's disease.

Chordee, a congenital curvature of the phallus usually associated with hypospadias, may rarely cause pain on erection. Currently, surgical correction of this cosmetic deformity is usually carried out before the boy enters kindergarten.

On occasion, *prior surgical procedures* on the phallus result in formation of skin adhesions or scar tissue which cause painful erections. Adhesions of residual prepucial tissue to the glans or fibrous scars of the investing tunics of the shaft of the phallus are not difficult to find on careful physical examination (Harrison et al., 1979).

Mechanical devices — penile rings — used to facilitate or prolong erections can be responsible for pain with erection. Prior trauma secondary to their use may result in an ongoing problem.

Inflammatory lesions of the urethra and internal male genitalia may, on occasion, cause painful erections. Generally, the pain elicited by these lesions occurs at a later point in the sexual act.

Pathology of Dyspareunia on Intromission

Pain on intromission or in association with the friction of mechanical stimulation of the erect phallus is commonly caused by many of the same processes which cause painful erections: *phimosis, paraphimosis, balanitis, balanoposthitis, frenular tethering, chordee,* and *scars of the skin or underlying tissues.*

Irritation of cutaneous lesions present before intercourse is begun may be aggravated. *Herpes progenitalis, scabies, eczematoid lesions,* and *preexistent traumatic abrasions* are common offenders. *Thrombophlebitis* of superficial veins in the coronal sulcus and penile shaft resulting from prior sexual trauma will cause pain upon subsequent sexual stimulation. *Mechanical abrasion* of the phallus during the sexual act can cause concomitent pain. Eczematoid cutaneous lesions with associated pain will often appear only following mechanical stimulation of the penile skin.

Pain is often caused by superimposed irritation of the urethra, where *urethritis* is already present. Nonspecific urethritis and gonococcal urethritis are the most common of the infectious urethritides. Excessive mechanical irritation of the urethra with sexual activities — intercourse, masturbation, or instrumentation — is most frequently responsible for non-infectious urethritis.

"Chemical urethritis," a cause of painful intercourse, can be determined by careful history-taking. Agents most commonly responsible for the pain are the contraceptive foams, jellies, and creams, the lubricants of condoms, soap, or any conceivable agent to which the urethra may be exposed. Sensitivity to vaginal secretions has also been reported.

EVALUATION

Evaluation of the male with the problem of pain associated with the sexual act is rather straightforward. A clear statement of the complaint in the physician's mind is mandatory.

History

The medical history is directed toward a statement of the current problem, its onset, and its natural history. The patient may recognize associated factors and may have made efforts at self-treatment; the physician's knowledge of such information is purposeful. Concomitant sexual dysfunction may exist. This information should be elicited. The history should also determine types of sexual activity, frequency, duration, partners, lubricants, contraceptives, and the relationship of any of these to the patient's symptoms. Is the patient on any drugs or has he had any surgical procedures which may relate? A detailed history of present voiding habits and symptoms, as well as prior urologic diseases — specifically urethritis, prostatitis, sexual transmitted diseases, and dermatologic disorders — is pertinent. Inquiry should be made regarding known problems or symptoms of sexual partners.

Physical Examination

On physical examination, cutaneous lesions are initially sought: Attention is focused on the inguinal area, external genitalia, and perineum, but skin lesions elsewhere should be noticed.

The inguinal areas are examined for hernias. On palpation of the external genitalia one searches for lesions deep to the skin, a Peyronie's plaque of the phallus or evidence of an epididymal or testicular lesion. The prepuce of the uncircumcised male must be retracted to check for phimosis and lesions on its underside. The urethral meatus should be carefully inspected, estimating adequacy of luminal size and looking for intrameatal inflammatory lesions.

On rectal examination one may find perianal or intraluminal lesions. Prostatic evaluation focuses on size, texture, symmetry, and sensitivity. Normal seminal vesicles are not palpable.

An abnormality of the patient's urinary stream as he voids may suggest the presence of an intraurethral lesion and need for further examination radiographically or with a cystoscopic examination.

Laboratory Findings

Microscopic examination of any urethral discharge with appropriate staining techniques and urinalysis with microscopic examination of the centrifuged sediment should be performed for all patients. A three glass urinalysis, examination of expressed prostatic secretions, and culture of urine, prostatic, or seminal fluid may be desirable.

The further diagnostic modalities of cystoscopic examination, intravenous pyelography, urethrography, vasography, and pelvic sonography or "CT scanning" might be applicable for particular patients.

REFERENCES

Ansell, J. S. Reasons for painful intercourse in men. *Medical Aspects of Human Sexuality*, 1982, 16:61.

Harrison, J. H., Gittes, R. F., Perlmutter, A. D., Stamey, T. A., & Walsh, P. C. (Eds.) *Urology*. Philadelphia: W. B. Saunders, 1979.

Kaplan, H. S. *Disorders of sexual desire*. New York: Brunner/Mazel, 1979.

Melman, A. Psychosexual reactions to urologic problems. *Medical Aspects of Human Sexuality*, 1982, *16*, 118.

8

THE UROLOGIC EVALUATION OF IMPOTENCE (MALE EXCITEMENT PHASE DISORDER)

Arnold Melman, M.D., and
Elliot Leiter, M.D.

Penile erection is of obvious importance to mankind for purposes of reproduction as well as sexual pleasure. Normal erection requires the integration of a complex series of events which necessarily begins with either an external or psychic stimulus. The resultant neural impulse is transmitted along the spinal cord to the autonomic nerves that innervate the blood vessels and smooth muscle that compose the erectile tissue of the penis. That event causes vascular engorgement and subsequent penile turgidity. The erection terminates with the rapid drainage of the additional blood from the cavernous spaces with a return to the flaccid state. However, the precise physiological mechanism responsible for a sufficiently rigid phallus permitting vaginal penetration is not well understood.

ANATOMY AND PHYSIOLOGY

Embryology

The penis develops in the normal 46 X,Y male fetus ten weeks after inception. The corpora cavernosa penis, columns which ultimately are responsible for tumescence, are paired mesenchymal bodies that grow in utero in response to hormones released by the fetal testes. A third mesenchymal column, the corpus cavernosum urethra, surrounds the urinary channel and fuses with the glans penis into a continuous structure, the corpus spongiosum. Although erectile activity is present in utero as well as throughout early childhood, penile growth does not occur again until puberty. At that time the concomitant rise in plasma testosterone causes both the corpora and the external genitalia to enlarge.

Anatomy

1) Corpora Cavernosa

The corpora are adherent structures in the pendulous portion of the penis. At the angle of pubic symphysis, the corpora diverge into two separate channels, the crura, which insert firmly into the ischiopubic rami of the pelvis (Figure 1). It is that insertion that provides stability to the pendulous portion of the penis during intercourse (Figure 2). Surrounding each crus is a thin skeletal muscle, the ischiocavernosus. This muscle is also present in lower mammalian species in whom it is believed to be of principal importance in increasing the intracorporal pressure during penile tumescence. In those animals the muscle contracts against the blood-filled crus in its rigid posterior fixation. The contraction forces blood into the pendulous portion of the corpora, thus raising the intracorporal pressures in the bull's penis, for example, to levels as high as 15,000 mm of mercury. In man, the muscle serves only a rudimentary function. Voluntary contractions of the ischiocavernosus will cause a minimal surge of blood into the pendulous

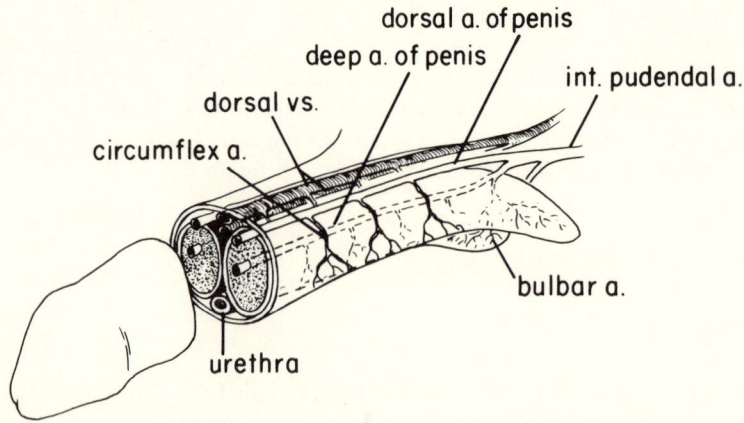

Figure 1. Basic anatomy and vasculature of the penis.

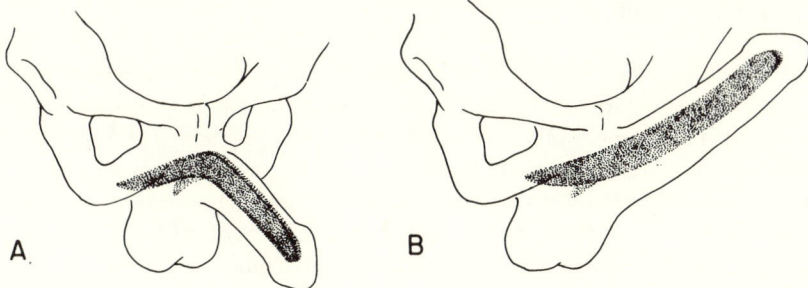

Figure 2. Relationship of the corpora to the pelvis during detumescence and full tumescence.

corpora and some movement of the penis itself. However, patients with complete spinal cord injury in which there is no longer any skeletal muscle activity can have entirely normal erections without the activity of the ischiocavernosus muscle.

a) Blood Supply

1) Arteries: The corpora cavernosa are supplied by two pairs of arteries: the artery of the corpora and the deep dorsal artery (Figure 1). The dorsal artery runs above the tunica albuginea beneath Buck's fascia. It gives off multiple circumflex arterial branches which communicate with the deep artery of the penis and the corpus spongiosum. The deep arteries enter the penis on the ventral surface of the crus. They give off nutrient vessels and the helical arteries. The latter are so named because they follow a wandering course as they travel through the corpora in the flaccid penis. Newman and Northrup (1981) reported finding them approximately three to a centimeter in the proximal half of the corpus cavernosa. They believe they each divide in treelike fashion into three or more subdivisions. It is from these arteries that the vascular spaces of the corpora are filled with blood during tumescence.

2) Veins: The venous drainage of the penis is unlike that of most other organ systems in the body, in which a major artery is accompanied by a corresponding vein throughout its course. In the penis, the central corporal artery is not accompanied by a specific vein. Instead, there are multiple short-channel, tissue emissary veins, which pierce the tunica albuginea and unite the cavernous spaces of the penis to a network of circumferential veins surrounding the corpora (Figure 1). These circumferential veins in turn empty into either a deep or superficial dorsal vein, which in turn drains into the veins of the pelvis.

b) Internal Structure

Each corpus is a cigar-shaped cylinder covered by a fibro-elastic layer of tissue 2–4 mm thick—the tunica albuginea (from the Greek, a coat resembling a boiled egg white). The tunica is one of the thickest fascial layers in the body and must support the internal pressures of the corpora during tumescence while resisting the counteracting external pressures of the vaginal wall during intercourse. The septum between both sides in the pendulous penis is incomplete. Thus, blood from one corpus drains freely into the adjacent side. The internal structure of the corpus is a composite of the helical arteries coursing from the central cavernous artery, smooth muscle cells which in turn lie in a stroma of collagenous tissue (Figure 3). Alongside

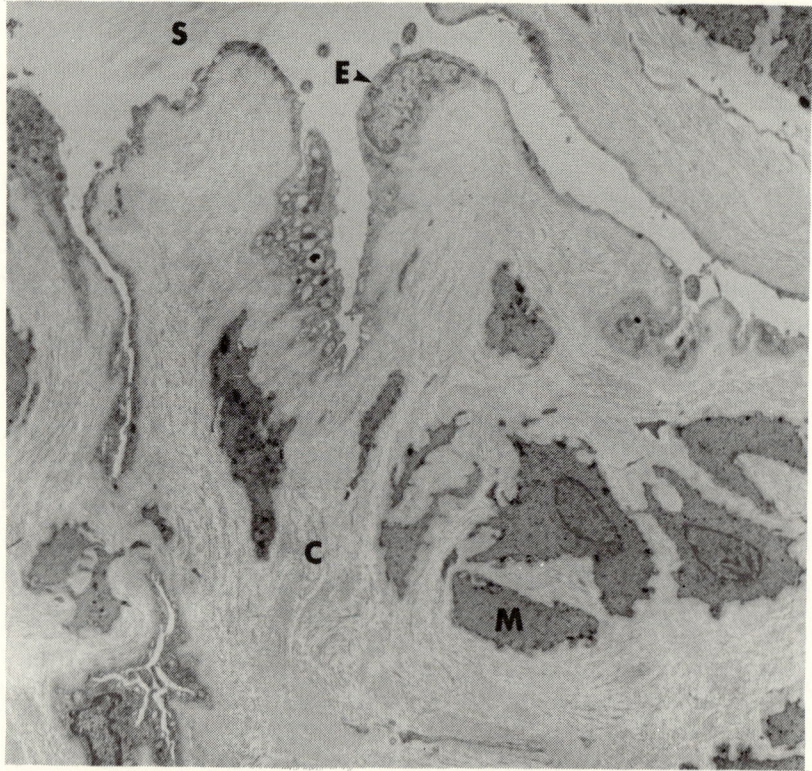

Figure 3. Electron neurograph of the corporal stroma, small muscle (M), collagen (C), cavernous sinus (S) lined by endothelial cells (E). Approximate magnification × 2500 (Courtesy Dr. Robert S. Bressler)

the arteries and smooth muscle cells are bundles of nerve fibers which innervate the blood vessels and smooth muscle cells of the corpora.

In humans, except in a case of injury with subsequent calcium formation of the injured tissue, there is no bony material in the corpora, as is present in lower mammalian species. In those animals the os penis or baculum is a bone which serves the purpose of supplying penile rigidity to the organ. The larger the os penis, the less erectile tissue is present (or necessary for penetration) in the corporal bodies.

c) Tumescence

The precise mechanism of tumescence is unknown. Experiments reported by Newman, Northrup and Devlin in 1964 demonstrated the presence of vascular shunts, at least 100 microns in diameter, between the arterial and venous system. The position of the anatomic shunts has not been histologically identified in man, however. Conti (1952) proposed that in the flaccid state blood was shunted outside the corpora, but was forced into the cavernous spaces during erection. The shunting mechanism, he and others believed, was aided by special cushions or pads which line the walls of the arteries in the penis and created greater resistance to the flow of blood when the vessels were constricted (Kiss, 1921; Muller, 1835; Stieve, 1930). However, more recent studies by Newman and Tchertkoff (1980) and Benson et al. (1981) suggest that these cushions do not play a role in erectile activity. They have not been found in the erectile tissue of children and appear to increase in size with aging. They more likely represent pathologic changes in aging vessels which have been subjected to stretch. Indeed, such changes have also been found in vessels in other parts of the body, particularly those which overlie joints and in the coronary arteries.

Increase in volume of the penis during erection has been estimated in two different ways. Shirai, Nakamura, Ishii, Mitsukawa, and Sawai (1976) utilized the injection of technetium tagged red blood cells into the corpora for that purpose. Patients were shown visually sexual stimulating movies and the increase in penile volume was estimated by measuring change in penile radioactivity. In the Japanese population the average increase in penile volume during tumescence was 60 ml of blood.

When saline was infused directly into the corpora of five unanesthetized men (Newman, Northrup, & Devlin, 1964), at rates between 20–50 ml per minute, a typical erection ensued. Once obtained, a flow of 12 ml per minute maintained the erection. The results of that experiment are not conclusive, however; one aspect of tumescence that remains unresolved is the question whether the additional volume of blood delivered to the corpora during erection is trapped and stagnant, or whether a continuing increased input and outflow of blood is needed to sustain the erection. There are reports from two laboratories in which an attempt was made to resolve this question. In each instance, radioactive xenon 133 was injected directly into the corpora of the flaccid penis. Unfortunately, the conclusions are contradictory. Shirai and Ishii (1981) report that, during erection, the washout of fluid from the corpora is enhanced, thus supporting a concept of increased flow through the corpora during tumescence. Wagner (1981), however, reports that the washout is reduced during erection. This latter concept is supported by considerable other evidence. Deysach (1939) theorized that a constriction of the emissary veins prevents blood from leaving from the corpora. His report has been criticized, but Wagner (1981) has documented reduction of venous outflow during erection with cineradiography. It is also a fact that blood from the turgid penis cannot be squeezed from the phallus during erection. These observations support the theory that blood is trapped within the cavernous spaces.

d) Tumescence Versus Rigidity

It is important to recognize that there are two phases of erection. There are specific differences between *tumescence* as a result of blood filling the cavernous spaces, with subsequent increase in penile circumference, and *rigidity*, in which intrapenile pressure rises to the level of arterial pressure (Figure 4). It is during the phase of rigidity that the penis straightens and becomes erect (Figure 2). Two laboratories (Metz & Wagner, 1981; Wein, Fishkein, Carpiniello, & Malloy, 1981) have now reported that, at the time of maximal increase in penile circumference, the penis is in fact flaccid and not capable of rigidity sufficient to effect vaginal penetration. Therefore, one should not equate maximal changes of circumference with penile rigidity. This subject will be addressed subsequently in the section on nocturnal penile tumescence.

2) *Neural Innervation of the Penis*

Electrical lesions placed in selected areas of the limbic system in monkey brain resulted in stimulation of penile erection (Dua & MacLean, 1964; MacLean & Ploog, 1962). It is unclear which segment of the brain inhibits erection. The effect of endogenous neurotransmitters within the brain upon sexual arousal (libido) and postejaculatory refractiveness has been studied in animal models (primarily rats) and man (Ambrosi, Travaglini, Gag-

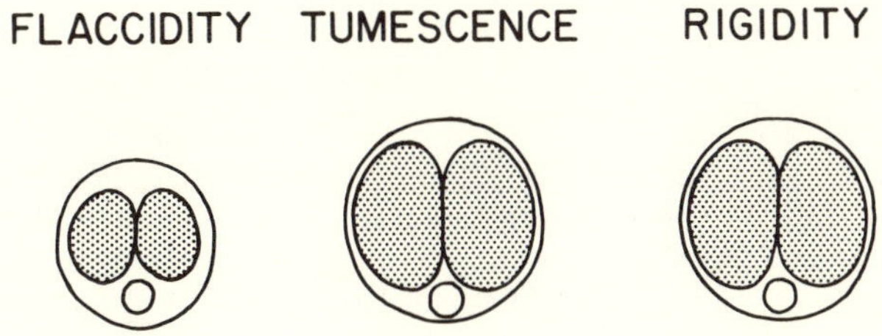

FLACCIDITY   TUMESCENCE   RIGIDITY

CIRCUMFERENCE	80 mm	110 mm	110 mm
INTRACAVERNOUS VOLUME	8 ml	60-70 ml	60-70 ml
INTRACAVERNOUS PRESSURE	5 mm Hg	< 90 mm Hg	> 90 mm Hg

Figure 4. Schematic of pressure-volume relationship within the penis during erection. (adapted from Wagner, 1981)

gini, Moriondo, Elli, Bara, & Faglia, 1979; Gessa & Paglietti, 1979; Gessa & Tagliamonte, 1974). The precise roles of these substances in man are poorly understood, but are listed for completeness (see Table 7).

Erection per se is a function of the autonomic nervous system that is reflexly, not voluntarily, initiated. In the past, tumescence was thought to be entirely a function of the parasympathetic nervous system mediated through the sacral roots of S2-4. There is recent evidence to suggest, however, that at least locally, within the corpora themselves, it is the sympathetic nervous system rather than the parasympathetic that is of greater significance in effecting penile erection (Melman & Henry, 1979).

This evidence is as follows:

a) Atropine even in high doses does not appear to cause impotence. Wagner has infused 0.35 mg./kg. of Atropine into normal patients without an effect on their erectile capacities (Wagner, 1981).
b) Choline acetyltransferase, the enzyme that manufactures acetylcholine, is not present in human erectile tissue (Melman, Henry, Felten, & O'Connor, 1980a).
c) Drugs that effect sympathetic nerve function cause erectile impotence.

A series of studies was conducted in our laboratory based upon the fact that the erectile bodies are composed of vascular smooth muscle (Melman

TABLE 7
Centrally Active Transmitters and Drugs

Substance	Effect	Drugs Which Alter Function
Enkephalin	Shortens Postejaculatory Period	Naloxone: Inhibits Morphine: Stimulates
Serotonin	Lengthens Postejaculatory Period, "Hypersexuality"	LSD, Methysergide, Metergoline: Inhibit
Dopamine	Increases Sexual Activity	Apomorphine, L-Dopa: Stimulate Haloperidol, Pimozide, Chlopro- mazine: Inhibit

& Henry, 1979; Melman, Henry, Felten, & O'Connor, 1980a, 1980b). It is known that the adrenergic nervous system is the principal moderator of vascular smooth muscle throughout (Marshall, 1977). The body tissue content of norepinephrine reflects the density of innervation of sympathetic nerves of a particular tissue (Euler, 1962). Therefore, we measured the tissue content of the principal neurotransmitter of the adrenergic nervous system, norepinephrine. The patients studied were those with normal reflex erections and from men impotent from a series of diseases. Figure 5 summarizes the result of those measurements.

Several conclusions can be reached from these studies:

1) Higher concentrations of norepinephrine are found in normal male erectile tissue than would be expected from the presence of vascular smooth muscle alone.
2) Confirmatory data from other laboratories have shown the presence of both alpha and beta adrenergic receptors in the corporal stroma (Levin & Wein, 1980). This suggests that tissue norepinephrine and its associated receptors are in fact functioning in a physiologic way within the corpora.
3) Norepinephrine content is altered by diseases or medications which are known to cause impotence.
4) The tentative conclusions derived from these studies suggest that one mechanism which may result in erectile dysfunction is mediated via sympathetic neurotransmission. Abnormal erection may occur as a result of adrenergic nerve damage with a reduction of neurotransmitter content, or alteration of either the release or the combining at the receptor level.

Because some patients with erectile impotence have a normal corporal norepinephrine content, we have speculated that norepinephrine may not be functioning alone, but along with other neurotransmitter substances within the corpora as a means of effecting penile turgidity and/or detumescence.

Recently, another substance, a vasoactive intestinal polypeptide (VIP), has been found in nonadrenergic, noncholinergic neurons within the corporal tissue. This substance is a potent vasodilating agent (Larsen, Ottesen, Fahrenkrug, & Fahrenkrug, 1981). It has been suggested as another potential regulator of intracorporal regional blood flow and muscle contractility in human erection.

Further studies are needed to establish the significance of these neurotransmitters in the regulation of erection.

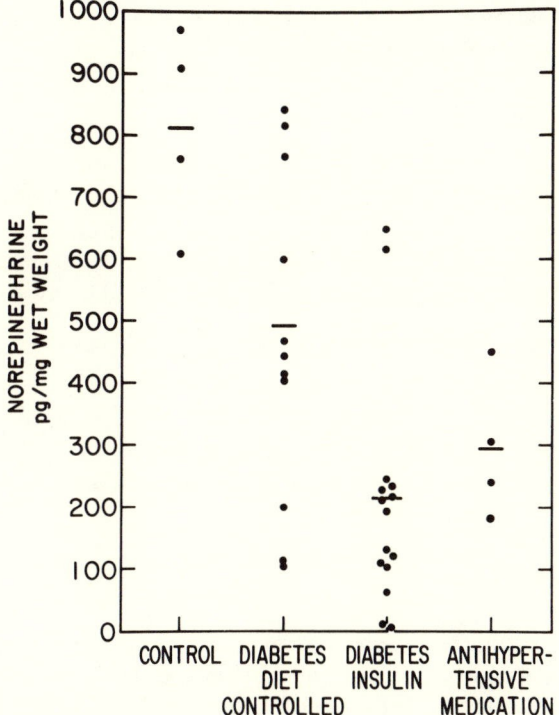

Figure 5. Graph of the norepinephrine content of the corporal tissue. Each closed circle represents one patient and the bar the mean of each group. (Reprinted with permission of *J. Urology*)

3) Hormones

Although changes in the sex-related hormones historically have generated the most attention, statistically they are the least common causes of erectile dysfunction and probably account for only 1–2 % of erectile impotence. The hormones in question are testosterone, prolactin and beta-estradiol. Testosterone is produced by the Leydig cells of the interstitium of the testis and to a lesser degree from the adrenal cortex. The hormone is released in intermittent bursts in response to the stimulus of luteinizing hormone produced from the anterior pituitary. The latter is in turn driven by the peptide, luteinizing hormone releasing hormone (LHRH), from the hypothalamus. Because of the intermittency of release of testosterone, there is a wide range of normal values — 300 to 1200 ng/ml of plasma in most laboratories. Although there seems to be a decrease in average plasma testosterone in men over age 60, there is a wide range of normal in the older age group. Therefore, there is no reason to believe that this decrease with aging is a cause of impotence in older men.

4) Aging

In the absence of disease, men can expect to maintain erectile capability throughout their entire life span. Karacan, Williams, Thornby, & Solis (1975) have shown that there is a gradual decline of nocturnal penile tumescence throughout the eighth decade of life. There are other changes that occur of which the physician and patient should be aware.

a) Penile Sensitivity

There is an increasing loss of penile sensation and vibratory sensitivity with age (Edwards & Husted, 1976; Solnick & Birren, 1977). These changes occur through the loss of nerve endings which are sensitive to both touch and vibration (Newman, 1970).

b) Rate of Response

In another study the rate of change of the penile circumference of patients shown a sexually stimulating movie was measured. Younger men (aged 19–30 years) responded six times faster than the older group (aged 48–65 years) in increases of penile circumference.

c) Lengthened Refractory Periods

With aging the period of time between erectile and orgastic events is increased. The mechanism is not known. These changes suggest that to obtain the same result, older men required a greater tactile stimulation, increased time to achieve the same degree of erectile potency than men 50 years of age or less.

5) Possible Mechanism of Normal Erection

Based on our studies and the results of other studies, a plausible mechanism of erection is as follows: During erection an increased volume of blood is forced into corporal spaces via a shunting mechanism controlled by the sympathetic nervous system. The blood, whether flowing at an increased rate or trapped, is present in increased volume (Figure 4). The smooth muscle of the corpora (under sympathetic control) then contracts thus increasing both the intra-corporal pressure and penile turgidity (Figure 6). Malfunction of this contractile ability would not allow sufficient penile turgidity to effect vaginal penetration. If this malfunction is secondary to the effects of disease of the sympathetic neurons and/or sympathetically derived neurotransmitter substances on the muscle cells themselves, one can account for the clinical picture of gradual onset of softening during tumescence. Those

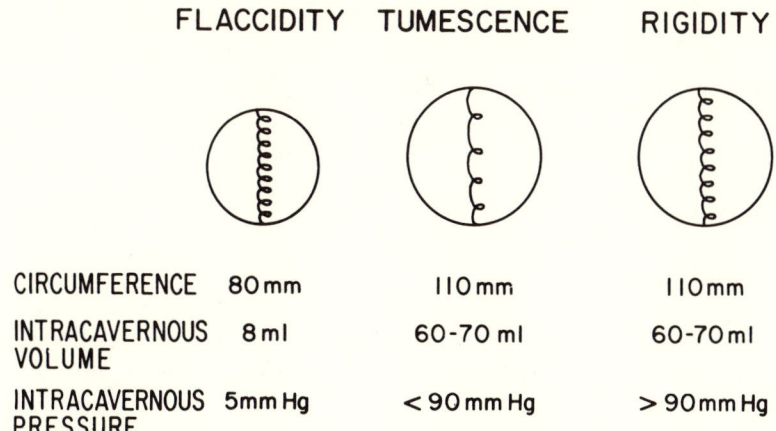

FLACCIDITY   TUMESCENCE   RIGIDITY

	FLACCIDITY	TUMESCENCE	RIGIDITY
CIRCUMFERENCE	80 mm	110 mm	110 mm
INTRACAVERNOUS VOLUME	8 ml	60-70 ml	60-70 ml
INTRACAVERNOUS PRESSURE	5 mm Hg	< 90 mm Hg	> 90 mm Hg

Figure 6. Schematic of pressure-tension relationships within the corpora during full erection. Contraction of the corporal smooth muscle is likened to increased tension of a spring in a close space.

clinicians involved with the care of patients having organic impotence will recognize that this is the symptom complex observed in most patients and is explained by the smooth muscle-neurotransmitter theory.

PATHOLOGY: DISEASE STATES AND DRUGS THAT MAY CAUSE ERECTILE FAILURE

Local Penile Anatomic Abnormalities

In this category, the most uncommon but self-evident abnormality would be that of total failure of penile development, as may occur in genetically normal (46 XY) men presenting without a penis. Less rare is inadequate development, such as seen with microphallus or occasionally with Klinefelter's syndrome.

A more common lesion is present in those boys born with hypospadias. The child may have normal corporal development but, because of abnormalities of the corpus spongiosum, the penis may be bent ventrally during erection (chordee). A similar problem occurs with the less common epispadias. However, in that condition, the corpora are abnormally splayed and there is dorsal flexion of the penis with erection. Some patients are born with a congenital lateral curvature of the penis — abnormal enlargement of one corpus. The large corpus allows a greater longitudinal expansion with tumescence, thus causing the curvature. This malfunction may cause either psychological difficulties or physically prevent the man from vaginal penetration. All of the deformities are diagnosed by inspection during erection and can be corrected with simple operative procedures.

Neurogenic

1) Multiple Sclerosis

Vas (1969) and Lilius, Valtonen, & Wikstrom (1976) reported that there is a 50% incidence of impotence associated with this disease. However, a careful separation of psychogenic versus organic origin is not available. There are no documented, quantified measurements of patients who have complaints of impotence secondary to this progressive disease of spinal cord demyelinization.

2) Spinal Cord Injury

Acute cervical spinal cord transection produces immediate erection. Men subjected to capital punishment by hanging and laboratory animals sacrificed with cervical dislocation have terminal erections. The implication is that either central inhibition of erection is released and erection created or that a sudden massive spinal cord stimulus generates an erectile response. There is ample experimental and clinical evidence to support the former supposition. Most patients with upper thoracic and lumbar spinal cord injuries are capable of penile erection. Reports indicate that 90% of men with thoracic spinal cord injuries are able to have erections (Karacan et al., 1975). The erection is reflexive — that is, stimulation of trigger points, either on the abdomen, perineum, thighs, or genitalia, will result in an erection of varying hardness and varying duration, depending upon the type and degree of injury (Comarr, 1970). The problem for the patient who may desire intercourse is that, because of its variability, the erection is not controllable and detumescence may occur at an inopportune moment.

3) Lower Motor Neuron Injuries

These are injuries to nerves that have already exited from the spinal cord or autonomic trunks. The mechanism of nerve destruction may be traumatic and can occur after pelvic trauma or at surgery. The nerve fibers that travel to the corpora course along the inferior half of the prostate gland and the ventral lateral surface of the corporal cylinders. Consequently, injuries to the pelvis, where prostato-urethral separation occurs, may result in erectile impotence. Similarly, nearly 100% of patients subjected to radical prostatectomy for cancer become impotent. When radiotherapy is given to the gland, also as a treatment for cancer, the incidence is nearly 50%. It should be emphasized that when benign lesions of the prostate are treated surgically either transurethrally or with anterior open resection, the nerve supply of the corpora is not disturbed and impotence is not an expected result. Surgery of the rectum and recto-sigmoid for cancer, colitis, or diverticulitis may result in impotence if those perineal nerves are destroyed. Surgery of the great vessels, performed to control bleeding, aneurysms, sympathectomies, or vena cava ligation, may cause destruction of the autonomic nerve trunks and subsequent impotence. Pure autonomic lesions, present in the Shay-Drager syndrome, are associated with impotence, but erectile potential of such patients has not been evaluated.

Vasculogenic

1) Priapism

Although usually not considered a vascular cause of impotence, priapism is caused by an abnormally sustained trapping of blood in the penile corpora. If treatment is not initiated rapidly, the final result can be impotence. The mechanism of priapism has not been established but it is thought that there is a blockage of the venous outflow from the corpora. It occurs in patients with sickle cell disease or leukemia. Other causes are known to occur after reversal of heparin therapy or in the presence of abdominal abscesses. Most cases are idiopathic, that is, of unknown etiology. After the erectile episode subsides, there is severe edema of the delicate fibromuscular stroma of the corpora, with subsequent fibrous scarring and inability of corporal spaces to expand with erection.

2) Atherosclerosis

Total occlusion of the distal aorta (Leriche syndrome) or of iliac, hypogastric, and/or pudendal arteries may result in erectile failure. The exact incidence of vascular occlusion as a cause of impotence is not known, but appears to be limited to fewer than 10% of cases. As a result of arteriographic studies it is known that atherosclerosis is a disease whose incidence increases with age. However, the presence of a partially narrowed vascular lumen does not mean that the vessel can no longer deliver ample blood for a satisfactory erection.

Several authors have described an external iliac artery "steal" syndrome (Metz & Mathiesen, 1979; Michal, Kramer, & Pospichal, 1978). Patients state that they have the ability to have erections, which tend to disappear when they assume a specific posture for coitus. The "steal" occurs because there is a need for blood in the ischemic gluteal muscles during pelvic thrusting. Blood is diverted from the pudendal arteries and diverted to the gluteal muscles. Thus, penile blood flow is limited during erectile activity and premature detumescence occurs. The decrease in penile blood pressure that occurs with pelvic motion can be measured by standard Doppler techniques (Abelson, 1977; Velchek et al., 1980).

3) Abnormal Drainage of the Corporal Bodies

Ebbehoj and Wagner (1979) reported four cases of men referred for "incomplete erection of the penis." They quite clearly demonstrated abnormal venous connections between the corpora cavernosa and glans penis. Under normal circumstances there are no vascular connections between the glans and the two corpora. Their thought was that the corpora should be considered a hydraulic system and that the abnormal drainage reduces cavernosal pressure. The diagnosis is made by cavernosography. Surgical ligation and cauterization of the small perforating vessels are curative.

Endocrine

1) Testosterone and Testicular Size

In our review of 150 male patients examined at the Center for Male Sexual Dysfunction at Beth Israel Medical Center, only three patients had plasma testosterone levels below 300 ng/dl. All the patients had normal testicular size (greater than 4.5 cm. in length). Three patients who had bilateral shrunken testes secondary to either trauma or adult mumps orchitis had normal plasma testes levels. The effect of testosterone per se upon the physiology of the erectile mechanism is unknown. Prepuberal castration does limit both the growth of external genitalia and libido; however, controlled studies of the effect of castration upon erectile function in sexually active men are obviously not possible. In patients with diabetes and presumed organic impotence, the testosterone levels have been reported as normal (Kolodny, Kahn, Goldstein, & Barnett, 1973). There is one report in the Norwegian literature describing the effect of castration upon criminals, in which as many as 25% of the sample reported continued sexual activity as long as one year after castration (Bremer, 1959).

2) Prolactin

Over the past several years, numerous reports have been published suggesting a causative association of hyperprolactinemia and impotence (Carter, Tyson, Tolis, Van Vliet, Faiman, & Friesen, 1978; Pont, Shelton, Odell, & Wilson, 1979; Spark, White, & Connolly, 1980). The mechanism of that impotence remains unknown. Indeed, the physiologic role of prolactin in man is an enigma. Of particular relevance is that in most reports associating elevated prolactin levels with impotence erectile activity was not studied. The exception is a single case report by Wasserman, Pollak, Spielman, and Weitzman (1980). In that patient, one erectile event per night was recorded before and after therapy. A post therapy erection observed by both patient and an observer was thought to have increased in firmness. Thus, the question remains whether the hormone affects erection, libido, or both.

Hyperprolactinemia is usually associated with concomitant low serum testosterone. Administration of exogenous testosterone alone reportedly does not cause a return of the sexual potency.

The incidence of hyperprolactinemia is not well established but probably varies with the population being studied. Spark et al. (1980) report eight of 102 men with a complaint of impotence had increased prolactin levels, whereas in our study only two of 150 men being evaluated for impotence had abnormal levels. Prolactin is secreted by the anterior pituitary gland under the control of the hypothalamus. It is released in a circadian rhythm with the acme during sleep. Secretion is pulsatile and the plasma half-life 15 to 20 minutes. The release is under the control of a negative inhibition of prolactin releasing inhibiting hormone (PRIH), which is similar in action to the adrenergic neurotransmitter dopamine.

There are multiple causes of hyperprolactinemia. Decreased metabolic clearance occurs with chronic renal failure and hypothyroidism. Overproduction results from pituitary adenomas, ectopic hormone production, psychotropic drugs (phenothiazines, butyrophenones, thioxanthenes), anti-hypertensives (alpha-methyldopa, reserpine), cimetidine, morphine and methadone.

Several reports describe the use of dopaminergic drugs as a treatment for impotence when the etiology of that impotence is undefined. In no study were the drugs effective in reversing the complaints of impotence in the absence of hyperprolactinemia (March, 1979; Thorner & Besser, 1978).

3) Beta-Estradiol

The effects upon erectile function of alterations of this hormone are not known. The hormone is produced either by the adrenal gland or by the testes. Patients with Cushing syndrome or adrenal carcinoma may produce excessive quantities of the hormone. In addition, patients with chronic alcoholism have increased peripheral conversion of testosterone to estradiol. A physical sign of this increase is gynecomastia. Recently, a study has shown a correlation with impotence and chronic digoxin therapy (Neri, Aygen, Zuckerman, & Bahary, 1980). Those patients had increased beta-estradiol levels, gynecomastia, and impotence. Specific studies of erectile function in patients with elevated beta-estradiol levels must be performed before definite conclusions can be made about the effect of this hormone.

4) Luteinizing Hormone Releasing Hormone (LHRH)

This hormone, a peptide released by the hypothalamus, is known to stimulate the anterior pituitary production and release of luteinizing hormone and follicle stimulating hormone. It has been described as enhancing the sexual ability of testosterone-primed castrated male rats. That observation has been extended to human beings after an initial successful report by Mortimer, McNeilly, Fisher, Murray, and Besser (1974). They stated that, in seven cases of men with associated gonadotropin deficiency, potency returned after seven to ten days of exogenous LHRH therapy. However, objective pre and postoperative study of erectile function was not performed.

In more recent studies, the drug was injected subcutaneously in 10 diabetic men without neuropathy, who complained of impotence from unknown but nonvascular causes, and in nine men complaining of diminution of their erectile powers (Ehrensing, Kastin, & Schally, 1981; Levitt, Vinik, Sive, Klaff, & Phillips, 1980). In neither was the drug different from placebo in effecting change of erectile ability. Therefore, its potential importance in male erectile responsiveness remains undefined and conjectural.

Diabetes Mellitus

Diabetes is a special case in the discussion of the causes of impotence. It is a common illness which affects five million men in the United States, of whom 50% suffer organic impotence (Rubin & Babbott, 1958). The disease is of two types: One is of hormonal origin, that is, a reduction of insulin secretion by the pancreas in the juvenile form of the disease; the other is seen in the adult form as a resistance to the effects of insulin on the cell membrane. Both forms of the disease have multiple and pervasive effects throughout the body.

1) Effects upon Nerve Function

Diabetes causes autonomic neuropathy, particularly in lower extremities (Martin, 1953; Rundles, 1945). Patients suffer hair loss, diminished sweat ability, and limited vasodilating ability. Ninety percent of diabetic patients with complaints of impotence have associated abnormalities of the nerves to both bladder and bowel (Ellenberg, 1971; Rydin, Lundberg, & Brattberg, 1981). In studies in our own laboratory we have shown that erectile tissues of men with impotence and diabetes have a reduction of norepinephrine content (Melman, Bressler, Henry, & Macadoo, 1981). Norepinephrine is the neurotransmitter of the sympathetic nervous system. In addition, electron microscopic evaluation of that same tissue shows a reduction in the presence of nerve fibers, as well as changes in the smooth muscle cells and the coating surrounding the cells of the penile corpora. The implication is that the generalized effects of diabetes may in fact be a cause of erectile dysfunction in diabetic men.

Impotence is often the first symptom of diabetes. A man with undiagnosed diabetes may complain that his penis gradually becomes softer over a period of months to years. He is eventually unable to have vaginal penetration despite the fact that an increase in penile circumference occurs. This concept is of primary importance. Penile rigidity is necessary for adequate vaginal penetration. In the evaluation in our Center for Male Sexual Dysfunction, patients with diabetes and concomitant impotence had nocturnal erections with increase in penile circumference but without rigidity. Only those men with psychogenic impotence did not develop *any* erectile activity! It is the inability to attain penile rigidity that is the most significant factor in diabetes-induced impotence. The highest correlation of impotence and the complication of diabetes is seen in patients with severe microangiopathy and symptomatic autonomic neuropathy (McCulloch, 1980).

Drugs

1) Iatrogenic

The major source of physician-induced impotence in the United States is antihypertensive medications. Those drugs may have a direct effect upon autonomic transmission by reducing levels of sympathetic neurotransmitters in the erectile tissue. Reserpine and guanethidine are two such agents. Other drugs, such as propanolol and alpha-methyldopa, may also cause impotence, but with central effects on the brain, by either inhibiting libido or interrupting afferent signals from the penis. These untoward side-effects have not been studied, despite the widespread use of antihypertensive medication in the United States.

2) Alcohol

It is estimated that problem drinkers comprise 10% of the adult male population of the United States. Briddel and Wilson (1976) and Smith, Lemere, and Dunn (1972) have emphasized that sexual dysfunction accompanying alcoholism may promulgate an increase in alcohol intake. In addition, they report that impotence in the male abstaining from alcohol may result in a return to alcoholism. The only objective data demonstrating decreased erectile capacity in this population has been from an acute study (Farkas & Rosen, 1976).

These reports suggest that the basis for the erectile impotence in patients with chronic alcoholism is organic and not psychological, but the mechanism by which erectile dysfunction occurs in chronic alcoholism has not been investigated. The specific effects of alcohol upon nerve function are not completely understood. There is evidence that alcohol may have an effect upon release of vesicles containing norepinephrine from sympathetic nerves and that there is a reduction of that nerve function by as much as 25–30%. However, the effects of chronic alcoholism on human erectile tissue have yet to be clarified. The influence of alcoholism on hormones associated with erectile activity also needs to be clarified. Patients with chronic alcoholism suffer from gonadal atrophy, feminization, infertility, and gynecomastia. These may all result from liver disease in the alcoholic. Specific hormonal changes include a reduction in plasma testosterone, FSH, and LH, with an increase in prolactin and in total plasma estrogen levels (Gordon, Altman, Southren, Rubin, & Lieber, 1976; Gordon, Southren, & Lieber, 1979).

3) Heroin, Methadone

Studies of impotence related to both heroin abuse and methadone maintenance have been by survey. In those reports, patients on heroin have reported a rate of impotence of up to 50%. Patients on methadone maintenance report half that value (Cicero, Bell, Wiest, Allison, Polakoski, & Robins, 1975; Cushman, 1972). The direct measurement of penile tumescence in patients receiving long-term methadone maintenance alone has not been reported. Within one year from the onset of treatment methadone alters the normal function of the hypothalamic pituitary gonadal axis. Patients receiving methadone over prolonged periods of time build up tolerance to the drug, with the exception of serum prolactin levels, which tend to remain high (Kreek & Khuri, 1979).

EVALUATION

History

The importance of a careful history cannot be overstated in the evaluation of men with sexual dysfunction. There are several key elements in the initial meeting of which the interviewer should be cognizant. These elements include:

1) Placement of the complaint into the correct category. The complaint should be identified as one of altered libido, erection, orgasm, ejaculation (including delayed or premature ejaculation).
2) Insuring that the patients understand their problem: Many patients

are not aware of the normal chain of physiologic events. Simple reassurance and education by the interviewer, for example, that it is normal for the penis to soften after ejaculation, or that increased tactile stimulation is necessary with aging, may be sufficient treatment of a worrisome problem.

3) Complete history of medication (including alcohol and other drugs of abuse), major illnesses and prior surgeries.
4) Is the problem a recurrent one?
5) Clearly establish the sexual preference of the patient.

Specific Erectile Dysfunction

Once it has been established that an erectile dysfunction is present, the interviewer can ask direct questions directed to the specific parameters of erection. The parameters are as follows:

1) The quality of erection, e.g., is the penis always flaccid or, if not, what percentage of normal does it attain?
2) Duration of problem — the patient who states that he has never had normal erections or that his erection becomes momentarily firm and then becomes flaccid within seconds, with or without attempts at intercourse, is a candidate for a corpora cavernosogram.
3) Is the problem an intermittent or continuous one?
4) Establish whether the patient's problem has plateaued, is increasing or decreasing in severity.
5) Specific questioning about penile trauma, as well as diseases or surgical procedures that may result in injury to the corpora.
   a) Priapism
   b) Gonorrhea
   c) Penile instrumentation
   d) Penile bands or other constrictive devices
6) Estimate of the quality of nocturnal or morning erections.
7) The quality of the erection with masturbation. Patients who are unable to have erections with attempted genital intercourse, but observe that they have normal erections at night, with masturbation, or at times of fantasy, almost always have psychogenic difficulties.
8) Ask patient to analyze the straightness of his penis during erection. This description will aid in the diagnosis of Peyronie's disease or suggest the presence of congenital malformation of the penis. The pa-

tient should be requested to bring in polaroid photographs taken at several angles of the penis during erection.

9) Is leg pain present, either from claudication secondary to vascular disease, or parathesias from diabetes or spinal cord injury?

10) Does the patient have difficulty voiding or defecating, suggesting other autonomic nerve disease?

This topic is also discussed in Sections I and III of this volume.

Physical Examination

The urologic examination for erectile impotence should not be restricted to the penis, but must include all of the components of a complete general physical examination. In that context, diseased entities known to be associated with erectile disorders can be specifically identified and the possibility of missing a diagnosis of a less common illness will be minimized.

Special emphasis should be given to the following:

1) Overall appearance, recent changes in weight, central versus peripheral obesity, skin striae, limbwasting, suggesting endocrine, renal or vascular disease.

2) Posture and gait, signs of spinal cord or other neurologic illness.

3) Blood pressure — hypertension suggests possible small vessel atherosclerosis.

4) Arrhythmias — indication of cardiovascular disease and possible peripheral vascular disease.

5) Retinopathy — indication of possible small vessel disease, diabetes, multiple sclerosis.

6) Gynecomastia — evidence of endocrine disease or a drug effect.

7) Abdomen — superficial caput medusa from liver disease or vena caval occlusion, aneurysm, obstruction of the femoral vessels.

8) Penis — careful examination of the corporal bodies and urethra for plaques of Peyronie's disease or other trauma, weakness of the wall of the tunica albuginea, or hypospadias.

9) Testis — examination for symmetry, size, texture, and possible endocrine active tumors.

10) Rectal exam — exam for anal tone, rectal masses, perineal sensation, pre-sacral dimpling.

11) Lower limbs — patella and ankle deep-tendon reflexes, possible clonus altered sensation, femoral, dorsalis pedis and posterior tibial artery, pulses, loss of hair, change in color of feet or toes.

Laboratory Findings

Laboratory findings relate primarily to endocrine abnormalities secondary to either primary endocrine diseases or medication and drugs of abuse.

1) Glucose Tolerance Test

Because of the occurrence of erectile impotence in 50 % of men with diabetes and the reports that in 13 % impotence is the first symptom of diabetes (Rubin & Babbott, 1958), it is necessary to establish the presence or absence of that disease. Criteria for that diagnosis include two or more fasting blood sugars greater than 140 mg %.

If the fasting blood sugar is normal, a 75 gm glucose tolerance test should be performed. The patient should be advised to take at least 200 gm/day of carbohydrates for three days prior to taking the test. The new criteria for the American Diabetes Association for the diagnosis of *diabetes* are fasting blood sugar of greater than 140 mg % on several occasions and greater than 200 mg % plasma glucose concentration at one and two hours. The diagnosis of *impaired glucose tolerance* is made when the fasting blood sugar is less than 140 mg %, but the one hour level is greater than 200 mg % and the two hour level is 140 to 200 mg %.

The diagnosis of impaired glucose tolerance signifies that there is an increased statistical probability that the person will develop overt diabetes, with its attendant complications. There is, at present, no proof that impaired glucose tolerance per se and impotence are associated. It is also important for the physician to recognize that, even if the diagnosis of diabetes is established, it should not be assumed that the disease is the cause of the impotence. In 15 of our patients in which a new diagnosis of diabetes was established, we found that in only seven was their impotence secondary to organic disease, while in the remaining eight the impotence was psychogenic in origin.

Special Procedures

1) Penile Blood Pressure

This test is best conducted by placing a pediatric blood pressure cuff around the base of the penis and using a Doppler 8-MHZ transducer probe to measure the systolic and diastolic pressures and flows of the penile arteries. Several measures have been used to analyze vascular potency. One is pressure itself, utilizing a ratio of penile systolic to brachial systolic pressure. In general it has been found that normal men have a ratio of greater than 0.8. Patients with presumed vascular impotence have ratios less than 0.6. Metz and Bengtsson (1981) report false classification in 20% using a reproducible technique. Several authors have utilized the Doppler flow pattern as a means of identifying those vessels in which obstruction has progressed to loss of typical pulsatile wave of the penile arteries. In those patients with abnormal pressure and/or flows, the lesion must be confirmed by arteriography. Wagner (1981) has shown that arteriographic evidence of damage to iliac and/or pudendal vessels does not necessarily correlate with erectile impotence. Therefore, one must be quite careful in document-ing decreased pressure and/or flow, vascular obliteration, and definite erectile impotence before stating a definite cause-effect relationship of a vascular lesion.

2) Corpus Cavernosogram

This test should be performed in any men who gives a history of *persistent* inability to either achieve or maintain (longer than 30–60 seconds) a rigid phallus. Patients of all ages are candidates and should not be excluded because they are too old or because the symptom is new.

The examination is performed under fluoroscopic control with spot x-ray capability. The penis is prepped with antiseptic and a 23 gauge butterfly needle inserted directly into *one* corpus. Anesthesia is neither needed or necessary — in fact, the injection of anesthesia is more painful than place-ment of the needle. Contrast media 15–40% iodine is injected slowly under low pressure. Abnormalities of drainage can be identified immediately on the fluoroscopic screen if the vessels within the glans penis are visualized. Spot x-rays can be taken for a permanent record. The needle is removed and no dressing is required.

3) Evoked Sacral Potential

In the early 1950s the bulbocavernosus reflex was described as a means of confirming a sensory reflex from the penis to the spinal cord peri-anal or of determining if bulbocavernosus striated muscle was intact. This test was positive in approximately 70% of normal men (Bors & Blenn, 1959). Im-proved technology increased the diagnostic accuracy of the test another 15% (Pierce, Roberge, & Newmann, 1960). The test is now performed by applying an electrical stimulus, less than 50 volts, to the penile skin. The reflex takes 35 to 40 milliseconds to traverse the spinal cord to return to the electrodes (Siroky, Sax, & Krane, 1980). It is important to understand that the nerve function being measured is peripheral and not autonomic. Therefore, the test measures peripheral nerve and spinal cord activity rather than the nerves directly associated with erectile function. We have found that the test is particularly useful in the following cases (Khan & Melman, 1981):

a) Decreased penile sensation.
b) Spinal cord disease, for example, history of Guillain-Barre syndrome, encephalitis, lumbar disc disease, multiple sclerosis, idiopathic spinal cord degeneration, or tumors.
c) Efferent nerve damage — diabetes, alcoholism, trauma, tumors invading the posterior prostatic area (thus destroying the nerves to the corpora) — all produce a prolonged latency time.

Again, as with all other indirect tests, the presence of a positive test does not mean a functional erectile lesion is present. That must be proven with other techniques.

4) Cystometrogram

Although Ellenberg (1971) reported a 90% incidence of abnormal cystometrograms in men who were diabetic and impotent, this test of bladder function is more useful in assessing the inability of the patient to urinate prior to the placement of a penile prosthesis than as a diagnostic modality for the assessment of erectile impotence. It should be used as an adjunct in men who are complaining of a slowing of the urinary stream.

5) Nocturnal Penile Tumescence

Fisher (1966; Fisher, Gross, & Zuch, 1965) and Karacan (1966) introduced the concept, in the American literature, of nocturnal erections associated with the rapid eye movement phase of sleep and dreaming, as a normal event present throughout the entire life span in men. Karacan has promulgated this test as a way of separating those men with organic impotence from those with impotence of psychogenic origin. The test has been considered the primary means of diagnosing impotence by many and has achieved a rapid rise in popularity. However, there are many problems with NPT that should be recognized by all of those who use its diagnostic results as a means of advising a course of therapy to their patients (Fisher, Schiavi, Edwards, Davis, Reitman, & Fine, 1979; Wasserman, Pollak, Spielman, & Weitzman, 1980).

According to these authors, the pitfalls are as follows:

a) About 20 % of the time normal men will not have REM erections in a clinical setting.
b) The strain gauge which is used to measure changes in penile circumference will not measure changes in penile hardness.
c) Two separate laboratories have quite clearly shown that maximal penile tumescence can be obtained before penile hardness occurs. That is, a patient who complains of penile flaccidity may accurately be describing his symptoms, although the nocturnal penile tumescence recording displays a significant change in penile circumference.
d) There is no uniform description of either maximal changes in penile circumference or penile hardness. Each patient is unique, so that maximal changes of penile circumference (not hardness) are variable from individual to individual. Thus, estimates of circumferential changes must be made by both an observer and the patient. The patient should be awakened from sleep to observe a particular erection.
e) Most patients who complain of impotence, be it organic or psychogenic, have some erectile activity at night. Very few patients have total absence of nocturnal erections. Therefore, the erectile event should be observed by a trained technician throughout the night(s) of study, in a private, quiet room. It is our feeling that it should not be attempted either on an outpatient basis, or in a hospital room without an independent observer. *

6) Visual Sexual Stimulation

This test has been used by many for various reasons to stimulate penile erection. We have shown a pornographic movie during one evening of study, prior to sleep, with simultaneous strain gauge monitoring of penile tumescence *and* technician observation. Nearly 20 % of the impotent patients whom we could not classify by means of history, physical examination, or nocturnal penile tumescence were diagnosed with the aid of visual sexual stimulation as having psychogenic impotence. Furthermore, the test can be used to confirm the degree of erectile malfunction caused by organic disease. For example, if a man claims that he has 50 % of his erectile capacity and then has repeated 50 % erections during the film, the diagnosis of organic dysfunction can be made with a greater degree of certainty. In ad-

---

*Considerable controversy exists regarding the merits of the portable monitor versus the inhospital procedure, and an alternative view on its clinical value is presented in Chapter 10 — *Ed.*

dition, when results of visual sexual stimulation also correlate with nocturnal penile tumescence, additional support for the diagnosis of organic disease can be made.

REFERENCES

Abelson, D. Diagnostic value of the penile pulse and blood pressure: A Doppler study of impotence in diabetes. *J. Urol.*, 1977, *113*, 636–639.

Ambrosi, B., Travaglini, P., Gaggini, M., Moriondo, P., Elli, R., Bara, R., & Faglia, G. Effects of serotonin antagonists in sexually impotent men. *Andrologia*, 1979, *6*, 475–477.

Benson, G. S., McConnell, J. A., & Schmidt, W. A. Penile "polsters": functional structures or atherosclerotic changes? *J. Urol.*, 1981, 125:800–803.

Bors, E., & Blenn, K. Bulbocavernosus reflex. *J. Urol.*, 1959, *82*, 128–130.

Bremer, J. *Asexualization. A follow-up study of 244 cases.* New York: MacMillan, 1959.

Briddell, D. W., & Wilson, G. T. Effects of alcohol and expectancy set on male sexual arousal. *Abnormal Psych.*, 1976, *85*, 225–234.

Carter, J. N., Tyson, J. E., Tolis, G., Van Vliet, S., Faiman, C., & Friesen, H. G. Prolactin-secreting tumors and hypogonadism in 22 men. *New England J. Med.*, 1978, *266*, 847–852.

Cicero, T. J., Bell, R. D., Wiest, W. G., Allison, J. H., Polakoski, T., & Robins, E. Function of the male sex organs in heroin and methadone users. *New England J. Med.*, 1975, *292*, 882–887.

Comarr, A. E. Sexual function among patients with spinal cord injury. *Urol. Int.*, 1970, *25*, 134–168.

Conti, G. L'erection du penis human et ses bases morphologico-vasculaires. *Acta Anatomica*, 1952, *24*, 217–252.

Cushman, P., Jr. Sexual behavior in heroin addiction and methadone maintenance. *N.Y.S. J. Med.*, 1972, *72*, 1261–1265.

Deysach, L. J. The comparative morphology of erectile tissue of the penis with especial emphasis on probable mechanism of erection. *Amer. J. Anat.*, 1939, *64*. 111–113.

Dua, S., & MacLean, P. D. Localization for penile erection in medial frontal lobe. *Am. J. Physiol.*, 1964, *207*, 1425–1434.

Ebbehoj, J., & Wagner, G. Insufficient penile erection due to abnormal drainage of cavernous bodies. *Urology*, 1979, *13*, 507–510.

Edwards, A. E., & Husted, J. R. Penile sensitivity, age and sexual behavior. *J. Clin. Psychol.*, 1976, *32*, 697–700.

Ehrensing, R. H., Kastin, A. J., & Schally, A. V. Behavioral and hormonal effects of prolonged high doses of LHRH in male impotency. *Peptides*, 1981, 2, Suppl. *1*, 115–121.

Ellenberg, M. Impotence in diabetes: The neurologic factor. *Ann Int. Med.*, 1971, 75, 212–219.

Euler, U. S. V. Physiology of catecholamines. In *Neurochemistry*, 2nd ed. K. A. C. Elliot, I. H. Page, & J. H. Quastel (Eds.) Springfield, Ill.: Charles C Thomas, 1962.

Farkas, G. M., & Rosen, R. C. Effect of alcohol on elicited male sexual response. *J. Studies Alcohol*, 1976, *37*, 265–271.

Fisher, C. Dreaming and sexuality. *Psychoanalysis – A general psychology.* R. M. Loewenstein, L. M. Newman, M. Schur, & A. J. Solnit (Eds.) New York: International Universities Press, 1966.

Fisher, C., Gross, J., & Zuch, J. Cycle of penile erection synchronous with dreaming (REM). *Sleep. Arch. Sen. Psych.*, 1965, *12*, 29–45.

Fisher, C., Schiavi, R. C., Edwards, A., Davis, D. M., Reitman, M., & Fine, J. Evaluation of nocturnal penile tumescence in the differential diagnosis of sexual impotence. *Arch. Gen. Psych.*, 1979, *36*, 431–441.

Gessa, G. L., & Paglietti, B. Induction of copulatory behavior in sexually inactive rats by naloxone. *Science*, 1979, *204*, 203–204.

Gessa, G. L., & Tagliamonte, A. Role of brain monoamines in male sexual behavior. *Life. Sci.*, 1974, *14*, 425–436.

Gordon, G. G., Altman, K., Southren, A. L., Rubin, E., & Lieber, C. S. Effect of alcohol (ethanol) administration of sex hormone metabolism in normal men. *New England J. Med.*, 1976, *295*, 793–797.

Gordon, G. G., Southren, A. L., & Lieber, C. S. Hypogonadism and feminization in the male: A triple effect of alcohol. *Alcoholism: Clin. and Exp. Res.*, 1979, *3*, 210–211.

Karacan, I. The developmental aspect and the effect of clinical conditions upon penile erection during sleep. *Excerpta. Medica. Inter. Congress*, 1966, *Series No. 150*, 2356–2359.

Karacan, I., Williams, R. L., Thornby, J. L., & Solis, P. J. Sleep related tumescence as a function of age. *Am. J. Psychiat.*, 1975, *132*, 932–937.

Khan, Z., & Melman, A. Use of evoked sacral potential in the diagnosis of male impotence. *Sexuality and Disability*, 1981, *4*, 105–107.

Kiss, F. Anatomisch-histologische untersuchungen uber die erektion. *Z. Anat.*, 1921, *61*, 455–521.

Kolodny, R. C., Kahn, C. B., Goldstein, H. H., & Barnett, D. M. Sexual dysfunction in diabetic men. *Diabetes*, 1973, *23*, 306–309.

Kreek, M. J., & Khuri, E. Effects of methadone maintenance on prolactin release. 61st Ann. Meeting Endocrin. Soc. P 289, June 1979.

Larsen, J., Ottesen, B., Fahrenkrug, J., & Fahrenkrug, L. Vasoactive intestinal polypeptide (VIP) in the male genitourinary tract concentration and motor effect. *Invest. Urology*, 1981, *19*, 211–213.

Levin, R. M., & Wein, A. J. Adrenergic alpha receptors outnumber beta receptors in human penile corpus cavernosum. *Invest. Urology*, 1980, *18*, 225–226.

Levitt, N. S., Vinik, A. I., Sive, A. A., Klaff, L. J., & Phillips, C. Synthetic luteinizing hormone-releasing hormone in impotent male diabetics. *South African Med. J.*, 1980, *57*, 701–704.

Lilius, H. G., Valtonen, E. J., & Wikstrom, J. Sexual problems in patients suffering from multiple sclerosis. *J. Chron. Dis.*, 1976, *29*, 643–647.

MacLean, P. D., & Ploog, D. W. Cerebral representation of penile erection. *J. Neurophysiol.*, 1962, *25*, 29–55.

March, C. M. Bromocriptine in the treatment of hypogonadism and male impotence. *Drugs*, 1979, *17*, 349–358.

Marshall, J. M. Modulation of smooth muscle activity by catecholamines. *Fed. Proc.*, 1977, *36*, 2450–2452.

Martin, M. M. Involvement of autonomic nerve-fibers in diabetic neuropathy. *Lancet*, 1953, *35*, 560–565.

McCulloch, D. K., Campbell, I. W., William, F. C., Prescott, R. J., & Clark, B. F. The prevalence of diabetic impotence. *Diabetologia*, 1980, *18*, 279–283.

Melman, A., Bressler, R. S., Henry, D. P., & Macadoo, V. K. Ultra-structure of human penile erectile tissue in patients with abnormal epinephrine content. *Invest. Urology*, 1981, *19*, 46–48.

Melman, A., & Henry, D. P. The possible role of the catecholamines of the corpora in penile erection. *J. Urology*, 1979, *121*, 419–423.

Melman, A., Henry, D. P., Felten, D. L., & O'Connor, B. L. Alteration of the penile corpora in patients with erectile impotence. *Invest. Urol.*, 1980(a), *17*, 474–477.

Melman, A., Henry, D. P., Felten, D. L., & O'Connor, B. Effect of diabetes upon penile nerves in impotent patients. *S. Med. J.*, 1980(b), *73*, 307–310.

Metz, P., & Bengtsson, J. Penile blood pressure. *Scand. J. Urol. Nephro.*, 1981, *15*, 161–164.

Metz, P., & Mathiesen, F. R. External iliac "steal syndrome" leading to a defect in penile erection and impotence. *Vascular Surgery*, 1979, *13*, 70–72.

Metz, P., & Wagner, G. Penile circumference and erection. *Urology*, 1981, *18*, 268–270.

Michal, V., Kramer, R., & Pospichal, J. External iliac "steal syndrome". *J. Cardiovascular Surgery*, 1978, *19*, 255–257.

Mortimer, C. H., McNeilly, A. S., Fisher, R. A., Murray, M. A., & Besser, G. M. Gonadotrophin-releasing hormone therapy in hypogonadal males with hypothalamic or pituitary dysfunction. *Brit. Med. J.*, 1974, *14*, 617–621.

Muller, J. Entdenkeeng der bei der erektion des mannlichen gleeles uverksomen anterior bei dem menschen und dem thieren. Arch Anat. Physiol. U Wiss Med., 1835, 202–213.

Neri, A., Aygen, M., Zuckerman, Z., & Bahary, C. Subjective assessment of sexual dysfunction of patients on long-term administration of digoxin. Arch. Sex. Behavior, 1980, 9, 343–347.

Newman, H. Vibratory sensitivity of the penis. Ferti. Steri., 1970, 21, 791–793.

Newman, H. F., & Northrup, J. D. Mechanism of human penile erection: An overview. Urology, 1981, 17, 399–408.

Newman, H. F., Northrup, J. D., & Devlin, J. Mechanism of human penile erection. Invest. Urol., 1964, 1, 350–353.

Newman, H. F., & Tchertkoff, V. Penile vascular cushions and erection. Invest. Urol., 1980, 18, 43–45.

Pierce, J. M., Roberge, J. T., & Neumann, M. M. Electromyographic demonstration of the bulbocavernosus reflex. J. Urol., 1960, 83, 319.

Pont, A., Shelton, R., Odell, W. D., & Wilson, C. B. Prolactin-secreting tumors in men: Surgical care. Annals. Internal. Med., 1979, 91, 211–213.

Rubin, A., & Babbott, D. Impotence and diabetes mellitus. JAMA, 1958, 168, 498–500.

Rundles, R. W. Diabetic neuropathy: Med., 1945, 24, 111–160.

Rydin, E., Lundberg, P. O., & Brattberg, A. Cystometry and mictometry as tools in diagnosing neurogenic impotence. Acta. Neurol., 1981, 63, 181–188.

Shirai, M., & Ishii, N. Hemodynamics of erection in man. Arch. of Andrology, 1981, 6, 27–32.

Shirai, M., Nakamura, M., Ishii, N., Mitsukawa, S., & Sawai, Y. Determination of intrapenial blood volume using ^{99m}Tc-labeled autologous red blood cells. Tohoku. J. Exp. Med., 1976, 120, 377–383.

Siroky, M. B., Sax, S. S., & Krane, R. J. Sacral signal tracing: The electrophysiology of the bulbocavernosus reflex. J. Urology., 1980, 122, 661–664.

Smith, J. W., Lemere, F. L., & Dunn, F. D. Impotence in alcoholism. Northwest Medicine, 1972, 71, 523–524.

Solnick, R. L., & Birren, J. E. Age and male erectile responsiveness. Arch. Sex. Behav., 1977, 6, 1–9.

Spark, R. F., White, R. A., & Connolly, P. B. Impotence is not always psychogenic. Newer insights into hypothalamic-pituitary-gonadal dysfunction. JAMA, 1980, 243, 750–755.

Stieve, H. Harn and geschlechts-apparat. Zweiter teil. Siebenter bar. Hand.d mikroskop. anat. d. menschen. Berlin: Springer, 1930.

Thorner, M. O., & Besser, G. M. Bromocriptine treatment of hyperprolactinaemic hypogonadism. Acta. Endocrinologica, Suppl. 216, 1978, 88, 131–146.

Vas, C. J. Sexual impotence and some autonomic disturbances in men with multiple sclerosis. Acta. Neurol. Scand., 1969, 45, 166–182.

Velcek, D., Sniderman, K. W., Vaughan, E. D., Jr., Sos, T. A., & Muecke, E. C. Penile flow index utilizing a Doppler pulse wave analysis to identify penile vascular insufficiency. J. Urology, 1980, 123, 669–673.

Wagner, G. Erection: physiology and endocrinology. In: Impotence: Physiological, psychological, surgical diagnosis and treatment. G. Wagner, & R. Green (Eds.) N.Y., London: Plenum Press, 1981.

Wasserman, M. D., Pollak, C. P., Spielman, A. J., & Weitzman, E. D. The differential diagnosis of impotence. The measurement of nocturnal tumescence. JAMA, 1980(a), 243, 2038–2042.

Wasserman, M. D., Pollak, C. P., Spielman, A. J., & Weitzman, E. D. Theoretical and technical problems in the measurement of nocturnal penile tumescence for the differential diagnosis of impotence. Psychosomatic. Med., 1980(b), 42, 575–585.

Wein, A. J., Fishkein, R., Carpiniello, V. L., & Malloy, T. R. Expansion without significant rigidity during nocturnal penile tumescence testing: A potential source of misinterpretation. J. Urol., 1981, 126, 343–346.

9

THE MEDICAL EVALUATION OF DISORDERS OF SEXUAL DESIRE IN MALES AND FEMALES

Melvin Horwith, M.D., and
Julianne Imperato-McGinley, M.D.

Physicians are often confronted with patients having problems with sexual function. These complaints are rather common and should be included in a thorough history. Initially, patients may be reluctant to discuss their sexual problems, but, when made aware of the possible relationship of sexual dysfunctions to other medical problems, they are grateful for the opportunity to discuss their concerns.

Recent advances in the understanding of reproductive and sex physiology, as well as hormone assay technology, have significantly improved our ability to assist patients with problems of sexual dysfunction (Crowley & Zemlay, 1981; Lipsett, 1980; Reichlin, 1981). Although the authors recognize the importance of the emotional components which interfere with normal sexual desire, this chapter is mainly concerned with the organic diseases and drugs which may contribute to patients' complaints of absent or decreased desire or libido. Any suggestion of waning interest or significant decrease in the frequency of sexual intercourse should be regarded as significant if it is an apparent change for that patient. Complaints of a change in the excitement phase (impotence) are thought to be the most common complaints presented to physicians, while complaints of decreased libido are most often presented to sex counselors. Usually the patients with complaints of decreased desire are male but, of course, females also complain of decreased sexuality. The preponderance of male patients may stem from the pervasive attitude that the male should be the aggressive partner. Thus, females with decreased sexual drive may not be as likely to seek medical help. Also, the nature of sexual arousal in the male is such that failure becomes painfully evident to the patient and his partner, while failure of arousal in the female is not as evident.

PATHOPHYSIOLOGY

We do not yet have a satisfactory understanding of the normal physiology of sexual desire. Sensory and psychic stimuli reaching the limbic system appear to be the important central mechanisms involved in libido (Reichlin, 1981). It is apparent that neurotransmitters play a role, but specific information is lacking. Generally, an increase in dopamine enhances libido (Gessa & Tagliamonte, 1974). Data that are available derive primarily from the pharmacologic effects of drugs which are known to affect the neurotransmitters.

From animal experiments it is now clear that in utero and/or early postpartum exposure to the appropriate sex steroids may be determinants of future sexuality (Beach, 1975; Gorski, Gordon, Shryne, & Southam, 1978). This is not yet unequivocally established for man. Although the peripheral effects of testosterone are dependent upon conversion of the testosterone to the 5α-reduced metabolite dihydrotestosterone, this compound does not appear to be of importance in the regulation of sexual desire (Imperato-McGinley, Guerrero, Gautier, & Peterson, 1974).

There are sufficient data, however, to indicate that, generally, in the adult male sexual desire is markedly reduced with a diminution in plasma testosterone. Occasionally, males with very low plasma testosterone claim to have a normal sexual desire, but this is rare. Most of the time, reduced sexual desire in a previously normal male correlates with decreased plasma testosterone levels associated with organic disease (Schiavi, 1981). A cycle or periodicity of testosterone secretion has been demonstrated in men (cycle of 20–22 days with wide variation); however, it is not possible to establish any link with libido or behavior (Doering, et al., 1975). Castrated males and hypogonadal males have been documented to have some sexual urge, especially if they were sexually active prior to the hypogonadal state (Bremer, 1959). This sexual drive is very minimal and is dramatically stimulated by androgen replacement. It should be recalled that the adrenal glands secrete androgenic steroids as well, which may be of importance in sustaining minimal sexual drive in the hypogonadal male. This may be significant in the female as well, as indicated by studies in females who have been castrated or adrenalectomized (Waxenberg, Drellich, & Sutherland, 1959). In fact, androgens may play the major role in women's sexual desire, while estrogen probably enhances female libido more indirectly. Sexual desire is increased during the pre-ovulatory period and diminished during the post-ovulatory phase of the cycle, and there is a rise in female-initiated sexual activity at midcycle. Both androgens and estrogens peak at that time (Adams, Gold, & Burt, 1978), but recent evidence suggests that it is the rise in *androgen* which is responsible for the increased sexual activity in females (Perski, Lief, Strauss, Miller, & O'Brien, 1978). Oophorectomized women and postmenopausal women do not develop hypoactive desire unless there are accompanying emotional or organic reasons (Lloyd, 1980). Perski et al. (1978) have suggested that the retention of sexual desire in postmenopausal women is due to adrenal androgens. Since reduced estrogen secretion leads to decreased vaginal lubrication and pliability, this may be considered an organic cause of decreased sexual desire, if, indeed, these problems are distressing to the patient. Estrogen replacement will generally correct these difficulties and may indirectly potentiate sexual desire.

Progesterone, on the other hand, is known to suppress sexual activity in nonhuman animals (Morin, 1977). It has been suggested that it is responsible for the decrease in desire during the post-ovulatory phase (Grant & Pryse-Davies, 1968).

When stimuli which were previously satisfactory for the individual now fail to create desire, one should consider further evaluation. Of course, new or varied stimuli might be tried, but this is often difficult to communicate to the patient. Loss of desire due to organic illness is usually universal; in contrast, emotional causes may be responsible for decreased interest in one partner, with normal desire for another.

PATHOLOGY: DISEASE STATES AND DRUGS THAT MAY IMPAIR LIBIDO

Abnormal Hypothalamic-Pituitary Function

Examples of abnormal hypothalamic-pituitary function with decreased secretion of the tropic hormones, in particular gonadotropins, leading to *decreased testosterone production* and/or *increased secretion of prolactin* are:

1) pituitary adenomata — either microadenomata or macroadenomata;

2) infiltrative disease such as hemochromatosis;
3) granulomatous disease such as sarcoidosis;
4) autoimmune disease of the pituitary leading to decreased pituitary function;
5) tumors such as craniopharyngioma or parasellar tumors such as meningioma or gliomas;
6) inherited abnormalities such as hypogonadotropic-hypogonadism alone or with anosmia (Kallman's syndrome).

Much has been written in the recent literature about the clinical features of *pituitary tumors* and *hyperprolactinemia* (Carter, Tyson, Tolis, Van Vliet, Faiman, & Friesen, 1978; Thorner & Besser, 1978). Male and female patients with hyperprolactinemia will commonly complain of impaired libido. In males this can occur despite the presence of normal circulating levels of plasma testosterone. In males with low circulating levels of plasma testosterone and hyperprolactinemia, testosterone administration alone fails to restore libido. However, administration of bromocryptine, a dopamine agonist which lowers prolactin concentration, is effective in restoring libido and sexual function.

Problems associated with primary testicular disease, elevated gonadotropins, and decreased plasma testosterone levels are:

1) chromosomal abnormalities such as Klinefelter's syndrome;
2) testicular atrophy secondary to autoimmune disease or vascular insufficiency;
3) infectious processes, which damage the gonads, e.g., mumps (in adulthood).

Systemic Diseases

There are a number of systemic diseases that alter the general metabolic state of the individual, thereby secondarily affecting testicular function and testosterone secretion directly or through alteration of hypothalamic-pituitary function. *Chronic renal failure* affects both gonadotropin secretion and testicular function (Holdsworth, Atkins, & de Kretser, 1977). Plasma testosterone levels decrease and the FSH and LH levels are disproportionately low. Response to HCG is decreased and prolactin levels are elevated (Frantz, Kleinberg, & Noel, 1972). Sexual desire and function may be improved by hemodialysis, but are still impaired when compared to functioning in normal males.

In patients with *cirrhosis*, gynecomastia and testicular atrophy frequently occur. There is a low testosterone level, with increased sex hormone binding globulin leading to low free testosterone. Estradiol and estrone are elevated (Kley, Nieschlag, & Kruskemper, 1975) and there is a blunted response to clomiphene indicating the presence of a hypothalamic-pituitary deficit as well (Distiller, Sage, & Dobowitz, 1976).

Alcohol

Apart from its action on the liver, *alcohol* also has a direct toxic effect on the gonads (Van Thiel & Lester, 1976). Altered metabolism of gonadal hormones takes place in the liver under the influence of alcohol, including increased testosterone metabolic clearance rate and the disappearance of pulsatile secretion of testosterone (Gordon, Altman, Southren, Rubin, & Lieber, 1976). Some patients have elevation of plasma LH with an increased response to LHRH and increased aromatization of androgens to estrogens; however, some patients do not have a compensatory increase in LH.

Endocrine Diseases

Cushing's syndrome is often associated with low plasma testosterone (in both hyperplasia and adenoma). Plasma FSH and LH range from normal to low (Luton, Thieblot, Valcke, Mahoudeau, & Bricaire, 1977). Many male patients complain of loss of libido, and atrophy of the testes is not uncommon. Similar endocrine abnormalities can be found by administering high doses of *exogenous cortisol* or other glucocorticoids (Doerr & Pirke, 1976). It is likely that glucocorticoid affects hypothalamic, pituitary and testicular function. *Adrenal insufficiency* adversely affects sexual desire. *Estrogen producing tumors* (adrenal or gonadal) cause feminization in the male with suppression of gonadotropins and testosterone and resultant sexual dysfunction.

In *hypothyroidism*, disorders of testicular function are not uncommon. Free estrogen and prolactin levels are normal or elevated (Barnes, Hayles, & Ryan, 1973). In *hyperthyroidism* FSH, LH, testosterone, and estradiol levels are elevated (Chopra & Tulchinsky, 1974).

Diabetes

The deleterious effects of diabetes mellitus on the sexual function in males is well documented; generally, diabetes has been regarded as affecting primarily erectile function. When impotence occurs, it is quite understandable that decreased libido will ensue with the frustration of not being capable of responding to the desires of the partner. Most men with diabetes mellitus initially complain of decreased erectile ability; however, after sustaining constant emotional frustration over the impotence, a progressive lack of interest in sex can develop. More recently, however, there have been some data to suggest that perhaps the less-commonly-complained-of loss of sexual interest may be a specific organic effect rather than a functional response to the impotence. There does not appear to be a good correlation with microangiopathy, nor does it appear that the endocrine functions of the pituitary or gonads are influential in the pathology of sexual dysfunction in the diabetic (Ellenberg, 1971, 1977). The explanation of the excitement and orgasm phase difficulty is believed to be a peripheral neuropathy, but no specific explanation for the decreased libido is apparent.

The effect of diabetes on female sexual function is unclear. Jensen (1981) reported that diabetic women and controls showed no significant difference in sexual dysfunction and that decreased libido was the most common complaint in controls as well as in diabetic women. Ellenberg (1971, 1977) discussed the differences of the effects of diabetes mellitus on sexual function in males and females but could not establish a reason for these differences, other than to suggest possible differences in criteria for evaluating dysfunction in both sexes.

Chronic Pain and Debilitating States

Patients with chronic pain without malignancy who are not on significant analgesics or narcotics may have deterioration of sexuality (Maruta, Osborne, Swanson, & Halling, 1981). These patients, however, may not have organic sexual problems, since marital and other adjustment problems often occur in the patient with chronic pain and may be responsible for the sexual maladjustment.

Among cerebral diseases, *temporal lobe epilepsy* and *stroke* are major conditions leading to altered or depressed sexuality. Here again the concomitant psychological effects may be more important than the organic illness. *Parkinson's disease* also lowers sexual drive, which may be improved by L-dopa therapy, which also improves the general well-being of the patient.

It must be appreciated that medical conditions which lead to *debility* may result in decreased sexual function, so that any acute or chronic illness may have consequent sexual dysfunction as a complaint. The debilitated patient with chronic illness, as well as the severely malnourished individual with generalized weakness, will evidence decreased desire.

Libido in the elderly certainly is still active and likely to remain so with aging, provided no organic cause for diminished sexuality supervenes and testosterone levels remain high enough to sustain libido (Martin, 1981). A pervasive factor affecting the degree of sexuality in the aged appears to be the degree of sexual activity during the preceding years. Martin's study of factors affecting sexual function in 60–79-year-old married males indicates that the strongest factor was motivation. Thus, an older individual is more likely to remain sexually active if he or she was more active at a younger age. Thus, it is very likely that future generations of older individuals will enjoy increased sexual activity based on progressively more liberal sexual attitudes during their earlier years.

Drugs

Although this chapter is primarily concerned with libido, it is difficult to completely separate libido (desire phase) from the excitement phase. This is particularly true when considering the deleterious effects of drugs on sexuality (Drugs That Cause Sexual Dysfunction, 1980; Hollister, 1975; Horowitz & Goble, 1979). Any patient with impotence from any cause can concomitantly develop difficulty with libido, either directly due to a drug effect or secondarily due to anxiety associated with the development of impotence. Drug effects leading to sexual dysfunction have been described primarily in the male but clearly can exist in the female as well.

Drugs which affect CNS function, e.g., alcohol, the tricyclic MAO inhibitors, opiates, etc. can affect desire and sexual performance. The effect of alcohol on sexual function is complex, since it is often consumed in an environment conducive to establishing sexual relationships. Although, in small amounts it may be responsible for release of inhibitions, when consumed in larger quantities it may significantly decrease desire and certainly decrease excitement. The chronic effects of alcohol on hepatic and CNS function and on the musculoskeletal system may also decrease libido.

Hypnotics also generally decrease desire, as will any drug which causes chronic central nervous system depression. Reserpine, as well as the antipsychotics, decreases dopaminergic transmission in the central nervous system, which may have a direct effect on decreasing sex drive. Cardiovascular and gastrointestinal system drugs are also an important group responsible for complaints of decreased libido and impotence. Marijuana and other hallucinogens have not been systematically studied and so it is difficult to be certain of the validity of various anecdotal reports. However, chronic marijuana use, as well as chronic opiate and methadone use has been associated with low plasma testosterone (Mirin, Meyer, Mendelson, & Ellingboe, 1980).

Elevations of prolactin have been associated with the phenothiazines, tricyclic antidepressants, butyrophenones, thioxanthene derivatives, meprobamate, chlordiazepoxide, reserpine, and α-methyldopa. This may be the mechanism for the commonly described decreased libido and sexual dysfunction among patients taking these medications. Reserpine depletes the brain of catecholamines and prevents their reuptake by nerve endings; phenothiazines interfere with the action of catecholamines at receptor sites and α-methyldopa inhibits the transformation of dopa into dopamine. The common effect of these drugs is a decrease in prolactin inhibiting factor, thus abolishing inhibition of prolactin secretion and increasing the prolactin level. Varied effects may depend on dose, route of administration, chronicity, environmental setting, and interaction among different drugs being used at once. Miscellaneous drugs, such as cimetidine (which has a weak anti-androgenic activity), clofibrate, and lithium, may also be responsible for decreased sexuality. A relatively new group of drugs, the alpha and beta blockers, may also affect sexual performance. The more frequently encountered drugs that may impair libido are listed in Table 8. (See also Table 16 in Chapter 10.)

EVALUATION

History

Evaluation of the patient for decrease or loss of desire should include a thorough review of medical, social, and family history. Also, a history of drug usage is mandatory. The medical history should include evidence of neurological as well as endocrinological disease. Areas in the medical history to be specifically considered are suggestions of:

1) intracranial disease with pituitary or hypothalamic dysfunction. The clinical clues suggesting primary intracranial disease, especially of the hypothalamus and/or pituitary, include headache, visual disturbances, thirst abnormalities, galactorrhea, acromegalic changes or evidence of target organ dysfunction, i.e., thyroid or adrenal;
2) gonadal dysfunction;
3) chronic debilitating illnesses;
4) diabetes mellitus, since early diabetes may lead to impotence and decreased libido before significant evidence of carbohydrate intolerance is present;

TABLE 8
Medications That May Impair Sexual Desire*

A. *Antihypertensives:*
Methyldopa (Aldomet)
Reserpine/hydralazine/Hydrochlorothiazides (individually or in combination as Ser-Ap-Es)
Chlorthiazide (Hygroton)
Clonidine (Catapres)
Spironolactone (Aldactone)

B. *Adrenergic-receptor blockers:*
Alpha: Phenoxybenzamine (dibenzyline)
Beta: Propranolol (Inderal, Lopressor)

C. *Antipsychotic Drugs* (rare):
Aliphatic phenothiazines (chlorpromazine: Thorazine, Chlor-72, and others; promazine: Sparine; triflupromazine: Vesprin)
Piperazine phenothiazines (prochlorperazine: Compazine and others; trifluoperazine: Stelazine and others)
Piperidine phenothiazines (thioridazine: Mellaril) Thioxanthenes (chlorprothixene: Taractan, Navane) Butyrophenone (haloperidol: Haldol)

D. *Antidepressant Drugs* (rare):
Tricyclics (amitriptyline and analogues: many manufacturers)
MAO inhibitors (Isocarboxazid: Marplan; Phenelzine: Nardil; Tranylcypromine: Paranate)
Lithium Carbonate (Eskalith and others)
Amitriptyline HCl (Elavil and others)
Doxepin (Adapin, Sinequan)

E. *Hypnotics and Antianxiety Agents:*
Alcohol
Antihistamines and Anticholinergics
Barbiturates
Benzodiazepines (chlordiazepoxide: librium and others; clorazepate: Azene, tranxene; diazepam: Valium; flurazepam: Dalmane; lorazepam: Ativan; oxazepam: Serax)

F. *Hallucinogens:*
LSD
Cannabis (Marijuana)

G. *Amphetamines and Cocaine*

H. *Narcotics:*
Heroin
Morphine
Codeine
Methadone

(*continued*)

TABLE 8 *(continued)*

I. *Endocrine Drugs:*
Glucocorticoids
Progestins
Estrogen in the male
Cyproterone acetate (anti-androgen)
Medroxyprogesterone (Provera)
Oral contraceptives

J. *Miscellaneous Drugs:*
Metronidazole (Flagyl)
Clofibrate (Atromid-S)
H_2-receptors (cimetidine: Tagamet)
Diethylpropion HCl (Tenuate, Tepanil)
Phentermine HCl and Resin (Fastin, Ionamin and others)
Fenfluramine (Pondimin and others)
Metoclopramide HCl (Reglan)

Although the drugs listed in this table can theoretically impair sexual desire, in actual clinical practice they rarely have this effect with the exception of 1) alcohol and narcotics abuse, 2) beta adrenergic blocker drugs, 3) centrally acting antihypertensive drugs, and 4) anti-androgen drugs.

5) effects of drugs;
6) testosterone deficiency including changes in hair and fat distribution, skin texture, and energy level.

Physical Examination

Physical examination should seek evidence of chronic disease, especially liver disease and the microangiopathy of diabetes mellitus. One should look for the presence or absence of an abnormality in visual fields, gynecomastia, galactorrhea, signs of hyper or hypothyroidism, acromegaly or Cushing's syndrome. Hyperpigmentation may suggest adrenal insufficiency or hemochromatosis. Evidence for androgen deficiency should be evaluated. In the male, this includes a decrease in beard and body hair and lack of temporal hairline recession. The size and consistency of the testes should be noted.

Laboratory Examinations

There are minimal laboratory studies which must be obtained as screening tests in patients complaining of decreased libido. If the patient is being seen in primary consultation, the patient should have a CBC, a standard automated chemical profile, and chest film. It is important to emphasize that a diagnosis of diabetes mellitus is made with a fasting blood sugar of 140 mg% or greater on two occasions or a two-hour postprandial blood sugar of 200 mg% or greater. Serum iron and total iron binding capacity are obtained to be certain that hemochromatosis is not present. With regard to special studies of the endocrine system, plasma testosterone, FSH, LH, and prolactin levels are ascertained. If there is any sign of other endocrine gland disturbances, as noted in the physical exam, the appropriate lab studies should be obtained. If there is any suspicion of intracranial disease, a coronal CAT scan with contrast should be done, as routine skull films are not accurate in diagnosing microadenomata. It is important to obtain formal visual fields as well.

CONCLUSION

Appropriate medical therapy may in itself correct deficient libido. Pharmacological replacement therapy with exogenous testosterone is indicated in certain selected patients seeking help for inadequate sexual desire. Males with low plasma testosterone levels because of gonadal, hypothalamic or pituitary failure should be treated with testosterone replacement. Females who have been castrated and adrenalectomized or who have abnormally low testosterone levels for other reasons may have improvement of libido when treated with relatively small amounts of androgens. One must be certain that underlying disease for which the ablative procedures were undertaken will not be exacerbated by the androgen replacement.* The postmenopausal female with complaints of a disturbing decrease in libido thought not to be psychological may be given estrogen replacement therapy as a therapeutic trial. If successful and prolonged therapy is contemplated, appropriate surveillance with periodic endometrial biopsy is indicated. If the patient has uterus intact, estrogen therapy should always be accompanied with cyclical progesterone therapy to induce monthly endometrial shedding. Bromocryptine therapy should be attempted for hyperprolactinemia when indicated.

REFERENCES

Adams, D. B., Gold, A. R., & Burt, A. D. Rise in female-initiated sexual activity at ovulation and its suppression by oral contraceptives. *N. Engl. J. Med.*, 1978, 299, 1145.
Barnes, N. D., Hayles, A. B., & Ryan, R. J. Sexual maturation in juvenile hypothyroidism. *Mayo Clin. Proc.*, 1973, 48, 849.

---

*Sex steroids alter the binding globulins, TBG and CBG. Therefore laboratory studies should be completed before commencing testosterone administration.

Beach, F. A. Hormonal modification of sexually dimorphic behavior. *Psychoneuroendocrinology*, 1975, *1*, 3.

Bremer, J. Asexualization. A follow-up study of 244 cases. New York: Macmillan, 1959.

Carter, J. N., Tyson, J. E., Tolis, G., Van Vliet, S., Faiman, C., & Friesen, H. G. Prolactin-secreting tumors and hypogonadism in 22 men. *New Engl. J. Med.*, 1978, *266*, 847.

Chopra, I. J., & Tulchinsky, D. Status of estrogen-androgen balance in hyperthyroid men with Grave's disease. *J. Clin. Endocrinol. Metab.*, 1974, *38*, 296.

Crowley, W. R., & Zemlay, F. P. The neurochemical control of mating behavior. In *Neuroendocrinology of reproduction — Physiology and behavior*. N. I. Adler (Ed.) New York: Plenum Press, 1981, 451.

Distiller, L. A., Sage, J., & Dobowitz, B: Pituitary-gonadal function in men with alcoholic cirrhosis of the liver. *Horm. Metab. Res.*, 1976, *8*, 461.

Doering, C. H., Kraemer, H. C., Brodie, H. K. H., & Hamburg, D. A. A cycle of plasma testosterone in the human male. *J. Clin. Endocrinol. Metab.*, 1975, *40*, 492.

Doerr, P., & Pirke, M. Cortisol-induced suppression of plasma testosterone in normal adult males. *J. Clin. Endocrinol. Metab.*, 1976, *43*, 622.

Drugs that cause sexual dysfunction. *The Medical Letter*, 1980, *22*, 108.

Ellenberg, M. Impotence in diabetes: The neurologic factor. *Ann. Intern. Med.*, 1971, *75*, 213.

Ellenberg, M. Sexual aspects of the female diabetic. *Mt. Sinai J. Med.*, 1977, *44*, 495.

Frantz, A. C., Kleinberg, D. L., & Noel, G. Studies on prolactin in man. *Recent Prog. Horm. Res.*, 1972, *28*, 527.

Gessa, G. L., & Tagliamonte, A. Role of brain monoamines in male sexual behavior. *Life Sci.*, 1974, *14*, 425.

Gordon, G. G., Altman, K., Southren, A. L., Rubin, E., & Lieber, C. S. Effect of alcohol (ethanol) administration on sex-hormone metabolism in normal men. *N. Engl. J. Med.*, 1976, *295*, 793.

Gorski, R. A., Gordon, J. H., Shryne, J. E., & Southam, A. M. Evidence for a morphological sex difference within the medial preoptic area of the rat brain. *Brain Res.*, 1978, *148*, 333.

Grant, E. C. G., & Pryse-Davies, J. Effect of oral contraceptives on depression, mood changes and on endometrial monoamine oxidase and phosphatases. *Br. Med. J.*, 1968, *2*, 777.

Holdsworth, S., Atkins, R. C., & de Kretser, D. M. The pituitary-testicular axis in men with chronic renal failure. *N. Engl. J. Med.*, 1977, *296*, 1245.

Horowitz, J. D., & Goble, A. J. Drugs and impaired male sexual function. *Drugs*, 1979, *18*, 206.

Hollister, L. E. Drugs and sexual behavior in man. *Life Sci.*, 1975, *17*, 661.

Imperato-McGinley, J., Guerrero, L. Gautier, T., & Peterson, R. E. Steroid 5α-reductase deficiency in man: An inherited form of male pseudohermaphroditism. *Science*, 1974, *186*, 1213.

Jensen, S. B. Diabetic sexual dysfunction: A comparative study of 160 insulin treated diabetic men and women and an age-matched control group. *Arch. Sex Behav.*, 1981, *10*, 493.

Kley, H. K., Nieschlag, E., & Kruskemper, H. L. Estrone, estradiol and testosterone in patients with cirrhosis of the liver: Effect of hCG. *Horm. Metab. Res.*, 1975, *7*, 99.

Lipsett, M. B. Physiology and pathology of the Leydig cell. *N. Engl. J. Med.*, 1980, *303*, 682.

Lloyd, C. W. Sexuality in the climateric. In *The menopause — comprehensive management* B. A. Eskin (Ed.) New York: Masson Publishing, 1980, p. 101.

Luton, J. P., Thieblot, P., Valcke, J. C., Mahoudeau, J. A., & Bricaire, H. Reversible gonadotropin deficiency in male Cushing's disease. *J. Clin. Endocrinol. Metab.*, 1977, *45*, 488.

Martin, C. E. Factors affecting sexual functioning in 60–79-year-old married males. *Arch. Sex Behav.*, 1981, *10*, 399.

Maruta, T., Osborne, D., Swanson, D. W., & Halling, J. M. Chronic pain patients and spouses. Marital and sexual adjustment. *Mayo Clin. Proc.*, 1981, *56*, 307.

Mirin, S. M., Meyer, R. E., Mendelson, J. H., & Ellingboe, J. Opiate use and sexual function. *Am. J. Psychiatry*, 1980, *137*, 8.

Morin, L. P. Progesterone: Inhibition of rodent sexual behavior. *Physiol. Behav.*, 1977, *18*, 701.

Perski, H., Lief, H. I., Strauss, D., Miller, W. R., & O'Brien, C. P. Plasma testosterone levels and sexual behavior. *Archives of Sexual Behavior*, 1978, *7*, 157.

Reichlin, S. Neuroendocrinology. In *Textbook of endocrinology*. R. H. Williams (Ed.) Philadelphia: W. B. Saunders Co., 1981, 620.
Schiavi, R. C. Male erectile disorders. *Annu. Rev. Med.*, 1981, *32*, 509.
Thorner, M. O., & Besser, G. M. Bromocriptine treatment of hyperprolactinaemic hypogonadism. *Acta. Endocrinol.*, 1978, Suppl. 216, *88*, 131.
Van Thiel, D. H., & Lester, R. Aicoholism: Its effect on hypothalamic pituitary gonadal function. *Gastroenterology*, 1976, *71*, 318.
Waxenberg, S. E., Drellich, M. G., & Sutherland, A. M. The role of hormones in human behavior. I. Changes in female sexuality after adrenalectomy. *J. Clin. Endocrinol. Metab.*, 1959, *19*, 193.

THE COMPREHENSIVE EVALUATION

In this final section, the psychological and medical aspects of the evaluation are brought together. The diagnostic criteria and clinical features of the psychosexual syndromes are described, and the medical and psychological aspects of the evaluation of each are summarized.

10

THE COMPREHENSIVE EVALUATION OF THE PSYCHOSEXUAL DISORDERS

Helen Singer Kaplan, M.D., Ph.D.

The sexual complaints a clinician is likely to encounter include the four syndromes which are subsumed in DSM-III under the category Psychosexual Disorders — the *Gender Identity Disorders*, the *Psychosexual Dysfunctions*, the *Paraphilias* (formerly called perversions, deviations, and sexual variations), and *Ego-dystonic Homosexuality* — and also *Sexual Phobias and Avoidance*, and *Unconsummated Marriage*.

I. GENDER IDENTITY DISORDERS (302.5x, 302.60, 302.85)

Diagnostic Criteria and Clinical Features

According to DSM-III, "the essential feature of the gender identity disorders is an incongruence between anatomic sex and gender identity." DSM-III describes three clinical subtypes of transsexuals — *asexual*, *homosexual*, and *heterosexual* — depending on the predominant sexual history. Gender disorders may occur in children or may surface later on in adult life. Fortunately, these are rare.

Gender identity disorders are not, strictly speaking, sexual complaints, since transsexuals may experience sexual pleasure and function well genitally. These patients are totally obsessed with being the "wrong" gender. They will tell you that ever since childhood they have felt that a "mistake" had been made, that they were born into the wrong body, that they ought to have been given the body of the opposite gender.

Transsexuals detest their own anatomical gender with an obsessive intensity. They deeply hate their genitals and, in the case of males, wish to get rid of them as though the penis were a phobic object. Conversely, the female transsexuals long obsessively for a penis.

Transsexuals are in considerable pain. They are deeply depressed, agitated, and preoccupied with their problem. Typically, they are convinced that if they could only change their sexual identity, they would become happy and fulfilled and find relief from the obsession which dominates their lives.

Evaluation

The etiology of transsexualism is regarded to be psychogenic and therefore the medical aspects do not have to be considered in the evaluation. Pathological family dynamics and confusing messages to the child about his gender have been implicated in the genesis of gender identity disorders by many authorities (Derogatis, Meyer, & Vazquez, 1978; Money & Ehrhardt, 1972; Stoller, 1968). The sad family histories of these patients support these hypotheses. I know of no transsexuals who grew up in stable, happy, normal families. Until recently, it had been believed that the essential damage to a person's sense of gender was done before the child was 18 months of age, but recent observations indicate that there may not be a specific critical period (Imperato-McGinley, Peterson, Gautier, & Sturla, 1981). These investigators studied males with a rare genetic abnormality which causes them to look like girls at birth, and who were therefore reared as females, whose male genitals emerged at puberty. These individuals were, albeit with some difficulties, able to assume a male gender identity that included marriage and fathering children.

Transsexuals require very special and expert management and most clinicians do not feel competent or interested in treating these patients. Therefore, only the specialist in these disorders needs to analyze the etiology of the transsexual problem in fine detail during the initial evaluation. However, for proper referral and patient management it is important for the clinician who sees patients with sexual problems to recognize transsexual patients and to differentiate them from those afflicted with other more prevalent conditions, such as homosexuality, transvestism, and schizophrenia. Patients with those disorders may also complain about their gender, along with other mental or emotional symptoms, but only in transsexualism is the central and core complaint the obsessive desire to change gender.

Treatment and Prognosis

Prognosis is generally poor for all treatment approaches that have been attempted up until now (Green & Money, 1969). Psychotherapeutic interventions of all kinds, including individual and family therapy, psychodynamic and behavioral approaches, seldom succeed in helping the patient to accept his or her anatomically correct gender with comfort and usually fail to diminish the patient's obsessive desire for sex reassignment. These poor results, together with the compassion felt for the intense suffering of these patients, has led to the adoption of *sex reassignment* as a therapeutic alternative. This entails surgical alteration of the patient's genitals to approximate those of the opposite gender, the administration of gender-specific hormones to modify secondary sex characteristics, and psychotherapeutic support for the assumption of a new sex and gender role. Despite early enthusiasm for the results of sex reassignment in terms of relieving psychic pain, recent follow-up studies are disappointing (Meyer & Reter, 1979). They indicate that, while some patients do seem to find peace, many remain depressed, sometimes suicidal, and deeply dissatisfied with their lives after undergoing this drastic and irreversible treatment.

The transsexual patient who is being evaluated is usually urgently trying to convince and pressure the examiner to recommend or authorize the surgical procedure immediately. However, there is a tendency today to engage the patient in extensive psychotherapeutic exploration of his underlying motivation. This evaluation process may take months or even years. If the patient still remains convinced that sex reassignment is the best alternative for him/her, some responsible authorities recommend, as the final evaluation procedure, that the patient undergo a trial of living in the desired identity. This entails wearing the clothes and taking the hormones and/or having electrolysis to create the appearance and secondary sexual characteristics of the desired gender for at least one year, before proceeding with irreversible surgical alteration of the genitals.

II. THE PSYCHOSEXUAL DYSFUNCTIONS

When an individual is experiencing intense conflict or stress, all three phases of his sexual response may be inhibited, with the result that he becomes entirely asexual. However, in clinical practice it is more usual to see the disruption of one phase with the sparing of the others. *The essential feature of the psychosexual dysfunctions is the impairment of the orgasm, excitement, or desire phase of the sexual response.*

1) THE ORGASM PHASE DISORDERS: IMPAIRED FEMALE ORGASM, RE AND PE

Orgasm phase disorders are highly prevalent. Among patients under 40, inhibition of the female orgasm and premature ejaculation in males are possibly the most common sexual complaints seen in clinical practice.

Impaired Female Orgasm (Inhibited Female Orgasm) (302.73)

Diagnostic Criteria and Clinical Features

DSM-III describes the following diagnostic criteria for *Impaired Female Orgasm* when this is due to psychological inhibition: *"Recurrent and persistent inhibition of the female orgasm as manifested by a delay in or absence of orgasm following a normal sexual excitement phase during sexual activity that is judged by the clinician to be adequate in focus, intensity, and duration"* (p. 279).

Patients in this diagnostic category are not "frigid" in any sense of that outdated term. They may be loving, care about men, be interested in sex, and have the capacity for erotic pleasure. During loveplay, they may feel sexual excitement and may lubricate. In other words, the desire and excitement phases of the sexual response are intact and *their chief complaint* is only that orgasm is difficult or impossible to achieve.

Women with orgasm problems will tell you: "I love him, I feel like having sex, I lubricate, I have really good sensations, but something happens. I get very excited but then at a certain point I just turn off. I reach a plateau. I get stuck and just can't seem to be able to let go."

The female orgasm threshold is distributed along a continuum (Kaplan, 1974). At one extreme are those rare women who can have an orgasm without any physical contact with the clitoral area, merely by engaging in erotic fantasies, kissing or stimulation of the breasts. Then there are the approximately 20 to 30% who are able to achieve orgasm through coitus alone without direct clitoral stimulation. Next on the continuum are women who can climax together with their partner but only if coitus is "assisted" by clitoral stimulation. Women who fall into the next segment of the distribution cannot reach orgasm in the presence of a partner, even if they receive clitoral stimulation. They can, however, stimulate themselves to orgasm when they are alone and employing erotic fantasies. At the pathological extreme of the orgasm threshold continuum are the totally anorgastic women who have never had an orgasm at all. These constitute approximately 8% of the U.S. female population (Fisher, 1973).

The demarcation between normalcy and pathology is a matter of some controversy. There is little disagreement that the last two response patterns are clearly pathological and that treatment should be recommended for such patients. But lesser degrees of inhibition are not as easily classified as to their normalcy and the appropriate method of therapeutic intervention. Some psychoanalytically oriented clinicians feel that all women who cannot reach a climax on penetration unless assisted by additional clitoral stimulation are abnormal and in need of treatment, even if they are orgastic with a partner. However, it is the consensus of current professional opinion that such a response pattern constitutes a normal variation of the female sexual response (DSM-III, 1980), and some therapists with a feminist orientation feel that such women should never be treated (Hite, 1976).

It has been my experience that some coitally anorgastic women can acquire a coital orgasmic response and should be given the opportunity for treatment, while it makes no sense to treat others. The distinction between who should be offered a trial of treatment and who should be reassured should be made during the evaluation.

The reaction of women and their partners to this dysfunction varies widely. In contrast to males, who are always distressed when sexual excitement does not lead to ejaculation, some women are perfectly content about not having orgasms and do not seem to suffer from tension or discomfort after sexual stimulation. In some cases this is denial, but there are women who simply find sex gratifying even if they do not experience a climax. This is not necessarily a sign of pathological passivity. It is my feeling that the person's point of view should be respected and that such women should not be pressured into treatment by husbands or by well meaning therapists. However, other anorgasmic women are desperate about their situation, sometimes to the point of obsession. They complain of tension, physical pelvic discomfort, and anger at their partner when the sex act always ends with a climax for him but never for her.

Sometimes the partner is more upset about his mate's orgasm problem than she is. Partner reaction is always an important diagnostic issue because, even though he may not have caused the patient's problem, his negative or pressuring response may create an obstacle to her cure, while his cooperation and support are invaluable for the success of sex therapy.

The Differential Diagnosis and the Medical Aspects of the Evaluation

The physiologic component of the female orgasm consists of a wave of reflexive rhythmic contractions (at the rate of 0.8 per second) of the muscles that surround the entrance of the vagina (Masters & Johnson, 1970). These contractions are experienced as exquisitely pleasurable. The sensory input that raises sexual tension and triggers climax is believed to derive primarily from nerve endings around the clitoris (Masters & Johnson, 1970), as well as from sensory receptors in the vagina (Gräfenberg, 1950; Hoch, 1980). The orgasm reflex is controlled by neural centers, located in the sacral portion of the spinal cord, which receive inhibitory as well as facilitative impulses from the higher brain. These neural connections are the conduits for psychological enhancement, as well as inhibition, of orgasm (Kaplan, 1974, 1979).

The female orgasm depends on the integrity of the anatomic structures mentioned above, so that theoretically any illness or drug that damages them or interferes with their proper functioning can impair orgasm. Actually, only a few drugs and illnesses impair orgasm in women and this syndrome is usually psychogenic. The most compelling evidence for this is the excellent response of approximately 90 % of anorgasmic women to sex therapy (Barbach, 1974; Masters & Johnson, 1970).

Nevertheless, a stunning variety of alleged physical causes have been proposed throughout the years. So far, none of these has been supported by scientific anatomic or clinical investigations. These include the claim that the pubococcygeal muscle (the muscle involved in the orgasm contractions) is weak in anorgastic women (Kegel, 1948, 1952, 1956; Kline-Graber & Graber, 1978) and that strengthening this muscle by "Kegel exercises" will improve orgasm. In my experience anorgastic women are not *cured* by exercising their vaginal muscles, but teaching a woman how to control these may in fact *enhance* her orgasmic experience, and so this is a worthwhile procedure in some cases.

Another totally unfounded hypothesis that had some popularity at one time is that anorgastic women suffer from clitoral adhesions which must be removed because they cover the clitoris and prevent its rotation and stimulation.

The newest sensational claim attributes anorgasmia to the neglect of the

"Gräfenberg" or "G" spot. It is claimed that stimulation of this spot, which is located in the anterior wall of the vagina, will produce a swelling and trigger orgasm and "female ejaculation" (Gräfenberg, 1950; Hoch, 1980; Ladas, Whipple & Perry, 1982). Actually the knowledge that many women have erotically sensitive areas in their vaginas which contribute to pleasure and orgasm is not new or controversial, but the claim of an anatomically distinct area and the existence of female "ejaculation" (as distinct from female urination during orgasm) has never been scientifically substantiated and is highly questionable, to say the least.

The most radical biological theory about and treatment of orgasm dysfunction have been proposed by J. C. Burt (Burt & Burt, 1975; Burt, 1977), who claims that many women cannot have orgasms on intercourse because at its natural anatomic location the clitoris does not receive enough friction from the thrusting penis. He has devised an operation which changes the clitoral/vaginal relationship. Many physicians, including this author, seriously question the wisdom of surgically altering the sexual organs of normal women.

Disease states and drugs

In my experience over half the women who complain of orgasm problems have a situational pattern, being able to have orgasm when they masturbate but not with a partner. It is not necessary to pursue physical causes in such cases. But for women who have no orgasms at all, the very rare but bona fide medical causes must be ruled out.

In otherwise *healthy* women, these include use of *MAO inhibitors* (antidepressants) and the *alpha adrenergic blocking agents* (used to treat hypertension), true *phimosis of the clitoris*, and very rare *congenital abnormalities*.

Neurological *degenerative diseases* or injuries or tumors that destroy the spinal centers and nerves that mediate the orgasm reflex, severe *damage to the genital organs* (as in radical pelvic surgery for cancer), and advanced *diabetes*, which may injure the sensory nerve endings of the clitoris, can also produce an absence or delay of orgasm. But women with these conditions *tend to be ill* and have other medical signs or symptoms.

The history of all totally anorgasmic women should include questions to rule out these drugs and diseases. A physical examination is also required to insure that the patient does not have one of the rare anatomic abnormalities of the genitals that can cause orgasm problems in women.*

---

*It will suffice if the patient has been found normal on a previous gynecological exam.

The risks of organicity are so low in the primary form of this syndrome that, when the medical history rules out the specific illnesses and drugs mentioned above the patient's genitals are normal, a trial of sex therapy without any further medical workup is safe. However, when a previously orgastic woman loses her capacity to climax, especially in the absence of a psychological crisis, there is a strong possibility that she has a medical problem, and the diseases and drugs that can cause orgasm impairment must be carefully ruled out, because serious and treatable illness, including diabetes, multiple sclerosis, spinal cord tumors and degenerative diseases, may otherwise be missed. Table 9 lists disease states and drugs that may impair female orgasm.

TABLE 9
Disease States and Drugs That May Impair Female Orgasm*

I. Neurological Disorders: Mechanical Disruption of Nerves That Mediate the Orgasm Reflex

1. *Neurological Disorders Affecting the Spinal Cord*

A. *Cause:* The mechanism of impaired orgasm in the following conditions is by irregular lesions in the spinal cord, interfering with sensory impulses in the pudendal nerve at the sacral level, and efferent nerves emerging from T11 and T12 (rare).
Multiple sclerosis
Alcoholic neuropathy
Tabes dorsalis
Syringomyelia
Amyotrophic lateral sclerosis
Myelitis
Severe malnutrition
Vitamin deficiencies

B. *Physical Exam:* Genitals are normal, neurological signs and symptoms

C. *Lab Findings:* Depend on disease

2. *Neurologic Disorders Causing Injury to Peripheral Nerves*

A. *Cause:* The mechanism of impairment is injury to the somatic and autonomic nerves controlling orgasm, the spinal reflexes in the lower cord (rare).
Alcoholic neuropathy
Herniated lumbar disc
Lumbar canal stenosis
Diabetes mellitus (severe neuropathy of the clitoris)

B. *Physical Exam:* Genitals are normal, neurological signs and symptoms

C. *Lab Findings:* Depend on disease

(continued)

TABLE 9 (*continued*)

---

3. *Surgical Injuries to the Spinal Cord and/or Peripheral Nerves*

A. *Cause:*	The mechanism is by interference with or disruption of the sympathetic pathways, or of sacral somatic nerves (rare).
	Thoraco-lumbar or lumbar sympathectomy
	Retroperitoneal lymphadenectomy
	Aorto-iliac surgery
B. *Physical Exam:*	Genitals are normal, neurological signs and symptoms
C. *Lab Findings:*	None

4. *Traumatic Injuries to the Spinal Cord and/or Peripheral Nerves*

A. *Cause:*	The mechanism is by interruption of the sensory pathways in a low transection, or disruption of the sympathetic pathways in a high lesion (rare).
	Paraplegia
	Posterior urethral rupture
B. *Physical Exam:*	Normal genitals; normal otherwise except for neurologic signs or operative scars.
C. *Lab Findings:*	None

II. Endocrine and Metabolic Disorders: Impaired Hormone Environment (rare)

A. *Cause:*	Testosterone deficiency—because this hormone is required by the sex centers; also by impairment of neural transmission and cellular response to the genitals; Thyroid deficiency—mechanism unknown; Adrenal disease—from interference with neural pathways of the brain and/or cellular response of the genitals; Pituitary disorders—same as adrenal disease.
B. *Physical Exam:*	Normal genitals—signs of endocrine disease.
C. *Lab Findings:*	Signs of endocrine disease.

III. Drugs: Chemical Disruption of Nerves That Mediate the Orgasm Reflex (common)

MAO inhibitor antidepressants, Alpha adrenergic blocking agents, High doses of sedatives, narcotics, and alcohol.

---

*This table was prepared by Sherwin A. Kaufman, M.D.

The Psychological Aspects of the Evaluation

Behavioral Analysis

If the patient cannot have an orgasm at all, the examiner needs a clear picture of what attempts she has made to become orgastic, and what her concept of orgasm is. Questions to be asked include:

Have you ever tried to have an orgasm? How? With your finger? How long did you use the vibrator? Where did you touch yourself? Have you used erotic fantasy while you were doing this? At what point do you stop stimulating yourself? What do you think having an orgasm feels like? Are you afraid to let go?

When the patient can climax alone on masturbation, but not in the presence of a partner, it is useful to obtain a clear picture of the contrast between her mental state and the technique she uses to stimulate herself when alone and what happens when she is with a man. Detailed descriptions of her masturbatory experiences and of the couple's sexual interaction provide information on this important diagnostic point. How does she masturbate? With her fingers? With a vibrator? Does she fantasize when she masturbates but not when she is with her lover? Does she like the way he touches her? Does it feel different when she touches herself? Does she receive enough stimulation during lovemaking? If not, can she tell him? Graciously? Does she get angry with him? Is she anxious with her partner? Is she too eager to please? Is she attracted to him? Is he reassuring? Sensitive? Does she trust him? Does she expect to have an orgasm on intercourse without clitoral stimulation? Does she think other women can climax more easily? That she is abnormal? Is she afraid her partner will reject her? Does it often feel like it is taking too long? That he is getting tired? At a certain point of arousal does she "cut off"? Can she abandon herself to her feelings? Can she identify her erotic sensations? Her feelings of tension? What sorts of thoughts enter her mind while she is making love? And how does her partner feel about her? How does he feel about stimulating her clitoris? Does he find it exciting, or sick, or a chore, or "second best"? Does he feel rejected if she does not climax on intercourse? Does he feel if he were a better lover he could make her come with his penis? Does she fantasize? What are her fantasies? What are his? Has she shared her sexual fantasies with her lover? Has he? Does he fulfill her fantasies?

The most common *immediate and current psychological mechanism* instrumental in the inhibition of the female orgasm is obsessive self-observation during lovemaking,* which will effectively interfere with the release of the orgasm reflex.

Another common simple cause is that the patient is not obtaining sufficient clitoral stimulation. This can happen when the couple has the unrealistic expectation that she should climax merely in response to rapid penile penetration without much foreplay and without clitoral contact. In other cases a woman will not let her partner know what she wants because of shame and insecurity.

Some anorgastic women are unable to fantasize or to use sexual imagery. Some report obsessive phenomena, that unwelcome thoughts or meaningless phrases or parts of songs, etc., enter their minds during sex. Others feel only neutral or even irritating sensations when the clitoris is touched and/or they are simply not aroused by clitoral stimulation. It may be speculated that these women have erected perceptual defenses against erotic sensations and are afraid of letting themselves go in sexual abandonment. These are the issues that become the focus of the behavioral aspects of treatment.

Analysis of the Intrapsychic Dynamics
and of the Couple's System

The patient's deeper intrapsychic problems in her relationship with her partner are inferred from her family and psychosexual history and from the assessment of the couple's relationship. Often inquiries into these areas elicit *no pathology* and simply psychological antecedents which operate in the "here and now" are the sole causes of the woman's orgasm problem. But there are those whose orgasm inhibition is the product of *deeper or unconscious sexual problems* which originate in the past and also in serious difficulties in the current relationship system.

Women who have difficulty only with orgasm but whose sexual response is otherwise good tend as a group to suffer the same kinds of underlying psychological and sexual difficulties and relationship problems as do women who have other types of psychosexual difficulties, but these tend to be milder (Kaplan, 1979). Conflicts due to strict childhood prohibitions against masturbation and other forms of sexual expression are often found in the histories of women with sexual problems. Most of these women did not masturbate in adolescence. A significant number had hostile or distant relationships with their mothers, who did not encourage their emerging sexuality.

---

*Masters and Johnson (1970) have termed this phenomenon "spectatoring."

Unconscious neurotic processes (oedipal conflicts), which cause the woman to develop a "father transference" towards her current partner, with attendant defenses against sexuality, are given a prominent place in the psychoanalytic literature on female sexual problems (Benedek, 1950; Deutsch, 1944, 1945; Freud, 1925, 1932; Lorand, 1939). In fact, overly close and/or ambivalent relationships with fathers are seen in some (but not all) women with sexual and relationship problems. Pleasure inhibitions and ambivalence about closeness and commitment to a man are often noted when reviewing these patient's relationships with the men in their current life. Some women with sexual problems are competitive with all men and may experience fear, ambivalence, and mistrust towards their current partner. This often comes from a sense of outrage at what is perceived by the woman as unfair advantages accorded to men in our culture. An over-controlling and compulsive personality style which makes it difficult for the patient to "let go" is commonly found among anorgastic women.

Treatment and Prognosis

Orgasm inhibition of women has an excellent prognosis with sex therapy. Almost all totally anorgastic women can learn to have orgasms, even when the symptom is associated with deeper intrapsychic and relationship problems. Whether the woman will be able to have orgasms with her partner is not as easily predictable, since this depends on the nature of the couple's system, and may require more complex conjoint therapy.

The problem of evaluating the coitally anorgastic woman for treatment requires special comment. If the analysis of her sexual experience reveals that a woman is easily orgastic on clitoral stimulation, is attracted to her partner, has no sexual anxieties, freely enjoys lovemaking, and that the partners make love in an adequate manner, but that coitus simply does not trigger her orgasm reflex, therapy will most probably not improve her already excellent sexual response. It makes sense to reassure such women and their partners as to their normalcy, and to tell them that a sexual pattern that includes clitoral stimulation to orgasm is not "second best." However, in other cases the inability to climax in response to coitus results from sexual anxiety, anger and conflict and/or inadequate lovemaking techniques. When her history suggests that a woman's orgasm threshold is elevated by emotional blocks, psychotherapeutic resolution of her sexual conflicts may help her become orgastic on intercourse. When technical problems are at fault, she may be a good candidate for behavioral sex therapy methods such as the "bridge maneuver," which helps some women to acquire a coital orgasmic response (Dagmar O'Connor, personal communication).

TABLE 10
The Evaluation of Delayed or Absent Female Orgasm

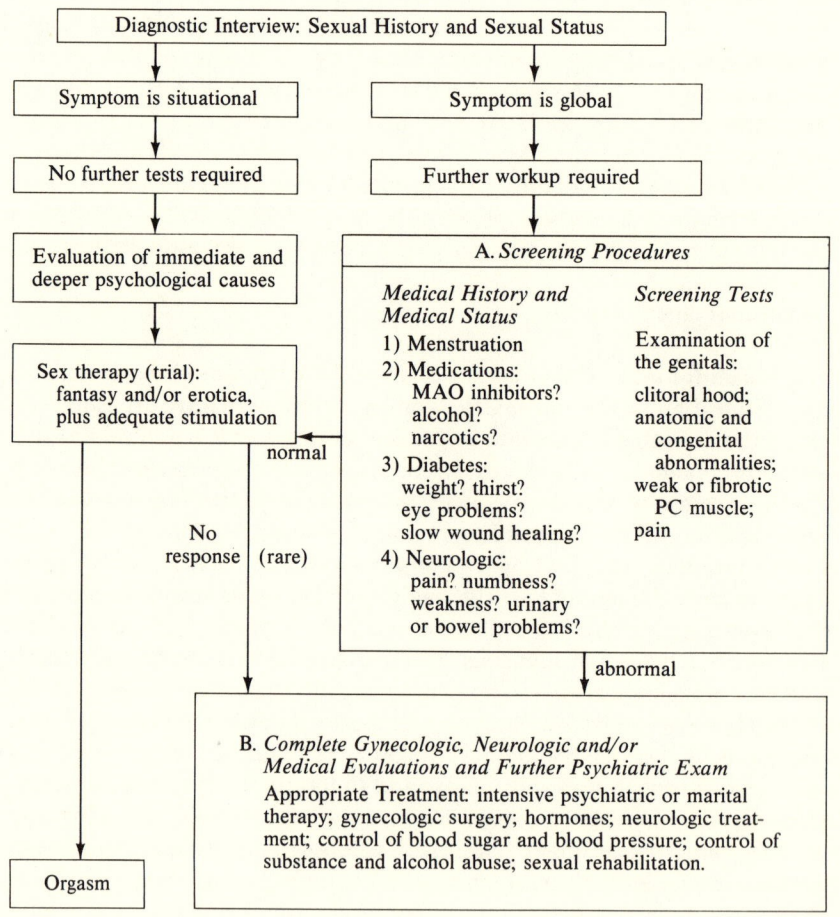

Orgasm Disorders of Males

There are three types of ejaculatory symptoms which may be either psychogenic or organic: *absent or delayed (retarded) ejaculation, absence of orgastic sensation or partially retarded ejaculation,* and *rapid (premature) ejaculation.* "Dry" orgasm is caused by *retrograde ejaculation** or by *anejaculatory orgasm,*** which are always due to organic causes.

Retarded Ejaculation or Inhibited Male Orgasm (302.74)

Diagnostic Criteria and Clinical Features

DSM-III describes the following criteria for inhibited male orgasm: *"Recurrent and persistent inhibition of the male orgasm as manifested by a delay in or absence of ejaculation following an adequate phase of sexual excitement"* (p. 280). This syndrome is analogous to inhibited female orgasm and the severity of the inhibition also ranges from very mild situational delays of ejaculation to total anorgasmia.

Patients who suffer from the most severe forms of retarded ejaculation (RE) complain that they have never experienced ejaculation in their lives. Some even inhibit themselves when they sense an impending nocturnal emission. Fortunately, this severe form is rare. Milder situational forms of RE are more common. Some patients can ejaculate only on masturbation when they are alone and immersed in erotic fantasy. Patients with still milder inhibitions can reach orgasm by self-manipulation in the presence of a partner or by manual and oral stimulation. They are unable, however, to reach orgasm inside the vagina. The mildest forms of retarded ejaculation are characterized by excessively long periods of intravaginal thrusting. Some men with a tendency towards ejaculatory inhibition experience a delay of orgasm only when they sense that their partner is not responsive or welcoming.

Desire and excitement are usually not impaired in this syndrome. Retarded ejaculators may have high sex drive and usually have no difficulties with erection. In these respects they are like anorgastic females. Only their orgasm is blocked or delayed.

---

*Patients with retrograde ejaculation experience normal orgasm sensation but no semen emerges from their penis because it enters the urinary bladder.

**Anejaculatory orgasm is also characterized by normal orgastic sensation without fluid. This syndrome occurs when no semen is produced or when the tubes which conduct the semen from the testes to the penis are blocked.

These men will describe their problem in terms similar to those used by women with inhibited orgasm, although males tend to react more uniformly with distress. In describing their sexual experience, such patients will tell you, "I get excited, I always get erections, I enjoy sex but I just can't seem to be able to come, I just can't let go. I reach a certain plateau — then nothing happens."

When questioned further, they will describe the precise conditions under which they can ejaculate: "When I do it myself, when I close my eyes, when she is not in the room it works all right." Or, "When I feel she is really loving I can come okay, but if I sense that she is holding back the least little bit, forget it."

Some males with this syndrome simulate orgasm and the partner may be completely unaware of her spouse's problem.* When she knows, however, she is usually distressed and may feel rejected by her mate's inability to ejaculate in her vagina. The partner response is always important in the dynamics and treatment of sexual dysfunction and should be carefully queried during the evaluation. In rare instances men experience retardation of their ejaculation only on masturbation or oral sex but can ejaculate intravaginally. This pattern of inhibition presents a clinical problem only when illness in the patient or his partner precludes intromission and requires that the patient ejaculate in response to oral or manual stimulation.

The Differential Diagnosis and the Medical Aspects of the Evaluation

Orgasm in the male, as in the female, is produced by pleasurable contractions of the genital muscles (0.8 per second), but the male orgasm is more complex, consisting of two subphases: emission and ejaculation. The female orgasm is analogous to the second phase only. During emission, reflex contractions of the smooth muscles of the internal male reproductive organs accumulate semen in the "pressure chamber" of the posterior urethra. This is followed a split second later by a wave of rhythmic contractions at the rate of 0.8 per second of the striated muscles at the base of the penis. The second phase is intensely pleasurable and causes the semen to be squirted out through the urethral opening.

The ejaculatory reflex can be delayed or blocked by emotional factors which influence the spinal centers, presumably via nerves descending from the brain. But orgasm in the male also requires the anatomic integrity of

---

*Simulation of male orgasm is sometimes discovered in the course of a fertility workup when a postcoital examination of the vagina fails to show semen.

the male reproductive organs, which include the testes that manufacture the sperm cells and an elaborate system of tubes which conduct the semen, an adequate hormone level, and an intact innervation system and blood supply. Any drugs or disease states which physically interfere with any of these can potentially impair orgasm. For this reason, although organic causes are extremely rare, they must be ruled out when evaluating patients with retarded ejaculation.

Actually, the differential diagnosis between organic and psychogenic RE is simple in the majority of cases. Most retarded ejaculators below the age of 50 can climax without difficulty on masturbation and organic factors do not have to be considered in these cases. In older men, the ejaculatory delay often occurs in all situations; then medical causes must be ruled out.

Ejaculation can be delayed or blocked by any physiologic stressors that impair the sex drive, including testosterone deficiencies, depression, and drugs which depress the central nervous system, such as alcohol, sedatives, and narcotics. Although these affect all three phases of the sexual response cycle, such patients are frequently unaware that their libido is diminished and may focus their concern on the difficulty they experience in reaching a climax.

Disease states and drugs

The *aging process*, which increases the refractory period of the male orgasm (Masters & Johnson, 1966), *alpha adrenergic blocking drugs** (e.g., clonidine [Catapres]), and also *thioridazine (Mellaril)*** are virtually the only organic causes which selectively impair the orgasm phase of the male sexual response cycle and produce no other sexual or medical disabilities.

Because primary RE is usually psychogenic, when an otherwise healthy man with a good libido who is taking no drugs complains of primary RE, a trial of sex therapy is warranted. The risk of missing a medical problem is negligible in such cases. However, *secondary ejaculation problems* carry a significant risk of organicity. When a man whose orgasms have previously been normal complains of delayed (or absent) ejaculation, *unless this is clearly the product of the normal aging process*, a thorough medical history and neurological workup is required because serious neurologic disease states may be associated with this symptom. The medications and disease states that may affect ejaculation are summarized in Table 11.

---

*Alpha adrenergic nerves control emission.
**Mellaril paralyzes the internal vescicle sphincter and causes retrograde ejaculation.

TABLE 11
Disease States and Drugs That May Impair Ejaculation*

1. Premature Ejaculation

A. *Cause:* No known organic cause for primary PE. Secondary to anxiety about pathologic states—commonly seen with impotence, also in association with symptoms of prostatitis or prostatism; neurological disease or trauma.

B. *Physical Exam:* Normal unless concurrent prostatitis or benign prostatic hypertrophy (B.P.H.) or neurological lesion.

C. *Lab Findings:* None unless urinary tract infection.

2. Retarded Ejaculation

A. *Cause:* Drugs: Sedatives, alcohol, butyrophenones (Haldol), ganglionic blockers, mood regulators, alpha adrenergic blockers (Catapres, Minipress).
Neurologic injury: tumor, multiple sclerosis, Parkinsonism, trauma, diabetes, alcoholism, uremia.

B. *Physical Exam:* Normal genitals; otherwise normal except for manifestations of neurologic process.

C. *Lab Findings:* Only as pertain to primary disease states as above.

3. Partially Retarded Ejaculation

A. *Cause:* No known organic cause except injury to or disease of spinal cord.

B. *Physical Exam:* Normal genitals; otherwise normal except for manifestation of neurologic process.

C. *Lab Findings:* None.

4. Retrograde Ejaculation

A. *Cause:* Surgical disruption of internal urinary sphincter by prostatectomy; diabetes mellitus, thioridazine (Mellaril).
Surgical disruption of sympathetic nervous system, typically: sympathectomy, abdominal aortic aneurysm, and retroperitoneal lymph node dissection.

B. *Physical Exam:* Normal genitals; normal otherwise unless surgical scars or diabetic damage to other organs.

C. *Lab Findings:* Semen in urine voided after ejaculation. Elevated blood sugar if diabetes not controlled, abnormal glucose tolerance.

5. Anejaculatory Orgasm:

A. *Cause:* Surgical disruption of sympathetic nervous system—see retarded ejaculation.

(*continued*)

TABLE 11 (*continued*)

	Alpha adrenergic blockade.
	Blockage of conducting tubes — vasectomy, infection and scarring, trauma.
	Severe endocrine abnormalities.
B. *Physical Exam:*	Normal genitals; normal otherwise unless surgical scars, signs of endocrine disorders.
C. *Lab Findings:*	No semen in urine voided after ejaculation.

*This table was prepared by Jon M. Reckler, M.D.

Surgical and traumatic injuries, tumors, disease of the spinal cord and of the pelvic nerves that mediate ejaculation, and advanced diabetes which injures the peripheral nerves can certainly cause ejaculatory difficulties. However, in such cases the patient either has a history of radical pelvic or abdominal surgery or spinal cord injury and/or will probably have other neurological signs and symptoms. These are likely to affect the motor and/or sensory functions of the lower extremities. And, since the spinal cord centers which control these reflexes are in close proximity, impairment of urinary and/or bowel control is often seen together with ejaculatory symptoms that are caused by neurological impairment.

For this reason all patients whose complaint involves globally delayed or absent ejaculations should be specifically asked about alpha blockers, Mellaril, pelvic or abdominal surgery, and bladder and bowel functions. If the medical history indicates that the patient has any of the above mentioned disease states, a thorough neurological evaluation is indicated.

When a patient complains that he experiences normal orgastic sensations but no fluid emerges from his penis, *anejaculatory orgasm* must be differentiated from *retrograde ejaculation*. This differential is not difficult, since the two syndromes are produced by different disease states and drugs. The most common causes of retrograde ejaculation are transurethral prostatectomy and Mellaril (thioridazine). Anejaculatory orgasm is caused by the failure to produce semen or by a blockage of the tubes which conduct semen from the testicles to the urethra. Vasectomy is currently the most common cause of anejaculatory orgasm.

The differential diagnosis between these two syndromes is made by examining a post orgasm urinary specimen under the microscope. Sperm cells will have entered the bladder and will be found in the urine of men with retrograde ejaculation, while the urine of anejaculatory patients will contain no sperm.

Sometimes it is difficult to differentiate severe retarded ejaculation and anejaculatory orgasm on the basis of the history. In such cases the situational nature of the symptom can sometimes be established by asking the patient to sleep with a condom each night with the hope of catching a nocturnal emission, which can then be examined under the microscope.

The Psychological Aspects of the Evaluation

Behavioral Analysis

A comparison of the patient's experiences when he is inhibited with those when he can ejaculate is useful for revealing the specific pathogenic mechanisms which must be modified in treatment. The examiner queries the retarded ejaculator about his mental processes during lovemaking. Does he "spectator"? Can he "let go" more easily on masturbation? Are his mental processes different when he is with a partner than when he is alone? Does he refrain from employing fantasy when he is with a partner?

The examiner asks: "How do you masturbate? What fantasies do you use? Do you ever have trouble coming on masturbation? When is that?" And, "What goes on in your mind when you are with your partner? Do you use your fantasy when you are with her?"

Retarded ejaculators are often exquisitely sensitive to their partner's response:"Can you tell when she is responsive? rejecting? Do you have more trouble coming when you are angry with her?"

The most common *immediate* psychological antecedent that blocks ejaculatory release is the same as in female orgasm inhibition — obsessive self-observation. The patient obsessively wonders: "Will I come? When will I come? Is she getting tired? Is she really enjoying this? Is she making love to me because she has to?" He is free of these obsessions when he masturbates and immerses himself in his sexual fantasies, and therefore has no trouble ejaculating in that situation.

Analysis of the Intrapsychic Dynamics and of the Couple's System

Deeper psychological problems include all the neurotic conflicts about sex and all the relationship difficulties that have been implicated in the other sexual disorders of males. It is my impression that ambivalence and rage towards women, which derive from unresolved childhood problems with mother, are particularly prevalent in this group. Fears of intimacy, commitment and pleasure are also common and are related to the same dynamics. Exploration of the patient's feelings towards women and a detailed analysis of his relationship with his mother, as well as with his current partner, often reveals neurotic processes that must be dealt with in treatment. Retarded ejaculators are frequently very angry at their current wives and lovers and involved in sadomasochistic systems with them. They "hold back" their orgasms along with their rage. During the evaluation of men with RE, it is particularly important to distinguish between appropriate anger towards a truly destructive partner and a generalized ambivalence towards women which would surface in any relationship. A rigid, compulsive, and overcontrolling personality with difficulty in handling anger is often seen in this patient population.

Treatment and Prognosis

The mildest situational forms of ejaculatory incompetence tend to be associated with relatively minor psychological problems and the prognosis for those patients is excellent with behaviorally oriented psychosexual therapy. But in my experience, the more severe forms of this syndrome tend to involve more serious underlying pathology and such patients are more difficult to treat with all modalities.

Partially Retarded Ejaculation

In this rare clinical variation of retarded ejaculation the emission phase of the ejaculatory reflex is normal but the pleasurable ejaculatory phase is inhibited (Kaplan, 1974). This is analogous to female "missed" orgasm, which is characterized by muscular contractions without pleasure.

Patients with this syndrome have normal erections. They will tell you that, after a period of stimulation and arousal, they feel a sense of "release" but they experience no real orgastic pleasure and no contractions and do not feel gratified after sex. Ejaculation in this patient population is characterized by a quiet "seepage" and not a pulsating "squirting" of semen from the penis. One of my patients has described this experience as "peeing" in contrast to a true orgasm. Another clinical characteristic of diagnostic importance is that the penis remains firm and erect for a fairly long time (five to ten minutes) after the seepage of emission, in contrast to the more rapid resolution of erection when the orgasm is normal.

In this syndrome there is a fascinating physiological "dissection," which by selective inhibition separates the emission from the ejaculatory phase of the male orgasm. From a psychodynamic vantage it is interesting that the nonpleasurable reproductive aspect is not disturbed but erotic pleasure and gratification are lost. The examiner should be alert to pleasure inhibitions when evaluating these patients.

TABLE 12
The Evaluation of Absent Ejaculation

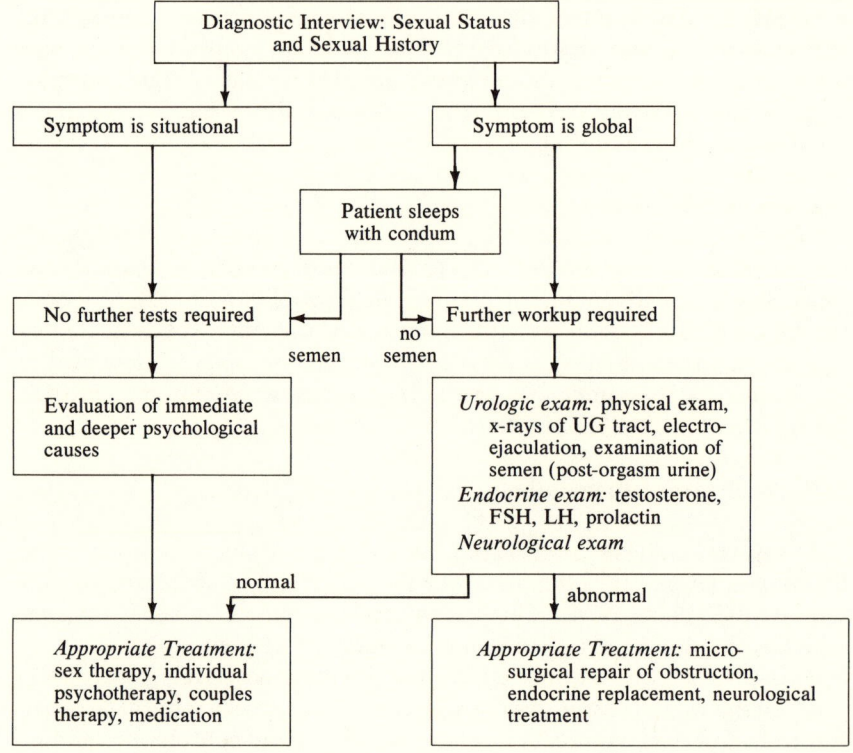

The Differential Diagnosis and Medical Aspects of the Evaluation

There are some urologic and neurologic diseases that can impair the ejaculatory phase only and leave the emission phase intact (see Table 11). However, my clinical impression, which is based on the few cases which I have studied and which have responded to psychological treatment, indicates that this syndrome can be caused by emotional factors as well. The diagnosis of psychogenic partial retardation is made on the basis of the clinical picture and by *exclusion* of neurological and urological causes by means of a thorough urological evaluation.

Premature Ejaculation (Inadequate Ejaculatory Control) (302.75)

Diagnostic Criteria and Clinical Features

DSM-III describes the following criteria for premature ejaculation: *"Ejaculation occurs before the individual wishes it, because of recurrent and persistent absence of reasonable voluntary control of ejaculation and orgasm during sexual activity. The judgment of 'reasonable control' is made by the clinician's taking into account factors that affect duration of the excitement phase, such as age, novelty of the sexual partner, and frequency and duration of coitus"* (p. 280).

The presenting complaint of the premature ejaculator is typical. He will tell you that he loves sex, he is attracted to his partner, he has no problem obtaining an erection (in fact, premature ejaculators often have a very strong sex drive). But as soon as he reaches a certain point of excitement, he ejaculates reflexively and rapidly.

"As soon as I enter I come, then it's all over." Or, "after two or three strokes," or "even before I enter," or "as soon as she starts moving, . . . I get excited very rapidly and come right away." "I tried everything — biting my cheek, condoms, anesthetic ointments, thinking of taxes — nothing works." One patient reported that he fantasizes lifting barbells while having intercourse in the attempt to delay his ejaculations.

Usually PE occurs with all partners because the man simply has not learned voluntary control over his ejaculatory reflexes. Sometimes control problems are situational and the symptom is more severe with a specific partner or a specific type of partner. Often control is better on masturbation, but the patient has not realized this. The examiner can test the patient's capacity for insight by asking him *why* he thinks he climaxes more rapidly when he is with a partner.

Premature ejaculators and their partners have diverse reactions to this problem. Some are unconcerned and are able to develop mutually enjoyable lovemaking patterns despite lacking control. The man may bring his partner to orgasm before intromission or after he has ejaculated. Very young men may compensate by making love several times. On the other end of the spectrum of reactions one sees very distressed couples. The wife may feel rejected and desperately unhappy because she (erroneously) concludes that her husband is either hostile to her or that he wishes to deprive her of pleasure. Or the partner of a premature ejaculator may become obsessed with the desire for coital orgasm which she fears will elude her forever because of the husband's rapid ejaculation. Such wives feel deprived and/or rejected, misinterpreting the rapid ejaculation as a sign of the husband's indifference, while he feels guilty and pressured, which does little to improve the situation.

Some men are very much invested in the duration of their excitement phase and feel like sexual failures because they cannot exert voluntary control. They are often obsessed about their rapid climax. They may develop a secondary pattern of sexual avoidance.

The Differential Diagnosis and the Medical Aspects of the Evaluation

The excellent response of this syndrome to sex therapy indicates that primary prematurity is rarely organic. However, there are some congenital conditions of the urinary tract and the spinal cord which can cause ejaculatory control difficulties on a physical basis. The most common of these is spina bifida. Such conditions are extraordinarily rare and tend to be associated with other signs and symptoms of medical and neurological disability.

Therefore, when a healthy young man who has a negative medical history complains that he has always come too rapidly, a trial of sex therapy without any further diagnostic procedures is a sensible diagnostic strategy. There is very little likelihood of missing a serious medical illness. (A urologic evaluation can safely be deferred for a few weeks to see if the patient will respond to sex therapy.)

By contrast, secondary prematurity is much more likely to be caused by an underlying medical disorder, especially when the loss of control is not associated with significant stress or a change in the patient's sexual relationship. A frequent case of late occurring premature ejaculation is organic impotence. The man who is progressively becoming impotent for a medical reason may "learn" to ejaculate rapidly before he loses his tenuous erection. Patients with secondary loss of ejaculatory control must always be questioned carefully about erections during the evaluation and sometimes nocturnal penile monitoring is required to establish erectile integrity. There is no drug that can cause rapid ejaculation, but some surgical procedures and spinal cord disorders can cause secondary PE by impairing the nerves and neural center that govern the ejaculatory reflex.* Therefore, when a man who had enjoyed good control complains that he is now coming rapidly, it is mandatory that he receive a careful neurologic or urologic evaluation,

---

*Dr. A. Zorgniotti has recently proposed that premature ejaculators have an abnormally low reflex threshold because their penile blood pressure is higher than normal (personal communication). Data to support this interesting hypothesis have not yet been offered and I doubt that organic causes will be discovered, because the fact remains that over 90% of premature ejaculators are cured rapidly with sex therapy.

lest a serious condition such as organic impotence or a spinal cord tumor or multiple sclerosis be missed.

The Psychological Aspects of the Evaluation

Behavioral Analysis

It is extremely important to obtain accurate information about the mental and sensory processes of the premature ejaculator during his sexual activity because the success of treatment depends on modifying and correcting these.

When one evaluates *premature ejaculation*, the patient is questioned closely about his subjective experiences as he becomes sexually excited: Does he become distracted, lost in, overwhelmed by his excitement? Does he have performance anxiety? Is he afraid that he will come too rapidly? Is he aware that he is tense? Is his control better on masturbation? on oral sex? How are the sensations different than when he is penetrating his wife? Is he able to "tolerate" pleasure in other spheres of life? Does he eat rapidly, move rapidly? Is he impatient in other areas apart from the sexual? In other words, is the prematurity an isolated symptom or is it part of his personality style? How does his partner react? Does she upset him? Does he tend to lose control when she becomes excited? When she starts to move actively? Is he insecure about his erections? Does he come quickly in order to avoid becoming flaccid?

The *sexual status* examination of premature ejaculators indicates that they are frequently not aware of the state of their sexual excitement or of their level of tension. These patients may obsessively focus on trying to control their ejaculation. Their excitement rises rapidly and they are not conscious of the sensations premonitory to orgasm. It has been postulated that this perceptual failure is the key to this syndrome (Kaplan, 1974). Sensory awareness and "sensory-sensory" integration are necessary for acquiring control of all voluntary reflexes, including ejaculation. On a deeper level, many premature ejaculators are conflicted about sexual gratification and pleasure and seem to *suppress* or *deny* their erotic sensations when these become "too" intensely pleasurable or last "too" long. The premature ejaculator's perceptual defenses thus interfere with this learning process.

Analysis of the Intrapsychic Dynamics and of the Couple's System

PE is often an isolated symptom, and no other psychological problem can be detected on the evaluation. In such cases the syndrome can be conceptualized as a *sexual learning disability* (Kaplan, 1974).

In other cases, prematurity is associated with deeper psychological problems and difficulties in the marital relationship. It has been postulated that premature ejaculators are hostile to women and that their symptom serves the unconscious purpose of depriving their partner of pleasure (Abraham, 1949; Fenichel, 1945). However, in my experience the psychological problems of these patients are not specific. One finds loving and kind as well as hostile men in this population; the partners also vary from loving to demanding. For this reason, the psychodynamics and relationship system of each patient must be carefully and individually evaluated.

Treatment and Prognosis

PE has an excellent prognosis with sex therapy that uses either the "squeeze" (Masters & Johnson, 1970) or the "stop-start" (pause) methods (Kaplan, 1974; Semans, 1956). The symptom can often be cured with these behavioral measures, even if it serves unconscious defensive functions. However, when prematurity plays a role in the patient's intrapsychic dynamics and/ or the couple's neurotic system, treatment is likely to be more complex. In such cases rapid improvement in sexual adequacy is apt to evoke anxiety and resistances to treatment that require psychotherapeutic interventions.

2) EXCITEMENT PHASE DISORDERS: IMPOTENCE AND IMPAIRED FEMALE EXCITEMENT

Sexual excitement in both males and females is caused by reflex vasodilation and congestion of the genital organs. This influx of blood changes them from the quiescent state and prepares them for their reproductive functioning. The excitement phase in males is marked by *penile erection* and in females by *vaginal lubrication* and *swelling*.

Impotence (Impaired Male Excitement, Inhibited Sexual Excitement in the Male (302.72))

Diagnostic Criteria and Clinical Features

DSM-III describes the following diagnostic criteria for *psychogenic* impotence or *inhibited sexual excitement of the male: "Recurrent and persistent inhibition of sexual excitement during sexual activity, manifested by . . . partial or complete failure to attain or maintain erection until completion of the sexual act"* (p. 279).

Impotent men retain their interest in sex and often can ejaculate with a flaccid penis. It is only the erectile aspect of the sexual response system that is impaired. However, some of these men develop a secondary avoidance of sex, so that it may look as though they are completely asexual. There are few other symptoms which are as threatening to the male.

Careful and meticulous questioning is often necessary to elicit the precise and detailed information about the specific circumstances under which the erectile difficulty appears that is needed to differentiate between organic and psychogenic impotence and also to formulate treatment strategies for psychologically impotent men. Some patients have morning erections, or can masturbate without difficulty when they are alone, but are impotent with a partner. Some complain they cannot *attain* an erection. Others *lose it* — when they take their clothes off, or are about to penetrate, or are inside the vagina or when there is a demand for performance, or when they are with certain types of women, or in an intimate or committed situation. Still others complain that their erections are not completely firm. The partners' reports are frequently helpful in clarifying these important diagnostic issues.

Women vary greatly in their reaction to their partner's impotence. Some are marvelously supportive and convey to the man the message that *he* is important to her — not his erect penis. Such loving attitudes rule out partner pressure as an etiological factor and are invaluable assets for sex therapy. At the other extreme are partners who are sexually demanding and critical and carry on when their man does not perform to their satisfaction. Some women insist on penetration as their only means of gratification, or object to their partner's use of erotica, or do not wish to stimulate his genitals. The pressure created for a man when he knows that his partner expects him to attain an erection rapidly and maintain it until she is satisfied heightens his performance anxiety and is likely to create or aggravate his potency problem.

The Differential Diagnosis and the Medical Aspects of the Evaluation

In terrestrial mammals* erection is produced by a reversible high blood pressure system in the penis. When a man becomes sexually aroused, the penile arteries dilate and a complicated system of shunts open between the penile blood vessel and the specialized sinuses in the corpora cavernosa. At the same time the penis outflow is constricted, thus trapping blood at a high

---

*The whale is equipped with an *os penis* (penis bone) which obviates the need for an erection. In a sense this is the mechanism of penile implant surgery.

pressure within the semiclosed penile chamber, producing penile rigidity and expansion, i.e., erection (Newman & Northrup, 1981).

A specialized neurophysiologic control system regulates the erectile mechanism. Erection is mediated by spinal reflex centers, which are ultimately under the control of cortical structures. These coordinate psychic and sensory input and form the biological substrate for the psychological enhancement or inhibition of erection.

Two spinal centers contain the final lower neuromechanisms that govern the erectile reflexes. The upper mediates psychoerotic inflow and the other tactile stimulation. When the complaint is incomplete erection or failure to erect spontaneously, the evaluator must ascertain whether the patient is using the full potential of both psychic and sensory stimulation. Young men are able to erect by psychic arousal alone, but older men usually need to supplement this with tactile stimulation.*

The highly complex erectile system depends on the integrity of the delicate penile anatomy, the pelvic blood vessels and nerves, the correct balance of neurotransmitters in the brain, a functional autonomic nervous system, an adequate hormonal environment, and, last but not least, a calm and erotically focused psyche. It is no wonder that erection is the most vulnerable part of the male sexual response and that impotence can be caused by a variety of drugs and disease states and emotional stressors.

Of all the psychosexual dysfunctions, impotence is the most likely to be caused by organic factors (Kolodny, 1974; Melman, Henry, Felten, & O'Connor, 1980; Spark, White, & Connolly, 1980). Since the physical manifestations of psychogenic and organic impotence are identical, *unless the symptom is clearly situational, organic factors must always be investigated and ruled out during the evaluation* before commencing sex therapy.

In men under the age of 40, psychogenic impotence is more common, while in older men there is a higher risk of organicity because of the greater incidence of circulatory problems and diabetes, as well as the more common usage of medications with sexual side-effects.

Although the modern evaluation of impotence has been greatly improved in recent years, it is not yet possible to make positive identifications of the more subtle causes of this disorder. Essentially, the diagnostic procedure consists of systematically ruling out the few disease states, such as diabetes and testosterone deficiency, that are known to cause obvious neurogenic,

---

*Many an impotent patient has been "cured" with the simple advice that increased physical stimulation of the penis is a normal requirement for erection after a certain age.

vasculogenic, and endocrine problems — a complex, costly, and far from precise procedure.

Actually only a small proportion of impotent patients require a complete urological workup. A skillful examiner who is knowledgeable about sexual medicine can probably rule out organicity in over 90 percent of psychologically impotent patients on the basis of the interview alone, simply by establishing that the difficulty *fluctuates with the patient's emotional state*. Patients whose erectile impairment has an organic basis do not have full erection at any time, while men whose problem is psychogenic may experience erectile difficulty only under emotionally demanding circumstances. For this reason impotent patients must be carefully questioned about spontaneous erections, erections on masturbation, as well as A.M. and nocturnal erections. If the patient or his partner recalls normal erections that are undiminished in quality and firm enough for penetration in any circumstance, organic factors do not have to be investigated further.

The role of NPT monitoring in the evaluation of impotence

Patients are often so anxious about their potency that they lose their objectivity and when this happens the diagnostic interview may fail to establish a definite fluctuating symptom pattern. In such cases the nocturnal penile tumescence monitor (NPT) can be used to establish this. The physically normal male has two to five full erections during his REM sleep (Karacan et al., 1975). These last from four to more than 20 minutes and are the result of an involuntary reflex (Karacan, Williams, Thornby, & Solis, 1975; Wasserman, Pollock, Spielman, & Weitzman, 1980). This response is reflexive and not associated with erotic dreams or thoughts. NPT measures and records penile tumescence during sleep, when negative psychic influences presumably are at a minimum. NPT monitoring takes advantage of this normal oscillation to establish the situational nature of the patient's difficulty. If a man who always has erection problems when he is awake has a normal pattern of tumescence when he is fast asleep, the situational nature of his symptoms and the physical competency of his erectile apparatus are established and no further medical diagnostic procedures are needed.

NPT monitoring is widely used today to test patients who are being considered for surgical penile implants since many urologists are reluctant to operate on men who have good sleep erections. NPT monitoring is also a valuable aid in differentiating organic from psychogenic impotence. In fact, sometimes this is the only means of obtaining this information because *the physical examinations, medical histories, and laboratory findings of many organically impotent patients are normal*, especially of those many patients whose impotence is due to small vessel disease of the penis or to subtle neurological deficits associated with the aging process. These patients may be falsely labeled as psychogenic by their physicians. Abnormalities on the *sleep test* may provide the only evidence of organicity. Therefore, to make the correct differential diagnosis between organic and psychogenic impotence, we consider it extremely important to monitor all patients who recall no erections adequate for penetration. Those with sleep records that are clearly normal in architecture, frequency, and duration are assumed to have sufficient erectile capacity for intercourse and are accepted for sex therapy, while those with abnormal sleep records are referred for a complete urologic evaluation.

Another valuable feature of the NPT is that it gives the clinician who becomes skilled at reading the recordings an indication of the extent and pattern of the physical disability when this is only partial. Some patients have *fewer* than normal erections, which occur only in the early morning; others have erections that are normal in architecture but very fleeting in duration; some have much better erections when they abstain from alcohol on one of the nights of testing. Such information about the physical limitations and vulnerabilities of a patient's sexual response is helpful for planning appropriate treatment and setting realistic goals.

A review of the sleep record with the patient can be a useful therapeutic experience. Seeing the objective evidence of erectile capacity during sleep has "cured" many patients without further therapy and has encouraged many couples to engage wholeheartedly in treatment.

There are still many unknowns in the area of NPT monitoring. For one, it has not been clearly established to what extent depression or intense stress may play a role in distorting a man's sleep erection pattern (Schiavi, 1981; Wasserman, Pollock, Spielman, & Weitzman, 1980). It has been our experience that some depressed patients have an abnormal sleep pattern which reverts to normal after the depression has lifted. For these reasons a clearly *normal sleep record is the most valuable finding*, as this constitutes proof of physical capacity, while abnormal findings do not establish organicity unequivocably.

Controversy also surrounds the use of the *portable monitor*, which the patient uses at home, versus *in-hospital monitoring*, during which both EEG and nocturnal erections are observed by a technician who is present during the entire night. The home monitor is obviously more convenient, much less costly, and also permits the patient to sleep under more normal conditions, while the in-hospital procedure provides the opportunity for visual inspection of the patient's erections by an objective observer.

It has been argued from a theoretical view that the "at home" procedure is unreliable (Chapter 8), but no objective data attesting to the superiority of either procedure are available. In our experience we have found the portable device *highly accurate for predicting response to sex therapy*, when this is used by an experienced clinician who integrates the sleep data with information from the sexual history and sexual status examinations, and providing certain precautions to insure validity are taken.* However, it should be stressed that false normals, such as in the rare "steal syndrome" (Wagner & Green, 1982) (which is readily diagnosed from the patient's history),** can theoretically occur with either procedure, even in the hands of a skilled clinician. For this reason, if a brief trial of sex therapy of a patient whose sleep record appeared normal fails to produce erections, the patient should be referred for further evaluation later on.†

An abnormal sleep record is considered by many clinicians as presumptive evidence of organicity. But this does not indicate what drug or disease state may be causing the problem and merely begins the medical aspects of diagnosis. The medical history is valuable in narrowing down the possible causes of the problem. In addition, simple laboratory procedures are available which will screen out the most common diagnosable medical causes of impotence: diabetes, testosterone deficiency, and the more obvious circulatory problems. The use of drugs with sexual side-effects is ruled out by the medical history.

Table 13 provides an extensive summary of the less common disease states and drugs that may cause impotence, and Table 14 depicts a flow chart which summarizes the sequence of the differential diagnosis and the medical aspects of the evaluation of the impotent patient.

The Psychological Aspects of the Evaluation

Psychological factors play a role in almost all cases of impotence, whether primarily organic or psychogenic. The patient who is partially impotent because of a mild circulatory deficiency frequently reacts to his diminished erectile capacity with panic, thereby worsening the physical disability. For

---

*For example, we guard against the possibility of false normal readings by checking the sleep record against a masturbatory measure. Unless the increase in penile circumference is clearly greater during sleep, the patient is not considered a good candidate for sex therapy. This method was suggested by Michael Perlman, Ph.D.

**Patients with this syndrome experience difficulty only in the male superior position and can function when they are on their back.

†A simple variant of NPT monitoring, the "postage stamp" test, is used by some clinicians as a screening method. This consists of a patient's pasting several postage stamps or "snap gauges" in a tight circle around his penis. If he wakes up with the stamps broken, this is evidence of sleep erection. This simple test sometimes has a beneficial effect of reassuring physically normal patients who are obsessively worried about their erections. Of course, this gives no information on duration and architecture of the erections, and is highly subject to false positive results.

TABLE 13
Disease States and Drugs That May Impair Erection

1. **Local Penile Abnormalities: Mechanical Impairment of Erectile Mechanism** (rare)

   A. *Cause:*   Congenital abnormalities, e.g., micropenis, absence of penis, traumatic and surgical injuries.

   B. *Physical Exam:* Will reveal the genital abnormality.

   C. *Lab Findings:*   None.

2. **Neurogenic: Mechanical Disruption of Nerves That Mediate the Erectile Reflex**

   A. *Cause:*   Multiple sclerosis, spinal cord injury, lower motor neuron injuries.

   B. *Physical Exam:* Genitals may be normal or there may be signs of neurologic symptoms.

   C. *Lab Findings:*   X-ray of injury, there may be a delay of the reflex.

3. **Vasculogenic: Impairment of Erectile Hemodynamics** (common)

   A. *Cause:*   Atherosclerosis of the small penile vessels; priapism due to trauma, sickle cell anemia; abnormal drainage of the corporal bodies; blockage of large vessels supplying penis.

   B. *Physical Exam:* Normal genitals. Normal otherwise; fundus may reflect atherosclerosis. Other signs and symptoms of circulatory deficits. In priapism, scarring in penis may be palpable.

   C. *Lab Findings:*   Penile blood flow studies may be abnormal; abnormal pelvic angiogram. Normal except for sickle cell leukemia if associated with priapism.

4. **Endocrine: Impaired Hormone Environment**

   A. *Cause:*   Testosterone deficiency, hyperprolactemia.

   B. *Physical Exam:* Genitals may be normal or testicular size may be abnormal; in severe deficiency states secondary sex characteristics may be deficient, signs of pituitary adenoma.

   C. *Lab Findings:*   Low testosterone, high prolactin, normal trophic hormones.

5. **Diabetes: Exact Mechanism Unknown; Impairs Vascular and Neurologic Components** (common)

   A. *Physical Exam:* Genitals are normal; otherwise may be normal or show symptoms of diabetic damage, e.g., neurological and eye signs.

   B. *Lab Findings:*   Glucose tolerance is abnormal, trophic and gonadal hormones are normal. There may be signs of diabetic damage, i.e., kidney abnormalities.

(*continued*)

TABLE 13 *(continued)*

---

6. Drugs: Chemical Disruption of Nerves That Mediate the Erectile Reflex (common)

Antihypertensive agents, alcohol, narcotics, beta adrenergic blockers.

---

this reason, the psychological aspects of the problem should be evaluated in all cases of erectile difficulty, even when the problem is clearly organic.

Behavioral Analysis

In most cases, the currently operating *immediate psychological cause* of psychogenic impotence is *performance anxiety* (Masters & Johnson, 1970).

An examination of the patient's mental processes when he attempts to make love will reveal this mechanism: "I wonder if it will work," or "I'm afraid I might not be able to have an erection," or "I don't think I can keep this erection until she comes," etc. Because of his obsessive concern about his erections, he is very likely to experience difficulty. The focus on performance to the exclusion of pleasure is threatening and, since the erectile response is very sensitive to emotion, the physiologic concomitants of the patient's performance anxiety will trigger the reflexes that drain the penis of the extra blood required for erection.

The recognition of the importance of performance anxiety in the etiology of psychogenic impotence is relatively new and is a substantial factor in the success of the new sex therapies in this disorder. Performance anxiety is highly amenable to behaviorally oriented and integrated sex therapy techniques; consequently, a significant element of performance anxiety is a favorable prognostic sign even when the patient also has deeper problems.

Analysis of the Intrapsychic Dynamics and of the Couple's System

Sometimes performance anxiety is "pure" and the psychological assessment of the couple reveals that the patient is free of emotional problems and that his relationship is good. In other cases the symptom serves as a defense against unconscious sexual conflict or plays a dynamic role in relationship difficulties. Such issues must be detected during the evaluation.

The psychopathology of the impotent patient is not specifically different from that of men with other sexual symptoms. Psychoanalytic theory postulates that unresolved oedipal problems and "castration anxiety" play a role in male sexual disorders (Fenichel, 1945; Freud, 1905, 1917; Mack &

TABLE 14
The Evaluation of Impotence

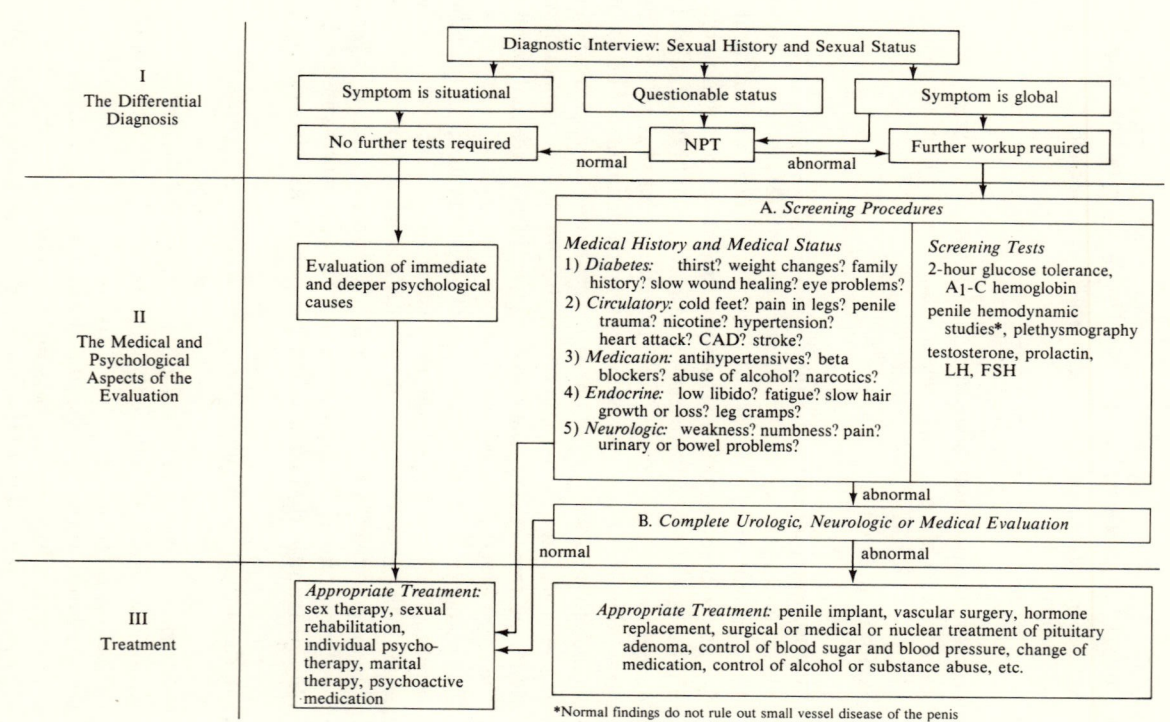

I The Differential Diagnosis	Diagnostic Interview: Sexual History and Sexual Status

Symptom is situational | Questionable status | Symptom is global

No further tests required | NPT | Further workup required

normal / abnormal

II

The Medical and Psychological Aspects of the Evaluation

Evaluation of immediate and deeper psychological causes

A. *Screening Procedures*

Medical History and Medical Status
1) *Diabetes:* thirst? weight changes? family history? slow wound healing? eye problems?
2) *Circulatory:* cold feet? pain in legs? penile trauma? nicotine? hypertension? heart attack? CAD? stroke?
3) *Medication:* antihypertensives? beta blockers? abuse of alcohol? narcotics?
4) *Endocrine:* low libido? fatigue? slow hair growth or loss? leg cramps?
5) *Neurologic:* weakness? numbness? pain? urinary or bowel problems?

Screening Tests
2-hour glucose tolerance, A$_1$-C hemoglobin

penile hemodynamic studies*, plethysmography

testosterone, prolactin, LH, FSH

abnormal

B. *Complete Urologic, Neurologic or Medical Evaluation*

normal | abnormal

III

Treatment

Appropriate Treatment: sex therapy, sexual rehabilitation, individual psychotherapy, marital therapy, psychoactive medication

Appropriate Treatment: penile implant, vascular surgery, hormone replacement, surgical or medical or nuclear treatment of pituitary adenoma, control of blood sugar and blood pressure, change of medication, control of alcohol or substance abuse, etc.

*Normal findings do not rule out small vessel disease of the penis

Semrad, 1967) and it is not uncommon to see evidence of ambivalence towards women and excessive sexual fears* in impotent men. "Oedipal" problems are recognized by investigating the patient's family dynamics and also by analyzing his adult sexual relationships. Was he overly close to or ambivalent toward his mother? Is he still too involved with her? Does he make "mothers" out of his current lovers or does he counterphobically avoid women who remind him of his mother? Is he overly competitive with or fearful of other men? Is his anxiety about sex excessive and impervious to realistic reassurance? The evaluation of impotent men frequently reveals that they are ambivalent about or openly hostile towards women and that they are still overly involved with their mothers.

Many men with erectile difficulties have received *negative messages* about sexual pleasure from those transmitters of our cultural values: their families, peers, and religious institutions. For this reason, it is important to assess the attitudes about sex and pleasure that prevailed in the impotent patient's family of origin.

Recently it has been postulated that aggressive sexual demands of the "new liberated woman" have caused an epidemic of "the new impotence" (Ginsberg, Frosch, & Shapiro, 1972). But this is not true. While both men and women are increasingly seeking help for their sexual problems, there is no evidence that there has been an actual increase of impotence. Also, the characteristics of the partners of impotent men argue against this hypothesis. The wives of impotent men often pressure their men for performance, but because they are hostile, neurotic or insecure — not because they are "liberated." The partners of impotent patients frequently are traditional, sexually passive women who will not accept clitorally induced orgasms and expect the man to take full responsibility for the sexual interaction. This puts these men under enormous performance pressure (Kaplan, 1977). Impotent men in such relationships improve when the partner becomes *more* "liberated," i.e., learns to be more active and stimulating and sexually responsible during the course of sex therapy.

This is not to say that a partner's aggressive sexual demands and critical attitudes do not play a causal role in impotence. Of course they do. An aggressive, nonsupportive partner who uses sex as a pawn in the marital struggle is often the critical element in impotence (and for that matter in other male and female psychosexual problems) and the success of treatment may

---

*In this discussion oedipal problems and castration anxiety are used metaphorically to describe sexual fears and ambivalences of which the patient is not aware and which can be traced to his early relationship to his parents.

depend on the improvement of the partner's attitudes. Therefore, the assessment of the couple's sexual system and of the partner's emotional characteristics (not her politics) is important in the evaluation of men with erectile problems.

Treatment and Prognosis

Patients whose impotence is the product of mild performance anxieties growing out of a lack of sexual confidence and partner pressure that is only due to ignorance and not a product of deep rooted hostility have an excellent and rapid response to sex therapy. Those whose symptoms reflect profound psychopathology and marital difficulties are, of course, more difficult to treat. It is important to assess the severity of the underlying problems during the evaluation in order to be able to give the patient a realistic estimate of his prognosis.

Evaluation for penile prosthesis

Some men and the wives of men who cannot have an erection adapt to this disability and learn to enjoy sex without coitus. After all, penetration is only one aspect of the sexual response and it is possible for both men and women to enjoy erotic desire, sensations, and orgastic pleasure without penetration. With judicious counseling, I have seen many couples develop a highly mutually gratifying sex life on this basis. However, for other men and for their partners, erection is very important and they do not choose to accept a permanently flaccid penis. For these, there are excellent penile prostheses available (Finney, Sharpe, & Sadlowski, 1980; Scott, Bradley, & Tim, 1973; Small, 1978).

In evaluating a patient for penile prosthesis or offering this alternative for his consideration, I have found the following issues useful in predicting a psychologically favorable outcome:

1) The patient is not a candidate for psychological treatment because: his condition is organic and irreversible; or he has a longstanding psychogenic impotence that is refractory to treatment; or he objects to sex therapy or psychotherapy.
2) The patient has realistic expectations and knows that the procedure is irreversible and will neither improve nor impair his ejaculation and libido or affect his basic relationship with women.
3) His partner (if he has one) is totally accepting of the procedure and has realistic expectations of the outcome.

4) He and his partner are free of major psychiatric pathology, such as depression or delusion.

5) He has no medical contraindications to the surgical procedures.

Impaired Female Excitement (Frigidity, Inhibited Sexual Excitement in Females (302.72))

Diagnostic Criteria and Clinical Features

DSM-III describes the following criteria for psychogenically impaired or *inhibited sexual excitement in females: "A recurrent and persistent inhibition of sexual excitement during sexual activity, manifested by . . . partial or complete failure to attain or maintain the lubrication-swelling response of sexual excitement until completion of the sexual act"* (p. 279). Women who meet the criteria for this syndrome feel the desire for sex and like lovemaking. Frequently they can have orgasms, especially when stimulated intensely with a vibrator. However, they remain dry when they are stimulated in a manner which would be adequate for most women. Penetration without normal lubrication and swelling can result in painful and uncomfortable intercourse. This may result in secondary problems such as dyspareunia, vaginismus, and loss of sexual desire. Partners of such patients often feel rejected and upset by what they take to be a personal sexual rejection or evidence that they are poor lovers. Others are oblivious.

The Differential Diagnosis and the Medical Aspects of the Evaluation

Like the male, the female's lubrication-swelling response is mediated by the autonomic nervous system, principally by its parasympathetic divisions. This mechanism is ultimately under the control of the cortex; therefore, theoretically female excitement should be as sensitive to emotional factors as male excitement. In actual fact, however, the psychogenic form of this disorder is uncommon. Apparently, a woman with sexual conflicts is more likely to lose her interest in sex or to develop orgasm difficulties than to become inhibited in the excitement phase. Most women who have a normal desire for sex and can reach orgasm but fail to lubricate are menopausal.

The vasocongestive phase of the female sexual response cycle is much more resistant to illness and drugs than male erection (Kolodny, 1971), because it involves simpler anatomic structures and does not depend on a complex hemodynamic high pressure system in the genitals. The increased pelvic vascularity which marks the female excitement phase merely causes a transudate to seep through the vaginal wall.

The only factor that makes female excitement vulnerable to physical stressors at all is that for proper vasocongestion and lubrication the vagina must be supplied with adequate levels of estrogen. When estrogen is deficient, the vaginal endothelium which transmits the fluid and its underlying network of blood vessels tend to atrophy. The most common cause of estrogen deficiency is menopause, due to the natural aging process or to the surgical removal of the ovaries. Although the senile ovary and the adrenal gland continue to make small amounts of estrogen in postmenopausal women, in most cases this is not sufficient to support the lubrication functions of the vagina. Therefore, all postmenopausal women, especially if they do not have regular intercourse, are likely to suffer from deficient vaginal lubrication.*

Estrogen deficiency is easily diagnosed. Normal menstruation is presumptive evidence of an adequate estrogen level and all patients who complain about vaginal dryness should be asked about the regularity and quality of their menses. In addition, all patients with this complaint should have a vaginal examination, which will reveal a dry and pale vaginal mucosa. Estrogen has a marked effect on the cells that line the vagina, and a microscopic examination of the patient's vaginal smear that has been specially stained will give a rapid (in the office), but not highly reliable, indication of whether estrogen is deficient. Advanced laboratory techniques for the measure of estradiol levels in the blood are now available for a much more reliable measure of estrogen.**

There are no other common organic causes of this symptom. The rare cases of vaginal dryness caused by post radiation vaginal atrophy and the rare vaginal infections and dermatological conditions that damage the vaginal epithelium are obvious on vaginal examination.

The Psychological Aspects of the Evaluation

A small number of young menstruating women do complain about vaginal dryness on a psychogenic basis. In some cases, this syndrome is clearly related to fear or conflict about intercourse or to poor lovemaking tech-

---

*Frequent and regular intercourse seems to protect some women from some of the effects on the vagina of estrogen deficiency.

**The deleterious effects of estrogen deficiency on the vagina are readily reversible by the topical (vaginal cream) or oral administration of premarin. The risks versus benefits of estrogen replacement must be carefully evaluated in each case. The most dangerous adversive effect of estrogen is an increase in endometrial cancer. In patients with an intact uterus this risk is minimized with cyclic progestrone administration and periodic examinations of the endometrium.

TABLE 15
Disease States and Drugs That May Impair Female Excitement*

I. Estrogen Deficiency States — Atrophic Vulvovaginitis

A. *Cause:*	By far the most *common cause* of impaired female sexual excitement is a disordered vasocongestive response from diminished lubrication, in turn caused by estrogen deficiency. This is found in:

> Menopause (without estrogen replacement)
> Oophorectomy
> Radical pelvic surgery
> Progestrone (progestins; some
> oral contraceptives)

B. *Physical Exam:*	Vagina is dry, inelastic and may show small fissures; other signs of estrogen deficiency, e.g., changes in fat distribution, skin tone, etc.
C. *Lab Findings:*	Parabasal cells in vaginal smear, low estrogen, high LH and FSH.

II. Neurogenic Disorders

A. *CNS Injury or Disease* (rare)

A. *Cause:*	While the following can interfere with female excitement by causing a longer arousal time or decreasing vaginal lubrication, it is emphasized that excitement phase disturbance is generally *not* the primary clinical complaint, due to the serious nature of the underlying condition.

> Head trauma — by injury to the sex centers, limbic system of parietal lobe
> Cerebrovascular accident — upon recovery, the chief mechanism is fear of recurrence.

In the following, the mechanism of excitement phase impairment is by interference with sex circuits:

> Hypothalamic lesions
> Pituitary tumor
> Psychomotor epilepsy.

B. *Physical Exam:*	Normal genitals; neurological symptoms, scars.
C. *Lab Findings:*	None.

B. *Neurogenic Disorders: Peripheral Nerves* (rare)

A. *Cause:*	The mechanism of impairment is by damage to nerves mediating vasocongestive reflexes:

> multiple sclerosis
> alcoholic neuropathy
> tabes dorsalis
> amyotrophic lateral sclerosis

(continued)

TABLE 15 *(continued)*

	syringomyelia
	myelitis
	severe malnutrition
	vitamin deficiencies
	primary autonomic degeneration
	traumatic paraplegia
B. *Physical Exam:*	Normal genitals; symptoms of disease
C. *Lab Findings:*	Depends on disease

III. Endocrine and Metabolic Disorders (rare)

A. *Cause:*	The following decrease libido, with secondary diminution of excitement:
	testosterone deficiency
	thyroid deficiency
	adrenal disease
	pituitary disorders
B. *Physical Exam:*	Normal genitals; otherwise depends on disease
C. *Lab Findings:*	Depends on disease

IV. Medications (rare)

Although the following drugs *may* theoretically cause vaginal dryness, they are rarely associated with excitement phase disturbance in clinical practice: antihistamines, anticholinergic drugs, antihypertensive agents, psychotropic agents.

---

*This table was prepared by Sherwin A. Kaufman, M.D.

niques that do not provide sufficient time and stimulation for an adequate response. But the clinical experience with this rare syndrome has been sparse and a specific set of immediate psychological antecedents has not yet been revealed for this disorder. Most of the patients with the psychogenic form of this disorder whom I have seen are ambivalent about intercourse because of significant deeper underlying sexual conflicts and problems in their marital relationships. These issues must be investigated during the portions of the evaluation that deal with the patient's family and psychosexual history and the analysis of the couple's relationship.

3) DESIRE PHASE DISORDERS: IMPAIRED SEXUAL DESIRE, THE PARAPHILIAS, AND EGO-DYSTONIC HOMOSEXUALITY

Diagnostic Criteria and Clinical Features

DSM-III describes the following diagnostic criteria for *deficient sexual desire when this is psychogenic: "Persistent and pervasive inhibition of sexual desire. The judgment of inhibition is made by the clinician's taking into account factors that affect sexual desire such as age, sex, health, intensity and frequency of sexual desire, and the context of the individual's life"* (p. 278). In other words, low sexual desire with an unsuitable person or in the absence of an attractive erotic situation is not to be regarded as a sexual disorder. I use the term *impaired sexual desire* to designate a deficient sex drive before the differentiation between psychogenic inhibition and organic impairment has been made.

DSM-III lists Inhibited Sexual Desire under the psychosexual dysfunctions, and places Ego-dystonic Homosexuality and the Paraphilias under two separate categories. But it makes more sense to me to subsume all these syndromes within the larger category of (situationally) inhibited sexual desire, because the behavioral and the psychodynamic features of all these variant arousal patterns are similar and all may respond to similar treatment strategies (Kaplan, 1982).

Situational ISD, homosexuality, and the paraphilias all have two essential components: low or absent desire for and gratification from sexual intercourse with a heterosexual partner in a committed and intimate relationship, with normal or intense desire and gratification in the variant situation. During the evaluation of all ISD patients, an attempt is made to understand the meaning of both these issues.

Both "straight" ISD patients and those with variant sexual desires will tell you that they experience no erotic feeling and may in fact feel discomfort, anxiety, or panic in an intimate sexual situation with an appropriate partner. However, they become highly aroused when they are engaged in their particular fantasy. Some enjoy sex only in the impersonal ambience of a massage parlor. Others "turn on" only when viewing certain kinds of erotica, when seducing a friend's wife, with group sex, with a stranger, or with a member of the same gender, or with a child. Or they need to abuse the partner or be abused or cross-dress or use a fetish or exhibit their genitals or observe a nude stranger in order to experience erotic pleasure. It is society's judgment, based on moral rather than on scientific or psychodynamic considerations, that has drawn distinctions among these atypically arousing situations, branding some as pathologic and others as normal.

An alternate view arranges the variant sexual interest along a continuum of severity of the underlying desire inhibition. Those with the most severe sexual conflict suffer from complete asexuality. Next are persons who use their atypical sexual fantasy to circumvent their underlying conflict. Persons with still milder inhibitions employ socially accepted impersonal sexual outlets and also choose partners far removed from their oedipal type (much older or younger partners, partners of a different class or race), while romantic sex within an intimate relationship is reserved for individuals who are conflict-free about sex.

In lower mammals, the sex hormones that are necessary for the activation of the brain's sex centers oscillate periodically. Female animals are receptive to sexual stimulation only during certain times (heat), while the males are sexually active only in the presence of a female of their species who is in estrus. Human beings are potentially receptive to erotic stimuli all the time, but most normal persons, even in good romantic relationships, experience some fluctuations in the intensity of their libido. Normal oscillation must be differentiated during the evaluation from pathologically deficient sexual desire.

When the sex drive is inhibited on a psychogenic basis, desire tends to be blocked only in *specific situations* or with a *specific partner*. The person retains interest in masturbating, in erotic fantasy, or in other sexual partners, but for reasons which are perplexing to him a specific partner ceases to be sexually attractive. When interest wanes for a clearly incompatible or unattractive person, one can hardly speak of a dysfunction. However, inhibited individuals do not feel moved to make love even when the partner is consciously perceived as suitable, attractive, loving, kind, attentive, skilled sexually, etc. A man may complain, "She's a wonderful woman; she looks terrific. I don't understand why I don't want sex with her."

Psychological inhibition of desire can also be global, so that the inhibited individual loses his erotic interest in all situations. In this form the syndrome is clinically indistinguishable from low libido caused by drugs or illness or depression. Patients with a global libido deficit or *sexual anorexia* will tell you that they do not desire sex with their partner and they have also lost their sexual appetite for all the situations which had elicited a sexual response in the past. "I don't look at pretty girls in the street anymore." "I try to make love to him; I really feel badly for him. He makes an effort to please me. He does all the right things but I really don't enjoy it." "I can't wait for it to be over." "It feels okay but there is not much to it and then I can't get myself to do it again for weeks." "I'm glad I got it over with, it's weird because when I do it it feels okay."

Many patients with a low drive can, providing they force themselves, function physically if their genitals are stimulated appropriately. But they must use intense fantasy to remove themselves from the inhibiting situation and usually they can experience only limited mechanical pleasure. Sometimes persons whose desire is inhibited enjoy the nonerotic aspects of physical contact and like "cuddling," kissing, and touching. Others come to dislike all manifestations of physical intimacy with the partner and experience intensely negative or aversive reactions to sex and to any sort of touch. Some may manage to get through the sex act but immediately afterwards are compelled to leave rapidly and cleanse themselves. In other cases the mere contemplation of sexual activity will evoke intense feelings of discomfort and deep revulsion and/or panic. Such patients develop sexual avoidance rituals. When they feel they are expected to have sex, they get "too busy," have headaches, have to make telephone calls, or simply get "lost." Avoiders tend to go to bed later or earlier than their spouse, bring home work from the office each night, become depressed and start arguments at bedtime. They are a highly motivated and ingenious population.

Sexual avoidance which is secondary to lack of desire must be differentiated from sexual avoidance which is motivated by a phobic reaction to sex and also from deliberate withholding of sex because of anger at or the wish to manipulate the partner. All these causes of *low sexual frequency* require different therapeutic approaches.

Some persons are not troubled by their loss of sexual desire and would not seek treatment except for their partner's frustration or pressure. Others are very distressed, fearing that their waning sexual interest signifies approaching old age and the end of their sexuality or means that they don't love their spouse.

The partners also react in diverse ways. Some, those with sexual problems of their own, are actually relieved when they are no longer "bothered" by their spouse's sexual demands. But others feel threatened and become preoccupied with the rejection, often to the point of obsession. A lack of desire on the partner's part can mobilize intense abandonment anxiety and feelings of insecurity and rage. Rejected partners may pressure obsessively for sex, which usually intensifies the symptomatic partner's sexual aversion.

The Differential Diagnosis and Medical Aspects of the Evaluation

To determine whether the loss of sexual desire is total or not, the patient is questioned closely about spontaneous erotic feelings and responses to erotic fantasy, literature, and pictures, as well as to persons other than the partner. If a woman can feel sexy if she is reading a romantic novel but turns off the minute her husband comes home, a psychogenic element has been clearly established.

But sexual desire, like other drives, has a physiologic basis; therefore, when the loss is global, illness, drugs and depression must be ruled out. Sexual desire depends on the activation of a specific system of circuits and nuclei in the brain. Lust is experienced when the "sex circuits" are activated. When the sex circuits are quiescent, the individual feels *no sexual interest*. Although all levels of the central nervous system are involved, the main regulatory mechanism is believed to be located in the most ancient part of the brain, the limbic system. Many details of the operation of the sexual drive system still need to be clarified, but it is known that adequate levels of testosterone and a proper balance of the neurotransmitters serotonin and dopamine and the catecholamines are necessary for the normal functioning of the brain sex circuits, both in males and females.

It has been known for some time that adequate levels of testosterone are required for the normal libido in males (Schiavi, 1976), and testosterone replacement has been the standard treatment for men whose sex drive is low because of testosterone deficiency. In the past it was believed that *estrogen* enhanced the female sex drive because this hormone supports the development of the female reproductive and secondary sexual organs, and because women tend to be most active sexually during the ovulatory period when estrogen is at its highest level (Benedek & Rubinstein, 1942). But recent evidence indicates that not estrogen but *testosterone is the libido hormone for women* (Persky, Charney, Lief, O'Brien, Miller, & Strauss, 1978; Persky, Dreisbach, Miller, O'Brien, Khan, Lief, Charney, & Strauss, 1982; Persky, Lief, O'Brien, Strauss, & Miller, 1977; Persky, Lief, Strauss, Miller, & O'Brien, 1978; Persky, Strauss, Lief, Miller, & O'Brien, 1980). Testosterone also peaks along with estrogen during ovulation and Persky has suggested that the higher testosterone levels account for the increased sexual activity of women during this time (Persky et al., 1982). This view is consistent with the fact that postmenopausal women, as well as those whose ovaries have been surgically removed and who thus have a low estrogen level, do *not* lose their desire for sex, while castrated women who are also *adrenalectomized*, and who therefore secrete no *testosterone*, become completely asexual (Waxenberg, Drellich, & Sutherland, 1959). Finally, support for the female libido-testosterone hypothesis derives from the common clinical experience that small amounts of testosterone dramatically increase the sex drive of testosterone deficient women, while estrogen has no such effect.

Apparently, all brains need testosterone for the proper activation and functioning of the sex circuits. However, women require smaller amounts of this substance than males. In females, testosterone or testosterone precursors are secreted by the ovaries and the adrenal cortex. After menopause and during the menstrual period, the ovarian portion of female testosterone diminishes while the adrenals continue to supply it. Adrenal androgens account for the sustained sex drive of most postmenopausal and perimenstrual females.*

Other substances are also involved in sexual activation. When prolactin is high, the sex drive is diminished even when the level of testosterone is normal (March, 1979; Spark et al., 1980). LHRF, a pituitary hormone that releases gonadal hormones, will by itself increase libido in some cases (Spark et al., 1980).

Disease states and drugs

Although the list of disease states and drugs that may impair desire is extensive (see Table 16), actually only a few organic causes are clinically significant. The examiner should be alert for two fairly common medical conditions which impair the sex drive which may occur in apparently healthy individuals who have no other medical signs and symptoms: testosterone deficiency and prolactin-secreting micro- and macro-adenoma of the pituitary gland. The sex centers are very sensitive to the sex hormones; consequently, libido can diminish before other androgen sensitive parts of the body, such as hair follicles, fat distribution, and skin texture, show any signs of testosterone deficiency. Prolactin-producing tumors and adenomas of the pituitary may be so small or slow growing that they can diminish the sex drive before any neurological manifestations appear. For this reason, all patients with a global loss of desire should have screening serum testosterone and prolactin determinations (Kolodny, Masters & Johnson, 1979) as well as LH and FSH. Patients who are either abnormally low in testosterone or high in prolactin or show abnormalities of these other pituitary hormones require thorough endocrine evaluations, because these chemical abnormalities may reflect serious and possibly treatable underlying illness, such as cancers of the gonads and the pituitary.

Chronic diseases may reduce libido by virtue of their general debilitating and depressing effect, but these are obvious from the patient's medical history. A large proportion of patients on kidney dialysis develop potency

---

*A small number of women experience a reduction of libido after menopause. This is probably due to several determinants, some emotional and some due to loss of ovarian testosterone.

TABLE 16
Disease States and Drugs That May Impair Sexual Desire*

---

1. Diseases Associated with Abnormal Hypothalmic Pituitary Function Leading to Decreased Secretion of Trophic Hormones

A. *Cause:* Pituitary diseases (common): pituitary adenoma, either macro or micro; infiltrative diseases; granulomatous diseases; autoimmune diseases; inherited abnormalities of the pituitary gland. Tumors compressing the pituitary gland (e.g., craniopharygiomas)

B. *Physical Exam:* May be normal (e.g., micro-adenoma of the pituitary, early macro-adenoma) or may show pathologic neurologic and/or endocrine signs.

C. *Lab Findings:* Abnormal pituitary hormones, e.g., high prolactin, low trophic hormones; low gonadal hormones. Enlargement of Sella Tursica on x-ray.

2. Primary Testicular Disease

A. *Cause:* Kleinfelter's syndrome; infections (e.g., mumps); tumors (e.g., seminoma); trauma, undescended testicles.

B. *Physical Exam:* May be normal; testes may be shrunken or absent; signs of testosterone deficiency (e.g., sparse facial hair, small genitals, etc.)

C. *Lab Findings:* High trophic hormones, low testosterone.

3. Systemic Diseases that Secondarily Affect Testicular Functioning

A. *Cause:* Chronic renal failure: cirrhosis; Cushing's syndrome; adrenal insufficiency; estrogen producing tumors; hypothyroidism; diabetes mellitus; *all debilitating diseases. Cerebral diseases*: temporal lobe epilepsy; stroke; Parkinson's disease.

B. *Physical Exam:* Varies from normal (e.g., early diabetes) to specific and severe signs and symptoms.

C. *Lab Findings:* Various findings associated with different disease states; trophic and gonadal hormones may be low or normal.

4. Drugs

  Alcohol and narcotics abuse; beta adrenergic blockers (e.g., Endoral); centrally acting antihypertensives (e.g., Aldomet); anti-androgens (e.g., Provera, Cyprosterone).

---

*See also Table 8.

and libido problems. Severe thyroid, liver, and other endocrine problems may also be accompanied by a low sex drive because of their general debilitating effects and the hormonal changes they produce. If the history reveals any of the above mentioned disease states, the patient must be referred for a complete medical and endocrine workup.

Evaluating the cardiac patient

Several studies have reported that sexual activity is reduced after heart attack, and that postcoronary patients have a lowered sex drive. The psychosexual evaluation of coronary infarction victims requires special comment because of the high prevalence of heart attack and the severe sexual problems of this population. Actually, the damage sustained to the heart is *not* responsible for the lowered sexual activity of these patients. This is caused by several other factors which must be sorted out during the evaluation:

1) Postcoronary patients are often depressed for as long as a year and a half after their life-threatening illness. Depression is a major cause of loss of sex drive.
2) Beta adrenergic blocking medication is now widely prescribed to prevent and diminish future heart attacks. This medication is notorious for diminishing libido.* Similar considerations apply to centrally acting antihypertensive agents which are used for the hypertensive postcoronary and CAD patient (these medications can sometimes be successfully substituted).
3) Postcoronary patients are often inhibited by the fear of another heart attack or sudden death during sexual activity. This can be minimized by the use of vasodilators** and by postcoronary stress testing to delineate the patient's safe physical capacity precisely. As a general rule, if a patient can safely walk up a flight of stairs, normal sexual activity (with a familiar partner), which has about the same oxygen requirements, is considered safe. Sex with a new partner is emotionally more stressful and physically more hazardous.

---

*Peripherally acting antihypertensive drugs have fewer side-effects and many of the new beta blockers do not cross the blood-brain barrier to the same extent that Endoral, the first beta blocker in use in this country, does. Calcium channel blockers can sometimes serve as substitutes for beta blockers.

**Short-acting vasodilators like nitroglycerine can be taken before sex, or long-acting preparations such as Isodil can be used on a constant basis.

Evaluating the patient for testosterone replacement

Two common causes of low testosterone in men are advancing age ("the male menopause") and functional endocrine imbalances. These conditions are not due to structural illness and such patients may be appropriate candidates for testosterone replacement therapy. Men with clear testosterone deficiency almost always respond to replacement testosterone with improvement of their sex drive. But some men with borderline or low normal level show a similar improvement, while others with the same laboratory values do not respond. Since I do not know any means of predicting the response to testosterone on clinical or laboratory grounds, it is my practice to recommend a trial of testosterone for male patients with low and borderline testosterone levels whose sex drive has gradually diminished for no apparent psychological reason and who have no medical contraindications.

When testosterone replacement is given to a male, it must be ascertained that he has no *carcinoma of the prostate.* Acid phosphate studies and a rectal exam are used for this diagnosis. In addition, the prostate must be checked at regular intervals so that the medication can be stopped if any prostatic *hypertrophy* is noted. The fluid retention that may accompany testosterone replacement makes this potentially hazardous for cardiac and hypertensive patients.

The use of testosterone in women is more controversial. Some clinicians prescribe small amounts of testosterone on an empirical basis to women whose sex drive and testosterone levels are low, with the caveat that irreversible masculinization (hair and voice) is a definite risk. In certain cases, these risks, which can be minimized by careful medical surveillance for signs of virilism, are outweighed by the benefits of increased vigor and libido which some women experience with testosterone treatment.

The medical contraindications for testosterone therapy may be summarized as follows:

1) increased red cell mass, e.g., polycythemia vera
2) prostatic hypertrophy
3) congestive heart failure
4) prostatic cancer
5) appearance of virilism in women

The many substances that can theoretically impair the sex drive are summarized in Table 15. From a practical point of view, only two kinds of drugs will depress libido to a clinically significant degree. The first are endocrine drugs that *block the action of testosterone* on the brain, which are not for the most part, in common use: cyprosterone, medroxyprogesterone, and estrogens at high levels. The second kind includes substances that *interfere with the neural activity entailed in the activation of the brain's sex circuits*. These drugs, which are widely consumed, include alcohol, the barbiturates, narcotics, centrally acting antihypertensive agents, and the beta adrenergic blocking drugs. Each patient who presents with a complaint of diminished frequency of sexual activity should be carefully and specifically questioned about these substances.

The Psychological Aspects of the Evaluation

Depression and Stress

The sex drive is extraordinarily sensitive to stress and one of the most common causes of globally reduced sexual desire is depression. In fact, libido may diminish before the patient shows any other signs of depression. Chronic and severe stress can likewise result in the syndrome. For this reason, it is important to rule out depression and to make sure the patient is not undergoing significant stress when assessing a low libido patient.

Behavioral Analysis

Unconscious and involuntary focus on negative aspects of the sexual situation is often an important defense mechanism against sexual arousal used by ISD patients. The inhibited person becomes highly critical and these self-induced negative thoughts and images "turn him off," presumably by tapping into the brain's natural inhibitor mechanisms (Kaplan, 1979). The following line of inquiry may reveal these mechanisms: "Do you feel tense or anxious before sex? What goes on in your mind just before you make love? When you make love? Do you ever have arguments before you make love? Do you focus on unpleasant or upsetting material — on her shortcomings, on your own, on extraneous problems — while making love?"

Some persons who depend on sexual fantasy or imagery to feel aroused will sabotage their sexual relationship by failing to use such fantasies while they are with their partner. This aspect of the sexual experience is also queried during the examination of such patients: "Do you have fantasies when you masturbate? What kind of fantasies? Do you use those fantasies when you make love to your partner? Why not? Have you shared your fantasies with your partner?"

The patients are also asked about the compatibility of their sexual fantasies: "What generally turns you on about a woman? What turns you off?

Does your wife do this? Is there anything about her that turns you off? Is she your sexual ideal? What is your sexual ideal? Have you ever been attracted to her? Have you ever been attracted to anyone? Describe her/him."

Avoidance of effective sexual stimulation and pleasurable erotic feeling in the presence of the partner or in the situation about which the patient is conflicted is a common feature of this syndrome. Inhibited patients will discharge their sexual impulses when they are not with the partner with whom they are blocked. They might masturbate when they feel sexual desire rather than make love with the partner. Some men, to their own puzzlement, quickly move away from their wives when they find themselves with an erection during the night.

When the sexual status examination reveals that the patient is putting on cold cream, not putting in her diaphragm, putting her hair in curlers, binging on food, or that he focuses on his taxes or on the children's problems, takes a drink, makes a phone call to his mother, starts to ruminate about her excess weight or on the fact that she leaves dirty dishes in the sink — the immediate defense mechanisms against sexuality become clear and can be confronted later on in therapy.

Analysis of the Intrapsychic Dynamics
and of the Couple's System

It is rare for these immediate and current defenses against sexual desire to exist in a "pure" state. Usually, they operate in the service of significant underlying or remote psychological conflicts which derive from the past. When compared to patients with impairment of the genital phases, ISD patients tend as a group to have more serious marital and intrapsychic problems. No specific psychopathologic conflicts characterize ISD patients and this syndrome may be associated with all the conflicts seen in the other dysfunctions. But certain issues appear to be somewhat more prevalent in this population and the examiner should be alert to these. Often ISD patients have major conflicts about *commitment* to one partner and fears of *intimacy* and *pleasure*. On an unconscious level they often harbor unresolved oedipal problems, along with unconscious fears of retaliation from the parent of the same gender and ambivalence toward and/or excessive attachments to the opposite gender parent. Therefore, the prognosis for patients with ISD is not as good as for those suffering from orgasm and erection problems. Even in successful cases treatment tends to be longer and stormier and the patients more resistant. Improvement appears to depend more on *insight* into and resolution of unconscious intrapsychic conflicts and re-

TABLE 17
The Evaluation of Low or Absent Sexual Desire

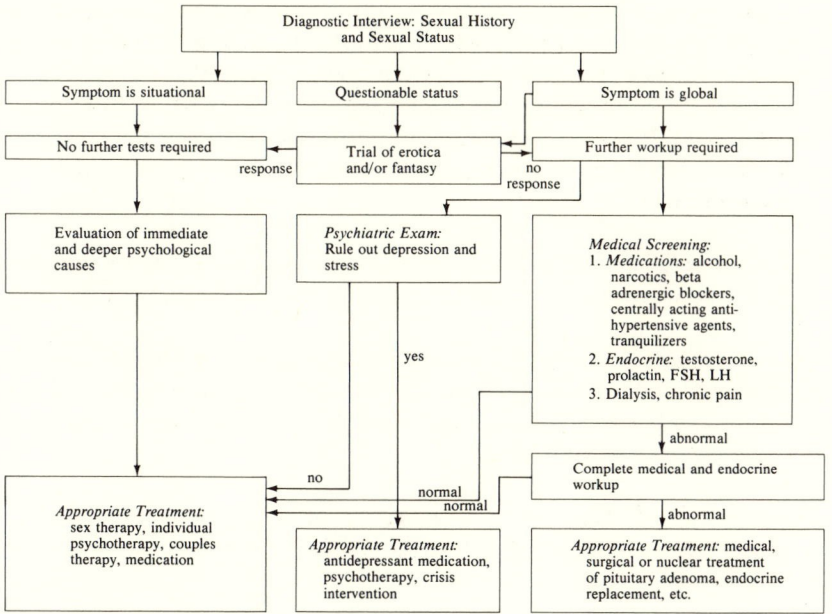

lationship problems than on the direct behavioral interventions which are so often effective in treating psychogenic impairments of the genital phases. For this reason, the assessment of the underlying psychodynamics, as well as of the motivation for treatment, assumes greater importance in the evaluation of ISD patients.

When making the decision whether to see the blocked patient alone, with an emphasis on insight into his intrapsychic conflicts, or whether to treat the couple in conjoint therapy, to try to improve the system, I am influenced by the historic pattern of the patient's romantic relationships. If the patient's blocked desire is a *repetitive pattern* which is likely to surface in any committed relationship (or with any woman whom he sees as his mother), it makes sense to work with him alone. But if he has demonstrated the capacity to combine intimacy and eroticism, therapy should focus on improving the current destructive relationship.

The Paraphilias (Perversions, Deviations, Variations)

Diagnostic Criteria and Clinical Features

"*The essential feature of disorders in this subclass is that unusual or bizarre imagery or acts are necessary for sexual excitement*" (DSM-III, p. 266). This arousal pattern is the repeatedly recurrent and preferred or more effective method of achieving sexual excitement. It is interesting to note that these conditions are seen almost exclusively in males.

DSM-III lists eight Paraphilias and has a ninth residual category of "atypical paraphilias":

Fetishism (302.81): "The use of nonliving objects (fetishes) is a repeatedly preferred or exclusive method of achieving sexual excitement" (p. 269).

Transvestism (302.30): "Recurrent and persistent cross-dressing by a heterosexual male" (p. 270). Cross-dressing is used for the purpose of sexual excitement. (The individual experiences intense frustration when cross-dressing is interfered with.)

Zoophilia (302.10): "The act or fantasy of engaging in sexual activity with animals is a repeatedly preferred or exclusive method of achieving sexual excitement" (p. 270).

Pedophilia (302.20): "The act or fantasy of engaging in sexual activity with prepubertal children is a repeatedly preferred or exclusive method of achieving sexual excitement" (pp. 271–272). Adults with this disorder may either desire children of the same gender or children of the opposite gender, but are more likely to be oriented toward children of the same gender.

Exhibitionism (302.40): "The essential feature is repetitive acts of exposing the genitals to an unsuspecting stranger for the purpose of achieving sexual excitement, with no attempt at further sexual activity with the stranger" (p. 272).

Voyeurism (302.82): "The individual repeatedly observes unsuspecting people who are naked, in the act of disrobing, or engaging in sexual activity and no sexual activity with the observed people is sought. The observing is the repeatedly preferred or exclusive method of achieving sexual excitement" (p. 273).

Sexual masochism (302.83): "The essential feature is . . . a preferred or exclusive mode of producing sexual excitement is to be humiliated, bound, beaten, or otherwise made to suffer" (p. 273). (Masochism is occasionally seen in women.)

Sexual sadism (302.84): "The essential feature is the infliction of physical or psychological suffering on another person in order to achieve sexual excitement" (p. 274).

Atypical paraphilia (302.90): "This is a residual category for individuals with Paraphilias . . . conditions include: Coprophilia (feces); Frotteurism (rubbing); Klismaphilia (enema); Mysophilia (filth); Necrophilia (corpse); Telephone Scatologia (lewdness); and Urophilia (urine)" (p. 275). One can add to this an almost infinite number of other "special interests" which do not have Greek or Latin names: exceedingly large breasts, exceedingly large buttocks, group sex, obesity, rubber, leather, long hair, fire, rape, exclusive anal or oral preoccupations, etc.

DSM-III also makes the important point that these variant arousal patterns may interfere with the capacity for reciprocal affectionate sexual activity.

Ego-dystonic Homosexuality (302.00)

Diagnostic Criteria and Clinical Features

Homosexuals experience very little if any sexual desire for members of the opposite gender, but find sex gratifying with members of the same gender.

According to DSM-III, homosexuality is classified as psychiatric disorder when it is "ego-dystonic": *"The essential features are a desire to acquire or increase heterosexual arousal, so that heterosexual relationships can be initiated or maintained, and a sustained pattern of overt homosexual arousal that the individual explicitly states has been unwanted and a persistent source of distress"* (p. 281).

Evaluation for Treatment

Many homosexuals are content with their sexual preference and consider homosexuality a normal variant (Bell & Weinberg, 1978; Marmor, 1980). Persons with this view are offended when one speaks of a "cause."

Alternate hypotheses suggest that homosexuality may have a biological basis. Genetic factors and inadequate fetal androgenization of the brain have been postulated, although endocrine studies of adult homosexuals have failed to demonstrate hormonal or physical abnormalities (Schiavi, 1976). Organic factors do not have to be considered during the evaluation of homosexuality.

Psychodynamic and learning theories consider homosexuality and the paraphilias as a form of or an adaptation to *inhibited heterosexual desire* (Bieber, 1967a, 1967b; Bieber et al., 1962; Feldman & MacCulloch, 1971; Kaplan, 1982; MacCulloch, Birtles, & Feldman, 1971; Masters & Johnson, 1979).

Most professionals, including myself, consider treatment inappropriate for homosexuals who are content with their preference. However, some homosexuals are very distressed about their homosexual feelings and seek treatment with the aim of acquiring the capacity to love a woman, to experience heterosexual gratification, and to enjoy a normal family life. Many clinicians, including this author, consider these persons eminently deserving of a trial of treatment.

Assessment of Motivation

The success of the treatment of ISD is contingent on a high degree of motivation and this should be evaluated very carefully. The homosexual who is in your office on account of pressures from his parents is no more likely to benefit from treatment than the turned off wife who is dragged there by her husband.

Behavioral Analysis

The patient who seeks help with unwelcome *homosexuality*, is asked to compare his homosexual with his heterosexual experiences. These differences often hold the key to effective treatment. For example, male homosexuals often feel intense performance anxiety when they are with a woman, but are seldom worried about their erections when with male partners, even though they are strangers and even though they occasionally have erectile or ejaculation difficulties with males. In such cases, the treatment of performance anxiety with women may open up the person to heterosexual pleasure (Masters & Johnson, 1979). And some lesbians report that caresses by their female lovers evoke feelings of tenderness and sensuous pleasure, while an identical kiss or touch from a male makes them feel furious and invaded. The exploration and resolution of the rage against men may be helpful with such patients.

The immediate psychic defenses associated with ISD have been described earlier. Male homosexuals seem to experience the same mental processes when they are with a woman. Avoidance of erotic stimulation, the focus on critical thoughts, intense performance anxiety, and withholding of effective erotic imagery are frequently reported by homosexual and paraphiliac males when they are with a heterosexual partner, but not in the variant situation.

Psychodynamic Evaluation

The psychodynamics of homosexuals also seem to be similar to those seen in "straight" ISD. Many homosexual patients who present themselves for treatment are phobic of and avoid commitment and intimacy with members of the opposite gender (Schwartz, 1982).

The histories of male homosexuals often reveal a difficulty with their male-male associations, beginning with poor relationships with their fathers in early childhood. They frequently report that they were very uncomfortable with boys of their own age (Bell & Weinberg, 1978; Bieber et al., 1962). Overinvolvement with the mother is also commonly seen, as is contempt for and distrust of women.

The dynamics and origins of lesbianism have been studied less extensively. It is my impression that intense hostility towards the mother with profound fears of retaliation and competitive feelings with males from early childhood on are often key dynamics. Also, the anticipation that they will be rejected or humiliated or exploited moves some of the women to avoid men. These issues become the focus of the psychodynamic aspects of treatment with these patients.

Treatment and Prognosis

In my experience, the male homosexual patient 1) who is below the age of 35, 2) whose history gives evidence that he has some capacity for heterosexual arousal which has been inhibited by fear and conflict, and 3) whose motivation is high enough and ego strong enough to withstand the anxiety and frustration entailed in treatment, has the best chance for success in psychosexual therapy. Patients who have been strongly effeminate since early childhood and who have never had any heterosexual fantasy or impulse and who cannot tolerate a high level of emotional stress, do not have a good prognosis. Similarly, the lesbian who is highly motivated and shows a clearcut anger at men, but who is otherwise psychologically healthy, has the best prognosis for treatment. Psychoanalytic, behavioral, and the sex therapies have all claimed some success with well motivated homosexuals and the treatment of choice is still controversial (Bieber et al., 1962; Feldman & MacCulloch, 1971; Masters & Johnson, 1979).

The results of traditional psychoanalytically oriented therapy with *paraphiliacs* have been diasppointing (Lorand & Balin, 1956), and behavior therapy seems to have done only a little better. The clinician who evaluates such patients should be aware that some promising innovative approaches that entail temporary chemical suppression of the sex drive, together with psychotherapy and/or behavioral therapy, are now available for the paraphiliac who runs afoul of the law at some experimental centers (Lanschett, 1973; Money, 1970).

Evaluation of sexual dysfunctions of homosexuals

Homosexuals suffer from the same orgasm and excitement phase dysfunctions as heterosexuals (Masters & Johnson, 1979). My experiences in studying and treating dysfunctional homosexual couples suggests that they are vulnerable to essentially the same physical and psychological stressors and have similar responses to sex therapy. For these reasons the principles and methods for the evaluation (and treatment) of genital phase dysfunctions are basically the same for hetero and homosexual couples.

4) SEXUAL PAIN AND DISORDERS ASSOCIATED WITH GENITAL MUSCLE SPASM: DYSPAREUNIA, UTERINE MUSCLE CRAMPS, VAGINISMUS AND EJACULATORY PAIN

The classification of this group of sexual disorders can be confusing. DSM-III places vaginismus and functional dyspareunia into two separate diagnostic categories. But from a clinical, as well as theoretical, point of view vaginismus belongs with a group of sexual symptoms that are caused by involuntary spasm of genital muscles, which can be painful, while other kinds of sexual pain are produced by different mechanisms.

In the following discussion, *dyspareunia* includes all types of sexual pain with the exception of syndromes that are caused by painful spasms of the genital muscles. These are described under the headings of *orgasmic uterine cramps, vaginismus* and *ejaculatory pain due to genital muscle spasm.* The differential diagnosis of *unconsummated marriage,* which is often caused by sexual pain, is discussed under a separate heading.

Dyspareunia (302.76)

DSM-III restricts functional dyspareunia to pain on coitus and gives the following criteria: *"recurrent and persistent genital pain, in either the male or the female"* (p. 280). We use the term to designate pain associated with orgasm and sexual excitement, as well as with intercourse, because the causes and treatment of all of these are similar.

Sex should not hurt and when it does something is wrong. Chronic sexual pain often has a deleterious effect on a couple's sex life and may also affect the entire relationship adversely.

The Differential Diagnosis and the Medical Aspects of the Evaluation

Dyspareunia can be a symptom of many gynecological and urological disorders; it can be produced by various psychic mechanisms. For this reason, the differential diagnosis is of utmost importance in the evaluation of sexual pain. Usually this is done by excluding physical causes. The most important diagnostic tool to differentiate organic from psychogenic sources of pain is a careful review of the character and location of the pain, when it occurs and what relieves it. As always, a situational symptom pattern suggests psychogenicity, but some painful gynecological conditions such as endometriosis or vaginal infections may fluctuate for biological reasons. Different medical problems have characteristic types of pain, and a detailed description will give the examiner who is knowledgeable about sexual medicine information about its etiology. The examiner should be alert to the fact that patients vary considerably with regard to the stoicism with which they bear their pain. Some endure too much pain for too long before they finally seek medical help. Others overreact to minor and insignificant discomfort.

The examiner should ask: "Where does it hurt? When does it hurt you? Durng ejaculation or orgasm? After ejaculation or orgasm or after sexual activity? Do you have pain on intercourse? When? Does it hurt when he enters? On deep thrusting? Does it ease after a while or does it become more severe with each thrust? What is the quality of pain? Does it burn, or poke, or stab? Is it just a little bit of discomfort or is it truly agonizing? Is it always in the same area? Is it worse in some positions? Do you sometimes have sex with no pain?"

A precise medical history will help narrow down the causes of the pain. Sexual pain in males is most frequently caused by local urologic disease, so that men who experience pain on ejaculation should be questioned about signs and symptoms of prostatitis, vesiculitis, and urinary difficulties which include pain on urination, frequency, and discharge. Women are questioned about signs and symptoms of the most common causes of female dyspareunia: endometriosis, vaginal infections, and a history of gonorrhea, which might indicate the presence of pelvic inflammatory disease.

A "wandering" pain is much more likely to be psychogenic than a localized, consistent pain or sensitivity. Of course, if it only hurts when the penis is the penetrating object, but the speculum or a tampon is comfortable, organicity is ruled out, as it is in any other situational complaint.

If the pain has no anatomic or pathophysiologic basis, psychogenicity may be suspected, especially if it seems to have symbolic meaning. Thus, for example, a patient complained that the glans of his penis hurt whenever he had intercourse or an ejaculation. There are no illnesses or drugs that can cause this complaint and, not surprisingly, numerous medical, urological, neurologic, and dermatologic examinations had proved negative in the past. Physical inspection of his penis showed a normal appearing organ. The psychological aspects of the examination revealed possible psychological causes. The patient was the middle child of a highly achieving family. His sister, brother, mother, father, uncles and cousins were all extremely accomplished. The pain on sex was a way he could gain attention and provided an excuse for not entering the "family olympics"* (Friedman, 1981).

However, many patients are erroneously assured by the gynecologist or urologist that "it's all in your head," when in fact their sexual pain is caused by subtle pathological conditions which may be missed on a routine examination. Small hypersensitive hymenal remnants, mild endometriosis, and fluctuating inflammations of the vagina or irritations of the labia are sometimes the real cause of the complaint. Therefore, every patient who complains about pain should receive a thorough examination of the painful area. During the examination one *looks for subtle pathology and tries to reproduce the pain*. Even if there is no obvious lesion, *if the pain can be replicated reliably by palpation of the same spot during the examination*, real organic pathology should be suspected and the patient may need further gynecological or dermatological evaluation. Conversely, if the characteristic pain cannot be elicited, the chances are that the patient has a psychogenic problem. The medical causes of dyspareunia are listed in Tables 18 and 19.

---

*The hypothesis proved correct when the patient went into psychotherapy, which helped him gain insight into the real meaning of the pain and improve his functioning in other areas of life.

TABLE 18
Disease States That May Cause Dyspareunia in the Female*

Causes of Pain on Stimulation

Labial pathology, infections, injury
Clitoral problems
   irritation, lesions, phimosis, hypersensitivity of clitoris

Causes of Pain on Entry

Vaginismus
Intact or rigid hymen, painful hymenal tags
Vulvovaginitis
   monilia
   trichomonas
   herpes
   atrophy
   chemical irritation and sensitivities
Bartholin and Skene glands
   cyst
   infection
Inadequate lubrication
Operative scarring
   tender episiotomy
   tight perineorrhaphy
   post-hysterectomy vault scars
   adhesions
   irradiation

Causes of Mid-vaginal Pain

Urethritis, trigonitis, cystitis ("honeymoon" cystitis)
Congenital shortened vagina

Causes of Pain on Deep Thrusting

Pelvic inflammatory disease
Endometriosis
Fixed uterine retroversion
Endometritis
Ovarian pathology: cysts, tumors
Pelvic congestion
Lower bowel disease
Parapelvic dyspareunia
   hip arthritis
   lumbosacral strain
   disc

(continued)

TABLE 18 *(continued)*

---

angina on effort
complications of IMD (perforation, infection, cramping)

Causes of Pain on Orgasm

Uterine contractions (from hypoestrogenic states)
Frictional vaginal discomfort
Spasm of abdominal muscles (infrequent)
Post-orgasm headache

---

*This table was prepared by Sherwin A. Kaufman, M.D.

The Psychological Aspects of the Evaluation

Sexual pain is often psychogenic and can be caused by several psychological mechanisms. *Hysterical or conversion pain* grows out of unconscious sexual conflicts. Such patients experience their sexual conflicts, guilts, and ambivalence as pain, and insight into the unconscious meaning of the symptom will often provide relief (Freud & Breuer, 1893). Intractable sexual pain is sometimes associated with *depression* (depression-pain syndrome). This can often be relieved with a treatment regime that includes antidepressant medication. Intractable pain is sometimes seen in latent schizophrenia (Kaplan, Schwartz, Kaye, & Glass, 1970), in which case antipsychotic agents are used. *Hypochondriacal preoccupations* and *obsessive overreactions* to normal physical sensations may cause patients to complain of sexual pain. Overreactions to minor physical problems are also seen in phobic-anxiety states.

Pain can also result from attempts at having intercourse when the woman is *insufficiently aroused and lubricated* and from *brutal, sadistic sexual practices*. Finally, sex can hurt on a psychophysiologic basis because of the painful genital muscle spasms of vaginismus and functional ejaculatory pain syndrome.

During the evaluation, it is necessary to rule out organic causes. It is also important to identify the precise psychological mechanisms of the pain because treatment will vary according to the psychiatric diagnosis. In all cases of dyspareunia, organic as well as psychogenic, it is essential to attempt to understand the psychic meaning of the patient's sexual avoidance, because such patients can often be helped by gaining insight into the role that sexual pain plays in their life.

TABLE 19
Disease States That May Cause Dyspareunia in the Male*

Causes of Painful Erections and Pain on Intromission

A. *Pathologic penile anatomy*
phimosis
paraphimosis
balanitis
balanoposthitis
frenular tethering
prior trauma — fracture, sickle cell anemia
Peyronie's disease
chordee
cancer of the penis (rare)

B. *Cutaneous Dermatologic Lesions:* pain on contact and friction
herpes progenitalis
scabies
eczematoid lesions
traumatic abrasion
thrombophlebitis
urethritis
nonspecific
gonococcal
traumatic
chemical
contraceptives
lubricants
soap
vaginal secretions(?)

Causes of Pain on Ejaculation

prostatitis
bacterial
congestive
urethritis and other urethral pathology
seminal vesiculitis
vasitis
epididymitis
inguinal hernia
cremaster spasm
post-ejaculatory headache
painful testicles
orchitis
tumor
trauma
tension of spermatic chord

(continued)

TABLE 19 *(continued)*

Other Conditions Causing Sex-related Pain

angina on effort
lower back pain on thrusting due to orthopedic problems
post-orgasm headache

---

*This table was prepared by Jon M. Reckler, M.D.

(Post) Orgasmic Uterine Cramps

The complaint of pain after or during orgasm is usually organic when it occurs in postmenopausal women. Estrogen deficiency will sometimes cause the uterus to become hypersensitive and react with painful spasms after orgasm. This is seldom a very serious problem and usually yields to reassurance.* A small number of patients have this complaint on a psychogenic basis.

Vaginismus (306.51)

Diagnostic Criteria and Clinical Features

Acccording to DSM-III, vaginismus is defined as follows: *"There is a history of recurrent and persistent involuntary spasm of the musculature of the outer third of the vagina that interferes with coitus"* (p. 280).

Ordinarily, when a woman is sexually aroused, the vaginal muscles relax and the introitus opens. But in vaginismic women the muscles snap together so tightly that penetration may be impossible. The husband will tell you, "I just can't get in, there is a block, an obstruction." When the vaginal muscle spasm is somewhat less severe, entry may be forcibly attained but the experience is painful for the woman. The patient has no voluntary control over her response, and on a conscious level vaginismic patients are often extremely distressed by their inability to have intercourse and children.

It is interesting to note that while some patients with this disorder also have other sexual problems, many have normal sexual desire, lubricate, and are orgasmic. In fact, I have seen some vaginismic women who are capable of having multiple orgasms. It is only penetration which is difficult, painful, or impossible.

---

*In those cases where the problem is severe, antiprostaglandin medication (Motrin) and/or estrogen replacement may be used.

In most cases, the vaginal muscles go into spasm in response to any attempt at vaginal penetration, so that the patient cannot use tampons and has great difficulty in undergoing a pelvic examination. Sometimes anesthesia is required for this purpose. A few patients have a specific vaginismus which only occurs during coital attempts and not at other attempts at vaginal penetrations. These patients can be examined without difficulty and this situational pattern rules out organic obstruction.

The Differential Diagnosis and the Medical Aspects of the Evaluation

Most patients find vaginal penetration difficult in all situations and must first have a vaginal examination to rule out organic obstruction and to establish that the vaginal muscles are in fact in spasm.

The examiner can palpate the vaginal muscles and confirm that they are tightly closed. Patients with vaginismus may feel pain when the examiner's finger(s) are first introduced, but if the examiner retains the examining fingers in the vagina while she quietly reassures or distracts the patient, the vaginal muscles of vaginismic patients will usually relax within 10 to 60 seconds. The patient then begins to feel comfortable with the speculum or the examiner's fingers inside her vagina. She has been confronted with the important fact that there is no structural abnormality and that the block was only due to her muscle spasm, which will diminish if she does not panic.

If the vaginal muscles are found to be tight, the next diagnostic question is whether the cause of the spasm is psychogenic or physical, because both can result in muscle spasm. Any gynecological disorder that makes sex painful can evoke a conditioned guarding response and vaginismus. Endometriosis, PID, vaginitis, herpes, birth and surgical injuries of the genitals are among the many painful medical disorders which can result in this syndrome.

For this reason, if the patient complains of *pain* during the vaginal examination, apart from that produced by the spastic vaginal muscle, a thorough gynecological evaluation is in order to insure that no treatable or dangerous gynecological conditions are missed.

The Psychological Aspects of the Evaluation

Behavioral Analysis

A reflex involuntary spasm of the muscles that guard the vaginal introitus is the immediate psychophysiological cause of vaginismus. At times the patient's sexual history reveals a specific precipitating trauma, such as incest or rape or a painful attempt at intercourse. Some have or have had a painful gynecological condition. Others are guilty and conflicted about sex. In many cases, however, the patient remembers nothing that could explain her symptom.

Analysis of the Intrapsychic Dynamics and of the Couple's System

Although vaginismus is very disabling and may make it difficult for the patient to lead a normal life, the underlying psychological causes range from the trivial to the serious. Vaginismus may occur as an isolated symptom in a basically healthy woman who is in a good relationship. Other vaginismic patients have severe neurotic conflicts about sex. Some are ambivalent about their marriage and/or about pregnancy or motherhood. Some are passive-aggressively punishing their husbands. Some have a panic disorder.

When evaluating the vaginismic patient it is important to gauge the severity of the underlying emotional problem, because this will determine how difficult treatment will be. In the more complex cases the symbolic meaning of the symptom and/or the role that the closed vagina plays in the relationship should be assessed, so that the therapist knows what psychological issues will have to be confronted during the psychodynamic aspects of treatment.

Many vaginismic patients develop a secondary phobic avoidance of vaginal penetration. This must be analyzed so it can be treated before the vaginal spasm, for one can hardly expect a patient to proceed with vaginal dilation if she panics at any approach to her vagina.

Treatment and Prognosis

Regardless of the severity of the associated emotional problems, the symptom of vaginismus has an excellent prognosis with treatment that includes progressive vaginal dilation. Although patients with more complex problems may resist during therapy, it is the rare vaginismic woman whose symptom cannot be cured with brief, direct, behavioral treatment.

Ejaculatory Pain Due to Muscle Spasm of the Male Genitals

This rather rare syndrome is analogous to vaginismus in the sense that it is caused by a painful and involuntary spasm of the muscles of the reproductive and sexual organs. In the male the cremasteric muscles and/or the smooth muscles of the internal male reproductive organs and/or the perineal muscles react with painful spasm as the man ejaculates or immediately thereafter. Patients typically experience a sharp cramp-like pain immediately upon ejaculation. This may be mild but can be excruciating and disabling. The pain is experienced in the perineum and in the shaft of the penis. It may be transient or last for hours and even days. The physical examination between episodes is normal and may also be normal while the patient is in pain. Sometimes, however, the scrotum is red, swollen, tender and tense during an attack.

Patients tend to be extremely distressed by this symptom and develop a fear of and avoidance of orgasm, which creates an intense conflict when they feel sexual tension. Some patients always experience the pain whenever they ejaculate, on masturbation as well as with a partner. In other cases the symptom is situational and is experienced only when they are ambivalent about ejaculating.

The Differential Diagnosis and the Medical Aspects of the Evaluation

Organic disorders, such as prostatitis, epididymitis, vesiculitis, diseases of the urethra and referred pain from other areas can theoretically cause ejaculatory pain, and evidence of these should be pursued during the medical history. Actually, organic ejaculatory pain is rare, but must nevertheless always be ruled out as it can be associated with dangerous disease states including penile cancer. The diagnosis of ejaculatory muscle spasm is made by the typical history of pain, by *exclusion* of organic causes, and by a trial of sexual therapy.

The Psychological Aspects of the Evaluation

My associates and I have treated only eight patients with this syndrome and I do not know how typical these were. However, their good response to sex therapy (which emphasizes confrontation of the psychological meaning of the symptom and psychotherapeutic support of sexual pleasure, combined stretching and relaxing the painful muscles with relaxation exercises and hot sitz baths and the concomitant use of muscle relaxants) indicates that this symptom is at least in some cases psychogenic. There is some evidence to suggest that the painful ejaculation syndrome lies on a continuum of ejaculatory inhibition which results from ambivalence about orgasm. At one extreme is retarded ejaculation, then partially retarded ejaculation, next is the syndrome of functional ejaculatory pain, while the orgastic experience of the least conflicted men merely lacks gratification and pleasure. * This syndrome may explain some of those puzzling cases of ejaculatory pain that remain undiagnosed and unimproved after repeated urological examinations.

---

*Suggested by J. Lawrence Moodie, M.D.

III. SEXUAL PHOBIAS AND AVOIDANCE

The avoidance of sex because of irrational fears and phobias is not, strictly speaking, a sexual disorder, because there may be nothing wrong with the phobic patient's sexual response. For this reason it is not included in DSM-III under the psychosexual disorders. However, sexual phobias are discussed here because these disabling syndromes are very common among patients with sexual complaints and are frequently amenable to sex therapy. Actually, some element of sexual avoidance is present in almost all sexual disorders, but it is the *essential feature* of sexual phobias.

The detection and analysis of a phobic component in any sexual problem are important aspects of the evaluation, because the patient's avoidance of sex must be resolved before the other aspects of the difficulty can be treated. For example, it is impossible to diminish an impotent man's performance anxiety with gentle sexual exercises if he panics whenever his lover touches him, and the importance of first resolving the phobic avoidance element in vaginismus has been discussed in the previous section.

*Diagnostic Criteria and Clinical Features**

The essential feature of a sexual phobia is the persistent and irrational fear of and compelling desire to avoid sexual feelings and/or experiences. The fear is recognized by the individual as excessive and unreasonable (see DSM-III, p. 225).

Phobic patients may avoid sex altogether or their anxiety and avoidance may be confined to specific aspects of sex: sexual failure, the genitals, sexual secretions and odors, sexual fantasies, various erotic activities such as kissing, oral sex and anal sex, masturbation, orgasm, undressing before the partner, seeing the partner nude, pregnancy, etc.

Fear and avoidance of sex are often highly distressing and may seriously interfere with the development of a normal sex life, romantic attachments, and marriage. The social and emotional life of such patients may become progressively constricted as a result of their avoidance of sexual situations. Some patients with sexual phobias remain virgins all their lives; many do not marry and some become socially isolated. Other phobic patients man-

---

*DSM-III lists these diagnostic criteria for other phobias, but specifically excludes sexual phobias. According to DSM-III, sexual phobias are classified under the term "Psychosexual Disorders Not Elsewhere Classified."

age to marry despite their phobias, but their lives are never easy. During the evaluation it is important to gain an understanding of the emotional damage which has resulted from the patient's phobic avoidance of sex, as this usually requires additional therapeutic intervention.

A typical phobic experience is: "By the afternoon I have already started to worry. I get edgy by two o'clock because I know he will want sex that night. Sometimes I take a drink before he comes home. I'll make any excuse. I'll be on the phone; I'll schedule a Cub Scout meeting; I'll drink; I'll binge; I'll zonk myself out with Valium. I'll pretend to be ill."

When she is "trapped" into a situation where sex can no longer be avoided on the pain of losing a valued partner or feeling guilt about frustrating a beloved one, the experience is extremely unpleasant. Phobic patients report that they feel panic or revulsion and sometimes rage during sex. A common experience is trying "to get it over with as quickly as possible."

Some partners of phobic patients are amazingly understanding, patient, and protective. Others are furious and threatened and try to manipulate and pressure the phobic patient for sex. The partner's reaction is a significant variable in planning therapy and in estimating the prognosis, because the cooperation of a gentle, nonpressuring partner is extremely helpful in treatment.

Sexual phobias must be differentiated from other kinds of problems which result in sexual avoidance. Some patients with ISD avoid sex because it gives them no pleasure. Others with anxiety about their sexual performance are afraid to face the humiliation and frustration of failure. Still other patients avoid intercourse because it is physically painful or uncomfortable, while some deliberately withhold sex to punish their partner. Again, the differential diagnosis between these different causes of low sexual frequency is important because in each case entirely different treatment approaches are required.

The Differential Diagnosis and the Medical Aspects of the Evaluation

Once the diagnosis of sexual phobia and avoidance has been made, the question of organic versus psychogenic etiology does not arise in the same way as for the psychosexual dysfunctions. However, many phobic patients complain about the physical symptoms of anxiety and panic, which include all the signs of sympathetic discharge: tremors, palpitations, dyspnea, vertigo, etc. Such complaints must be carefully investigated from a medical perspective because they can be produced by a variety of serious and treatable physical conditions, including hypoglycemia, heart failure, hyperthyroidism, as well as the abuse of stimulants and the withdrawal of sedative substances such as barbiturates and alcohol. Many patients with panic disorders also suffer from prolapse of the mitral valve (Gorman, Fyer, Glicklich, King, & Klein, 1981). These patients will respond to antipanic drugs just as phobic patients with normal heart valves.* For this reason it is my practice to recommend echo-cardiograms for all patients with panic disorder.**

The Psychological Aspects of the Evaluation

Differentiating Simple Sexual Phobias from Sexual Phobias Associated with Panic Disorder

Patients with sexual phobias are frequently afflicted with panic disorder (phobic anxiety syndrome). Such patients have an abnormally low threshold for panic on a psychophysiological basis. They experience panic attacks and tend to develop multiple phobias (Klein, 1964, 1980; Roth & Myers, 1969), including sexual ones (Kaplan et al., 1982).

Persons whose fear or panic threshold is *normal* may also develop sexual phobias. These irrational fears are presumably acquired on a learned or neurotic basis. That is not to say, of course, that patients with panic disorder do not learn to be afraid or are not subject to neurotic processes. On the contrary, they are probably more vulnerable to these because of their propensity to panic. †

The differentiation between "simple" sexual phobia and phobia associated with panic disorder is of utmost importance during the evaluation because patients with panic disorders are not amenable to psychological therapies alone and require antipanic medication (Kelly, Guiruis, Fromer, Michell-Heggs, & Sargent, 1970; Leibowitz & Klein, 1979; Muskin & Fyer, 1981; Tyrer, Candy, & Nelly, 1973; Zitrin, Klein, & Woerner, 1978), while those with simple sexual phobias respond to a variety of psychotherapeutic approaches and should not be medicated (Kaplan et al., 1982). Simple phobias are highly amenable to sex therapy while phobic patients with

---

*It may be speculated that the frequent association between the two syndromes is not a causal one but is due to a genetic linkage, that is, the gene for mitral valve prolapse and the one for panic disorder may be located on the same chromosome.

**Echo-cardiogram is the only means of confirming the diagnosis of mitral value prolapse.

†According to learning theory, sexual phobias are caused by conditioning, that is, by the temporal association of sex with pain or danger or guilt. Psychoanalytic theory favors the explanation that phobias are the product of unconscious neurotic processes acquired during childhood. According to that model, sex evokes panic because symbolically it has become a dangerous, incestuous, sinful, or competitive act.

panic disorders may actually become worse in sex therapy unless they are protected from panic attacks with antipanic medication.* In our experience, the prognosis for sexual complaints related to phobias is excellent when the appropriate combination of medication and sex therapy is employed.

The clinical criteria which will predict which sexually phobic patients will require antipanic medication and which ones will not respond to drugs have not yet been delineated precisely. In our experience, if a patient has multiple phobias and avoidances and/or a history of panic attacks, as well as separation anxiety and/or a family history of phobic anxiety syndrome, a trial of antipanic medication makes sense. When sexual phobia and avoidance occur as isolated symptoms in an otherwise calm and basically non-anxious person, medication is not likely to be effective (Kaplan et al., 1982).

When the diagnostic interview leaves doubt about whether the patient is in fact suffering from a panic disorder or not, it is my opinion that a trial of antipanic medication is indicated. The risk of not medicating a patient who will not recover without the drug seems greater in terms of human suffering than that posed by medicating a person who does not really need it.

Behavioral Analysis

Whether the patient is drug responsive or not, it is extremely important to analyze the behavioral dimensions of the phobic reaction precisely in order to be able to plan desensitization, which is used in the treatment of phobias and the phobic elements of all disorders (Barlow, 1981; Wolpe, 1962). A detailed analysis of the specific circumstances that evoke the patient's panic and of the contingencies that reinforce the avoidance behavior is required for this process.

The examiner should ask: "Does she panic at any mention of sex? At any physical intimacy? Or is the phobic reaction specific to kissing, to genitals, oral sex, penetration, orgasm? How does the patient avoid the phobically feared situation? Does she realize that she is panicked by sex? That she avoids sex?"

---

*The antipanic medication currently favored is Tofranil (imipramine), a tricyclic antidepressant, because the experience is most extensive with this agent. However, clinical evidence indicates that other tricyclics and MAO inhibitors also block panic effectively (Tyrer et al., 1973) and recent experience suggests that some of the newer antidepressant and antianxiety agents, notably, Xanax (alprazolam) and Desyril (trazodone) and also some of the tetracyclic antidepressants, such as Ludiomil, may also have antipanic properties. The lesser toxicity of these new drugs may make them the treatment of choice in the future (Risch & Janowsky, 1981).

Analysis of the Intrapsychic Dynamics and of the Couple's System

The examiner should also attempt to gain an understanding of the symbolic meaning of the phobic reaction if, in fact, this seems relevant. The patient's avoidance of sex may have unconscious symbolic meaning and/or serve as a defense mechanism. The phobia may also play a dynamic role in the couple's relationship. The recognition and understanding of such dynamics are helpful in dealing with resistances to the extinction of the fear response, which often emerge when the avoidance of sex serves as a defense against the patient's unconscious conflicts about sexual pleasure, commitment and intimacy, or as a weapon in her battle with her spouse.

Treatment and Prognosis

Avoidance of sex can have many causes, including painful intercourse due to an undiagnosed gynecologic condition, a view of the partner as repulsive, or a neurotic conflict about sexual pleasure. Or the patient may have developed the avoidance pattern on account of an unrecognized phobic anxiety syndrome (panic disorder). Phobic avoidance of sex resulting from each of these etiologies has in most cases a good prognosis, but only if the pathogenic agent is correctly identified, and only if appropriate medical and/or psychological therapy is instituted.

IV. UNCONSUMMATED MARRIAGE

The inability to have intercourse can be the product of any number of physical and psychological determinants. Couples who cannot consummate a sexual relationship are among the most distressed and troubed one sees in clinical practice (and when they are helped, among the most grateful). They are frequently embarrassed about what they consider a shameful inadequacy and tend to be secretive about their problem. They may irrationally blame themselves for their difficulty, feeling that they are being punished for masturbation or for other "forbidden" sexual acts.

The Differential Diagnosis and the Medical Aspects of the Evaluation

The multiple physical and psychological causes that can interfere with consummation of sexual intercourse range from major irreversible ones (fortunately rare) to the much more common minor and treatable types of problems (see Table 20). Accurate diagnosis is particularly important when a complaint can result from such a diversity of causes.

Among the more common anatomic abnormalities of the genitals that can preclude coitus are an imperforate or rigid hymen and severe chordee of the penis. Rare anatomic causes include vaginal agenesis and micropenis. Organic impotence may also be implicated, as may painful and disabling vaginal disorders. The psychological causes show the same diversity and range from sexual avoidance in an otherwise normal woman to extremely severe psychopathological and relationship problems.

TABLE 20
Disease States That Can Prevent Sexual Intercourse

A. On the Part of the Female

1. *Vaginal Obstructions*

    imperforate or rigid hymen
    vaginal agenesis or other congenital genital abnormalities
    vaginismus
    pelvic and abdominal tumors impinging on vagina
    foreign bodies in vagina
    uterine prolapse

2. *Painful Gynecological Conditions* (Also see Table 18)

    atrophic vaginitis (estrogen deficiency plus irradiation)

TABLE 20 (*continued*)

infected Bartholin cyst
vaginal infections
PID
genital allergies and irritations
endometriosis
painful pelvic and abdominal tumors and inflammations
infected IUD

3. *Other Painful and Obstructive Conditions*

severe skeletal and pelvic deformities
neurological conditions causing spasm and/or abnormal movements (e.g.,
  cerebral palsy)
extreme obesity

B. On the Part of the Male

1. *Inadequate Phallus* (Also see Table 19)

absent penis, micropenis and other congenital genital abnormalities
loss or damage to penis due to injury or surgery
penile deformities
  chordee
  hypospadias
  phimosis
organic impotence
organic anejaculation

2. *Painful Urological Conditions*

infections (e.g., herpes) of penis, genital warts
genital allergies and irritations
testicular tumor or infection
hernia

3. *Other Medical Conditions*

severe skeletal and pelvic deformities
arthritis
neurological injuries and diseases (e.g., spinal cord injuries and diseases; cerebral palsy; degenerative diseases, etc.)
extreme obesity

C. Incompatible Size of Partners' Genitals

A diagnostic interview that emphasizes a detailed description of the couple's current sexual status and their sexual history is the examiner's most valuable diagnostic tool. It narrows down the possible organic and psychological causes that must be pursued and illuminates the immediate physical and emotional obstacles to successful intercourse.

Has either had successful intercourse with another partner? If one has, the other is the obstacle. Has he had a medical or urologic examination? If so, he has no gross anatomic abnormality.

The examiner should inquire: "Tell me what happens when you try to have intercourse. Does she have pain? Can she insert anything into her vagina—a tampon, a finger? Has she had a gynecological exam? (If so, we have eliminated physical obstacles to penetration, but perhaps she has vaginismus.) Does she tighten up when he tries to enter? (Phobic avoidance of penetration is among our differential diagnoses.) Does she panic? Does she scream and yell and move away from him in bed? Or is the obstacle to the consummation of marriage *his* problem? Does he masturbate? Can he have an erection? Does he have a sexual dysfunction? Does he lose his erection, does he lose his desire, does he ejaculate before he can enter? Can he ejaculate at all? Does he avoid sex?"

Unless the complaint is clearly situational (both have had intercourse with other partners), all patients who complain of not being able to have intercourse must also have physical examinations of their genitals to rule out organic factors or report normal findings on a recent examination before commencing psychological treatment.

The Psychological Aspects of the Evaluation

In psychogenic unconsummated marriage the behavioral, psychodynamic, and systems aspects of the symptom must be evaluation and the precise psychic mechanism must be detected and understood for proper treatment. Table 21 lists the psychological causes of the failure to consummate a sexual relationship.

Treatment and Prognosis

This book has stressed the importance of evaluating sexual disorders comprehensively and precisely for planning appropriate and effective treatment. There can be no better illustration of this than the complaint of unconsummated marriage, which can result from diverse physical and psychological difficulties. The inability to engage in a successful sexual union can be highly traumatic, and the great majority of these unhappy couples can be treated successfully, but only if the underlying causes have been accurately identified.

TABLE 21
Psychogenic Problems That Can Prevent Sexual Intercourse

A. On the Part of the Female

psychogenic dyspareunia
ISD
vaginismus
phobic avoidance of intercourse, on the basic of panic disorder or simple phobia
ambivalence about or rejection of the partner
unconscious conflict about sex, commitment, pregnancy, motherhood, fear of injury during sex and/or childbirth
psychotic delusions about penetration
deliberate avoidance of intercourse

B. On the Part of the Male

psychogenic dyspareunia
ISD
performance anxiety
impotence (which may be specific to penetration attempts)
premature ejaculation which may be so severe the patient ejaculates before entering
phobic avoidance of intercourse on the basis of panic disorder or simple phobia
ambivalence about or rejection of the partner
unconscious conflict about sex, commitment, parenthood, fear of injuring the partner
pathological passivity which prevents active thrusting
psychotic delusions about penetration (vagina dentada)
deliberate avoidance of intercourse
mental retardation

C. Problems in the Relationship

poor sexual techniques
lack of information
poor communications
neurotic interactions: power struggles, contractual disappointments, mutual parental transferences
incompatible sexual fantasies
incompatible marriage
relationship problems secondary to alcoholism and substance abuse

REFERENCES FOR SECTION III

Abraham, K. Ejaculation praecox. In *Selected papers on psychoanalysis*. London: Hogarth Press, 1949, 280–310.

American Psychiatric Association *Diagnostic and statistical manual*. Third Edition. Washington, D.C.: American Psychiatric Association, 1980.

Ayd, F. J. Introduction: New antidepressant drugs. *Psychiatric Annals*, 1981, II, 11.

Barbach, L. G. Group treatment of preorgasmic women. *Journal of Sexual and Marital Therapy*, 1974, *I*, 139–149.

Barlow, D. (Ed.) *Behavioral assessment of adult disorders*. New York: Guilford, 1981.

Bell, A. P., & Weinberg, M. S. *Homosexualities*. New York: Simon & Schuster, 1978.

Benedek, T. The functions of the sexual apparatus and their disturbances. In *Psychosomatic medicine*. F. Alexander (Ed.) New York: W. W. Norton, 1950.

Benedek, T., & Rubinstein, B. B. *The sexual cycle in women: The relation between ovarian and psychodynamic processes*. Washington, D.C.: National Research Council, 1942.

Bieber, I. Sexual deviations I: Introduction. In *Comprehensive textbook of psychiatry*, 1st Ed. A. M. Freedman & H. L. Kaplan (Eds.) Baltimore: Williams & Wilkins, 1967(a), 959–962.

Bieber, I. Sexual deviations II: Homosexuality. In *Comprehensive textbook of psychiatry*, 1st Ed. A. M. Freedman & H. L. Kaplan (Eds.) Baltimore: Williams & Wilkins, 1967(b), 963–976.

Bieber, I., Dain, J. J., Diuce, P. R., Drelich, M. G., Grand, H. G., Grundlach, R. H., Kremer, M. W., Rifkin, A.H., Wilbur, C. B., & Bieber, T. B. *Homosexuality*. New York: Basic Books, 1962.

Burt, J. C. Presentation, Annual meeting of the scientific study of sex. Las Vegas, 1977.

Burt, J. E., & Burt, J. C. *The surgery of love*. New York: Carlton Press, 1975.

Derogatis, L. R., Meyer, J. K., & Vazquez, V. A psychological profile of the transsexual: I. The male. *Journal of Nervous and Mental Diseases*, 1978, *196*, 234–254.

Deutsch, H. *Psychology of women: A psychoanalytic interpretation*. New York: Grune & Stratton, 1944 (Vol. I), 1945 (Vol. II).

Feldman, M. P., & MacCulloch, M. J. *Homosexual behavior.* Oxford: Pergamon Press, 1971.

Fenichel, O. *The psychoanalytic theory of neurosis.* New York: Norton, 1945.

Finney, R. P., Sharpe, J. R., & Sadlowski, R. W. Finney hinged penile implant. Experience with 100 cases. *Journal of Urology,* 1980, *124,* 205–207.

Fisher, S. *The female orgasm.* New York: Basic Books, 1973.

Freud, S. Three essays on the theory of sexuality. In *The complete psychological works of Sigmund Freud, Vol. VII* (1905) London: Hogarth Press, 1953, 125.

Freud, S. Introductory lectures in psychoanalysis (lectures 20 & 21). In *The complete psychological works of Sigmund Freud, Vol. XV* (1917). London: Hogarth Press, 1953, 303–339.

Freud, S. Some psychical consequences of the anatomical distinction between the sexes. In *The complete psychological works of Sigmund Freud, Vol. XIX* (1925). London: Hogarth Press, 1953, 243.

Freud, S. Female sexuality. *International Journal of Psychoanalysis,* 1932, 281–296.

Freud, S., & Breuer, J. Studies in hysteria. In *The complete psychological works of Sigmund Freud, Vol. 11.* (1893). London: Hogarth Press, 1953.

Friedman, M. *Overcoming the fear of success.* New York: Warner, 1981.

Ginsberg, G. L., Frosch, W. A., & Shapiro, T. The new impotence. *Arch. Gen. Psychiat.,* 1972, *26:3,* 218–220.

Gorman, J. M., Fyer, A. J., Glicklich, T., King, D., & Klein, D. F. Effects of sodium lactate on panic disorder patients with mitral valve prolapse. *Am. J. Psych.,* 1981, *138,* 247–249.

Gräfenberg, E. The role of the urethra in female orgasm. *International Journal of Sexology,* 1950, *3,* 145–148.

Green, R., & Money, J. (Eds.) *Transsexualism and sex reassignment.* Baltimore: Johns Hopkins U. Press, 1969.

Hite, S. *The Hite report.* New York: Macmillan, 1976.

Hoch, Z. The sensory arm of the female orgasm reflex. *Journal of Sex Education and Therapy,* 1980, *6,* 4–7.

Imperato-McGinley, J., Peterson, R. E., Gautier, T., & Sturla, E. The impact of androgens on the evaluation of male gender identity. In *Pediatric audiology, clinics in audiology, Vol. 7.* S. J. Kogan, & E. S. Hafez (Eds.) Hague/Boston/London: Martinus Midhoff Press, 1981, 99–108.

Kaplan, H. S. *The new sex therapy, vol. I. New York: Brunner/Mazel, 1974.*

Kaplan, H. S. *The myth of the new impotence.* Presented at the American Academy of Psychoanalysis, Toronto, 1977 (Unpublished).

Kaplan, H. S. *Disorders of sexual desire: The new sex therapy vol. II.* New York: Brunner/Mazel, 1979.

Kaplan, H. S. *ISD: A model for the treatment of egodystonic homosexuality.* Presented at the 2nd Symposium in the Integrative Psychiatry Series, N.Y. Medical College, Jan. 1982 (Unpublished).

Kaplan, H. S., Fyer, A. J., & Novick, A. The treatment of sexual phobias: The combined use of anti-panic medication and sex therapy. *Journal of Sex and Marital Therapy,* 1982, *8,* 3–28.

Kaplan, H. S., Schwartz, S., Kaye, A., & Glass, J. B. J. Post gastrectomy pain and schizophrenia. *Psychosomatics,* 1970, *II.*

Karacan, I., Williams, R. L., Thornby, J. L., & Solis, P. J. Sleep related tumescence as a function of age. *American Journal of Psychiatry,* 1975, *132,* 932–937.

Kegel, A. H. Progressive resistance in the functional restoration of the perineal muscle. *American Journal of Obstetric Gynecology,* 1948, *56,* 238–248.

Kegel, A. H. Sexual functions of the pubococcygens muscle. *Western Journal of Surgical Obstetrics and Gynecology,* 1952, *57,* 527–535.

Kegel, A. H. Sexual functions of the pubococcygens muscle. *Western Journal of Surgery,* 1956, *60,* 521–524.

Kelly, D., Guiruis, W., Fromer, E., Michell-Heggs, W., & Sargent, W. Treatment of phobic states with antidepressants. *British Journal of Psychiatry,* 1970, *116,* 387–398.

Klein, D. F. Delineation of two drug responsive anxiety syndromes. *Psychopharmacology,* 1964, *5,* 397–408.

Klein, D. F. Anxiety reconceptualized. In *Anxiety: New research and changing concepts*. D. F. Klein, & J. G. Rabkin (Eds.) New York: Raven Press, 1980, 235–241.

Kline-Graber, G., & Graber, B. Diagnosis and treatment procedures of pubococcygens deficiencies in women. In *Handbook of sex therapy*. LoPiccolo & LoPiccolo (Eds.) New York: Plenum Press, 1978.

Kolodny, R. C. Sexual dysfunction in diabetic females. *Diabetes*, 1971, *20*, 557–559.

Kolodny, R. C. Sexual dysfunction in diabetic males. *Diabetes*, 1974, *23*, 306–309.

Kolodny, R. C., Masters, W. H., & Johnson, V. *Textbook of sexual medicine*. Boston: Little, Brown, 1979.

Ladas, A. K., Whipple, B., & Perry, J. D. *The G spot and other recent discoveries about human sexuality*. New York: Holt, Rinehart & Winston, 1982.

Lanschett, U. Antiandrogen in the treatment of sex offenders: Mode of action and therapeutic outcome. In *Contemporary sexual behavior: Critical issues in the 1970s*. J. Zubin, & J. Money (Eds.) Baltimore: Johns Hopkins University Press, 1973.

Leibowitz, M. R., & Klein, D. F. Treatment and assessment of phobic anxiety. *Journal of Clinical Psychology*, 1979, *40*, 486–492.

Lief, H. I. What's new in sex research? Inhibited sexual desire. *Medical Aspects of Human Sexuality*, 1977, *11:7*, 94–95.

Lief, H. I. Sexual problems in medical practice. Monroe, Wis: Amer. Medical Association, 1981.

Lorand, S. Contributions to the problem of vaginal orgasm. *International Journal of Psychoanalysis*, 1939, *20*, 432–438.

Lorand, S., & Balin, M. (Eds.) *Perversions: Psychodynamics and psychotherapy*. New York: Random House, 1956.

MacCulloch, M. J., Birtles, C. J., & Feldman, M. P. Anticipatory avoidance learning for the treatment of homosexuality: Recent developments and an automatic aversion therapy system. *Behavior Therapy*, 1971, *2*, 151–169.

Mack, J. E., & Semrad, E. V. Classical psychoanalysis. In *Comprehensive textbook of psychiatry*. 1st ed. A. M. Freedman, & H. L. Kaplan (Eds.) Baltimore: Williams & Wilkins, 1967, 269–320.

March, C. M. Bromocriptine in the treatment of hypogonadism and male impotence. *Drugs*, 1979, *17*, 349–358.

Marmor, J. (Ed.) *Homosexual behavior*. New York: Basic Books, 1980.

Masters, W. H., & Johnson, V. *The human sexual response*. Boston: Little, Brown, 1966.

Masters, W. H., & Johnson, V. *Human sexual inadequacy*. Boston: Little, Brown, 1970.

Masters, W. H., & Johnson, V. *Homosexuality in perspective*. Boston: Little, Brown, 1979.

Melman, A., Henry, D. P., Felten, D. L., & O'Connor, B. Effect of diabetes upon penile nerves in impotent patients. *S. Med. J.*, 1980, *73*, 307–310.

Meyer, J. K., & Reter, D. Sex reassignment: Follow-up. *Archives of General Psychiatry*, 1979, *36*, 1010–1015.

Money, J. The use of androgen-depleting hormone in the treatment of male sex offenders. *Journal of Sex Research*, 1970, *6*, 165–172.

Money, J., & Ehrhardt, A. A. *Man and woman/boy and girl — the differentiation and dimorphism of gender identity from conception to maturity*. Baltimore: Johns Hopkins University Press, 1972.

Money, J., Hampson, J. G., & Hamson, J. L. Hermaphrodism: Recommendations concerning assignment of sex, change of sex, and psychological management. *Bull. Johns Hopkins Hospital*, 1955, *97*, 284–300.

Muskin, P., & Fyer, A. J. Treatment of panic disorder. *Journal Clinical Psychopharmocology*, 1981, *1*, 81–90.

Newman, H. F., & Northrup, J. D. Mechanism of human penile erection: An overview. *Urology*, 1981, *17*, 399–408.

O'Connor, J. F., & Stern, L. O. Results of treatment in functional sexual disorders. *New York State Journal of Internal Medicine*, 1972, *72*, 1927–1934.

Perls, F. S. *Gestalt therapy*. New York, Grove Press, 1961.

Persky, H., Charney, N., Lief, H. I., O'Brien, C. P., Miller, W. R., & Strauss, D. The relationship of plasma estradiol level to sexual behavior in young women. *Psychosomatic Medicine*, 1978, *40*, 7.

Persky, H., Dreisbach, M. S., Miller, R. W., O'Brien, C. P., Khan, M. A., Lief, H. I., Charney, N., & Strauss, D. The relation of plasma androgen levels to sexual behaviors and attitudes of women. *Psychosomatic Medicine*, 1982 (In press).

Persky, H., Lief, H. I., O'Brien, C. P., Strauss, D., & Miller, W. Reproductive hormone levels and sexual behavior of young couples during the menstrual cycle. In *Progress in sexology*. R. Geme, & C. Wheeler (Eds.) New York: Plenum, 1977.

Persky, H., Lief, H. I., Strauss, D., Miller W. R., & O'Brien, C. P. Plasma testosterone levels and sexual behavior of couples. *Archives of Sexual Behavior*, 1978, *7*, 3.

Persky, H., Strauss, D., Lief, H. I., Miller, W. R., & O'Brien, C. P. Effect of the research process on human sexual behavior. *Journal of Psychiatric Research*, 1980, *16*, 41–52.

Risch, S. C., & Janowsky, D. S. Trazodone. *Psychiatric Annals*, 1981, *II*, 11.

Roth, M., & Myers, D. H. Anxiety neurosis and phobic states: Diagnosis and management. *British Medical Journal*, 1969, *1*, 559–562.

Schiavi, R. C. Androgens and male sexual function: A review of human studies. *Journal of Sexual and Marital Therapy*, 1976, *II*, 3.

Schiavi, R. C. Male erectile disorders. *Annual Review of Medicine*, 1981, *32*, 509.

Schwartz, M. The Masters and Johnson approach to homosexuality. Presented at the 2nd symposium in the Integrative Psychiatry Series, New York Medical College, New York, January, 1982.

Scott, F. B., Bradley, W., & Tim, G. W. Management of erectile impotence. *Urology*, 1973, *2*, 80–82.

Semans, J. H. Premature ejaculation: A new approach. *Southern Medical Journal*, 1956, *49*, 353–359.

Sheenan, D. V. Panic attacks and phobias. *New England Journal of Medicine*, 1982, 307:3, 156–158.

Small, M. P. Small-Carrion prostheses: A report on 160 cases and review of the literature. *Journal of Urology*, 1978, *119*, 365–368.

Spark, R. F., White, R. A., & Connolly, P. B. Impotence is not always psychogenic: Hypothalmic-pituitary gonadal dysfunction. *Journal of the American Medical Association*, 1980, *243*, 750–755.

Stoller, R. *Sex and gender: On development of masculinity and feminity*. New York: Science House, 1968.

Strayhorn, J. M., Jr. *Foundations of clinical psychiatry*. Chicago: Year Book Medical Publishers, Inc., 1982.

Tyrer, P., Candy, J., & Nelly, D. A. A study of the effects of phenelzine and placebo in the treatment of phobic anxiety. *Psychopharmacology*, 1973, *32*, 237–254.

Wagner, G., & Green, R. *Impotence*. New York: Plenum Press, 1982.

Wasserman, M. D. The differential diagnosis of impotence: The measurement of nocturnal penile tumescence. *Journal of the American Medical Association*, 1980, *243*, 203–242.

Wasserman, M. D., Pollock, C. P., Spielman, A. J., & Weitzman, E. D. Theoretical and technical problems in the measurement of nocturnal penile tumescence for the differential diagnosis of impotence. *Psychosomatic Medicine*, 1980, *42*, 575–585.

Waxenberg, S. E., Drellich, M. G., & Sutherland, A. M. The role of hormones in human behavior. I: Changes in female sexuality after adrenalectomy. *Journal of Clinical Endocrinol. Metab.*, 1959, *19*, 193.

Wolpe, J. The experimental foundations of some new psychotherapeutic methods. In *Experimental foundations of clinical psychology*. A. J. Bachrach (Ed.) New York: Basic Books, 1962.

Zorgniotti, A. W., & Rossi, G. *Vasculogenic impotence*. Springfield, IL.: Charles C Thomas, 1980.

Zitrin, C. M., Klein, D. F., & Woerner, M. G. Behavior therapy, supportive therapy, imipramine and phobias. *Archives of General Psychology*, 1978, *35*, 307–316.

INDEX

Epilepsy:
  psychomotor, 124, 237
  temporal lobe, 188, 244
Episiotomy, 257
Erection, simultaneity of with orgasm, 140
Ergot alkaloids, 121
Erikson, E. H., 56, 111n.
Estradiol, 123, 170, 187
Estrogen, 85, 126, 173. *See also* Hormones;
    Testosterone
  cyclical production of, 185
  deficiency states, 10, 20, 27, 132, 236
    and female excitement disorders, 122–
      24
    and frigidity, 236–37
    and menopause, 122–23
    replacement, 25
    and sexual desire, 242
    and vaginal cells, 236
    and vaginal lubrication, 122
Estrone, 123, 187
Euler, U. S. V., 162, 180n.
Evoked sacral potential, 177–78
Excitement disorders, female, 79, 122–26,
    235–38
  anatomy and physiology of, 122–23
  and drugs, 126
  and estrogen deficiency, 122–24
  and medical disorders, 124–26
Exhibitionism, 51, 250
Extramarital sexuality, 100

Faglia, G., 161, 180n.
Fahrenkrug, J., 163, 181n.
Faiman, C., 169, 180n., 186, 194n.
Family:
  antisexual attitudes in, 98
  family history, 96–102
Fantasy, sexual, 42, 79, 106
  incompatibility of, 66, 272
Farkas, G. M., 172, 180n.
Feldman, M. P., 252, 254, 274n., 275n.
Felten, D. L., 161, 162, 181n., 226, 275n.
Female excitement disorders. *See* Excite-
    ment disorders, female
Fenichel, O., 56, 111n., 224, 231, 274n.
Fetishism, 250
Fibrosis, 151
Fields, D. H., 134, 138n.
Fine, J., 178, 180n.
Finney, R. P., 234, 274n.
Fisher, C., 178, 180n.
Fisher, R. A., 171, 181n.
Fisher, S., 204, 274n.
Fishkein, R., 160, 182n.
Fithian, M., 90, 112n.

Folliculitis, 131
Foreskin, infection of, 152
Frantz, A. C., 186, 194n.
Frei test, 132
Frenular tethering, 151, 153, 259
Freud, S., 56, 111n., 211, 231,
    258, 247n.
Friedman, M., 49, 111n., 256, 274n.
Friesen, H. G., 169, 180n., 186, 194n.
Frigidity, 7, 235–38
  and estrogen, 236, 237
  and neurogenic disorders, 237
Fromer, F., 266, 274n.
Frosch, W. A., 233, 274n.
FSH, 92
Fundoscopic examination, 119–20
Furlow, W. L., 140, 149n.
Fyer, A. J., 26n., 111n., 266, 275n.

Gaggini, M., 160–61, 180n.
Galactorrhea, 192
Gautier, T., 184, 194n., 200, 274n.
Gender identity disorders, DSM-III cate-
    gory, 200–202
  evaluation of, 200–201
  treatment and prognosis of, 201–202
Genital reflexes, 125
Gessa, G. L., 161, 180n., 184, 194n.
Gilman, A., 146, 149n.
Ginsberg, G. L., 233, 274n.
Gittes, R. F., 142, 149n.
Glans penis, 156
Glass, J. B. J., 258, 274n.
Glicklich, T., 26n., 111n., 266, 274n.
Glucose tolerance test, 85, 176, 230
  diabetic curve on, 119
Glycosuria, 119
Goble, A. J., 189, 194n.
Gold, A. R., 185, 193n.
Goldstein, H. H., 169, 181n.
Gonadotropins, 186
Gonorrhea, 174, 256
Goodman, L. S., 146, 149n.
Gordon, G. G., 173, 181n., 187, 194n.
Gordon, J. H., 184, 194n.
Gorman, J. M., 26n., 111n., 266, 274n.
Gorski, R. A., 184, 194n.
Graber, B., 205, 275n.
Gräfenberg, E., 205, 206, 274n.
Gräfenberg ("G") spot, 206
Grant, E. C. G., 185, 194n.
Granuloma injuinale, 132
Granulomatous disease, 186
Green, R., 23n., 25, 113n., 201, 229, 274n.,
    276n.
Gross, J., 178, 180n.

Group therapy, sexually oriented, 72
Grundlach, R. H., 68, 112n.
"G" spot, 206
Guanethidine, 121, 146, 172
Guerrero, L., 184, 194n.
Guilt, 4, 82, 97
Guiruis, W., 266, 274n.
Gynecomastia, 170, 192
  and impotence, 175

Haldol (haloperidol), 145, 162
Halling, J. M., 188, 194n.
Hallucinogens, 146
Haloperidol (Haldol), 145, 162
Harrison, J. H., 142, 144, 149n., 152, 154n.
Hartman, W. E., 90, 112n.
Hayles, A. B., 187, 193n.
Headache, post orgasmic, 137
Head trauma, 124
Hematuria, 120
Hemochromatosis, 186, 192
Hemophilus bacteria, 130
Hemorrhages, 118, 120, 123
Hemorrhoids, 136
Henry, D. P., 161, 162, 171, 181n., 275n.
Heparin therapy, 168
Hepatitis, 120, 125
  postmononucleosis, 125–26
Hernias, 25, 118, 151, 154
Heroin, 173
Herpes, 21, 25, 130–31, 153, 257, 259, 261
Hexamethonium, 145
Hite, S., 204, 274n.
Hoch, Z., 205, 206, 274n.
Holdsworth, S., 186, 194n.
Hollister, L. E., 189, 194n.
Homework, 62
  for nonorgastic women, 43–44
Homosexuality, 26, 200
  ego-dystonic, 8, 73, 239, 251–54
    behavioral analysis of, 252–53
  and heterosexual capacity with sex therapy, 8
Hormones, 4
  and impotence, 164, 169–71
  and sexual desire, 240–43
Horowitz, J. D., 189, 194n.
Horwith, M., 183–93
Husted, J. R., 164, 180n.
Hygiene, genital, 132
Hymen:
  intact or rigid, 129
  obstruction of, 21
Hyperpigmentation, 192
Hyperplasia, 142, 144
  benign prostatic, 150

Hyperprolactinemia, 170, 186, 193
Hypertension, 26, 119, 125
Hyperthyroidism, 187, 265
Hypertrophy, cardiac, 120
Hypnosis, 94
Hypnotic drugs, 121, 189
Hypochondriasis, 258
Hypoglycemia, 265
Hypogonadism, 184, 186
Hypopituitarism, 120, 125
Hypospadias, 91, 152, 166, 270
Hypothalamus, 139, 170
  and desire, 185–86
  lesions of, 124, 237
Hypothyroidism, 170, 192
Hysterectomy, 133
Hysteria, 258

Iliac artery steal syndrome, 168
Imipramine (Tofranil), 121, 145, 267n.
Impaired female orgasm, 117–21, 203–12.
    See also Orgasm disorders
  differential diagnosis of, 205–206
  treatment and prognosis of, 211
Impaired sexual desire. *See also* Desire disorders
Imperato-McGinley, J., 183–93, 194n., 200, 274n.
Impotence, 7, 10, 20, 24, 50–52, 87, 142, 155–80
  and aging, 164
  anatomical-physiological aspects of, 156–66
  assessment of basis of, 3–4
  and blood pressure, 175
  and depression, 95–96
  diabetes mellitus based, 171–72
  diagnosis of, 224–29
  drug-based, 172–73
  embryological aspects of, 155–56
  endocrine based, 169–71
    laboratory findings on, 176
  evaluation of, 173–80, 224–35
    erectile dysfunction, 174–75
    history, 173–74
    laboratory findings, 176–80
    physical examination, 175
  and hormones, 164, 169–71
  and libido, 26
  and local penile abnormalities, 166
  and masturbation, 50, 174
  neurogenic, 166–67
  and nocturnal penile tumescence monitoring, 227–29
  organic basis of, 5, 226, 270
  psychoanalysis on, 231–32